The
Country Antiques
Companion

The
Country Antiques
Companion

DAN D'IMPERIO

ILLUSTRATED WITH PHOTOGRAPHS

DODD, MEAD & COMPANY · New York

The author is grateful to the National Gallery of Art, Index of American Design, for permission to reproduce the photographs in this book.

Library of Congress Cataloging in Publication Data

D'Imperio, Dan.
    The country antiques companion.

    Includes index.
        1. Antiques. I. Title.
NK1125.D44   745.1'0973   76–48063
ISBN 0–396–07377–8

For Margaret, Daniel & Dolores

Introduction

Country antiques offer beginning and seasoned collectors alike an opportunity to acquire objects related to our country's rich heritage. Simple utilitarian articles, once commonplace in every farmhouse, now command the attention of antique aficionados everywhere. The term "country antiques" is used here in its broadest sense. It encompasses a myriad of mementos made or used in rural communities from the 17th century through the 19th century, articles invariably conjuring up a sense of home and hearth and reflecting the resourcefulness of early settlers. Early handcrafted items are discussed along with later factory-produced pieces.

This book, which covers the subject from A to Z, was designed with the beginning collector in mind. Every attempt has been made to help the novice recognize and evaluate antiques with greater confidence. Since many collectors seek data pertaining to prices, a convenient value guide accompanies most entries. The price quotations are based on actual sales transactions obtained from a nationwide survey of antique shops, shows, estate sales, auctions, flea markets and other outlets. Retail prices fluctuate depending on condition and geographical location, and prices are quoted for items in salable condition, unless otherwise indicated. Certain museum-quality pieces, infrequently traded in the antique marketplace due to scarcity, have been listed as "extremely rare."

Because of the widespread appeal of country antiques, the novice competes with the museum curator for existing examples. A knowledgeable buyer always has the edge, and it is hoped that with this book as your antiquing companion, your future will be full of fortunate finds. Happy hunting!

The
Country Antiques
Companion

A

AGATEWARE. Country folk visiting the Philadelphia Centennial Exposition of 1876 were impressed with the elaborate displays of a new iron cookware called agateware. Shortly thereafter, local emporiums boasted a complete line of agateware kitchen and bathroom accessories in mottled colors, including blue, black, green, brown, turquoise and gray. Advertisements proclaiming its light weight and durability referred to it as granite steelware, granite ironware, enamelware and glazed ware. Many present-day collectors prefer the term graniteware. Most manufacturers marked their output with paper labels, which have disappeared with time. The solid white agateware edged in blue, introduced in the early 1900s, is more available than mottled pieces of the same vintage. Agateware value guide: colander, gray, 10" diameter, $11; coffeepot, blue, $22; gravy ladle, gray, $8; teakettle, green, $25.

ALFORD & COMPANY. Arba Alford became a partner in the reorganized Lambert Hitchcock chair factory in 1832. Chairs made under the ensuing Hitchcock, Alford partnership were signed "Hitchcock, Alford & Co., Hitchcocksville, Conn.—Warranted." The signature was utilized until 1843, when Lambert severed his relationship with Arba to open another factory. The scarcity of signed examples can be attributed to repeated refinishing and repainting. Arba acquired another partner, and together they continued shipping chairs to many different parts of the country, labeling them "Alford & Company." They currently earn a nod of approval from the country chair contingent. Alford & Company value guide: caned seat, stenciled decoration, circa 1835, $225; wooden seat, fruit stenciling, "Alford & Company," circa 1845, $265.

ALMANACS. The ever-reliable almanac was always close at hand in farmhouses from the late 1600s onward. By consulting one of these illustrated pamphlets the reader could keep track of days, weeks, phases of the moon, weather predictions, calculations of measures and volumes, and other information of daily importance. The number of pages and illustrations varied depending on the publisher, with the larger ones having forty or more pages. Many early almanacs also contained data pertaining to post routes, stagecoach routes and college commencement dates. Often an almanac included riddles, articles and propaganda for various causes. As might be expected, they generally show vigorous usage since most were consulted 365 days per year. Almanac value guide: *An Astronomical Diary for 1789*, Nathaniel Low, $25; *Bickerstaff's New England Almanac*, 1783, $30; *Farmer's Almanac*, 1845, Robert B. Thomas, $8; *New England Almanac*, 1815, Nathan Daball, $18.

AMELUNG, JOHN FREDERICK. Every country antique enthusiast dreams of finding a piece of early American glassware from the renowned New Bremen Glass Manufactory. The factory was founded in 1785 near Frederick, Maryland, by John Frederick Amelung. Amelung glass is characterized by superb copper wheel engraving and a smoky hue. Bottles, window glass, tableware articles and presentation items originated at the factory. Trained workmen were imported from Germany to decorate the glass in a truly Continental manner. The glass bears engraved motifs of birds, ciphers, festoons, wreaths, coat of arms and inscriptions. The colored glassware in shades of green, blue and purple is coveted. Amelung overestimated the American market, forcing himself into debt and bankruptcy by 1795. It is extremely difficult to positively attribute pieces to Amelung. Amelung value guide: scent bottle, Amelung type, $250; wine glass, Amelung type, engraved birds, $185.

AMERICAN STANDARD ROCKERS. This rocking chair revolutionized the chair industry when it rocked onto the scene in the 1870s. It represented a distinct departure from earlier styles, as the base remained stationary while the chair rocked on its spring-type mechanism. Thus even repeated rocking failed to wear out a carpet. What other chair offered maximum comfort combined with money-saving advantages? Platform or spring rockers were greeted as welcome additions to country parlors of the 1880s and 1890s. The country-made versions were simple adaptations of the factory-made rockers. Many were made of oak, and those possessing Eastlake details are particularly prized. Long recognized as a thrift shop staple, the platform rocker has become a bona fide antique. American standard rocker value guide: oak, circa 1885, $125; walnut, Eastlake details, circa 1890, $140.

ANDIRONS. Logs have been supported in American fireplaces since the Colonial period by pairs of andirons made of wrought iron, cast iron, bronze, brass and other materials. The early blacksmith fashioned wrought-iron andirons with flattened or twisted shafts, usually terminating in solid ball, or ball with ring finials. George Washington, Adam and Eve, Hessian soldiers, eagles, owls, dogs and Gothic fretwork designs were among the popular hearthside companions of the 18th and 19th centuries. Since the same subject was often cast by more than one foundry, minor differences become apparent only upon close inspection. As a guide to dating, most andirons followed contemporary furniture styles: therefore those displaying Queen Anne, Chippendale or Classical influences may be dated accordingly. Andiron value guide: bronze, Hessian soldiers, circa 1850, $360; brass, ball top, arched scroll supports, circa 1830, $340; brass, ball top, circa 1820, $260; wrought iron, goose neck, circa 1820, $250.

APOTHECARY CHESTS. More than one early apothecary chest has traveled the storeroom-to-living-room route. These druggists' chests were simply constructed, with the number of storage compartments varying according to the needs of the owner. Pine was the

George Washington cast-iron andiron
National Gallery of Art, Washington

3

favorite wood. Some chests have seven or more levels of three square drawers with plain wooden knobs. A potential buyer should exercise caution as many chests have been cut down to a smaller size. Those made by the Shakers are held in high esteem. Another type of apothecary chest is the smaller herb storage chest. It was popular in kitchens and stores throughout the 19th century. Various preparations were stored in these chests, which are especially in demand by space-conscious collectors. Apothecary chest value guide: Shaker, maple, sixteen drawers, circa 1840, $700; pine, original labels, twelve drawers, wooden knobs, circa 1850, $580.

APPLE-BUTTER ACCESSORIES. The pursuer of apple-butter-making accessories may be rewarded by uncovering a brass or copper apple-butter kettle, once used to boil fruit. Apple-butter stirrers, some approaching shovel size, are other finds in this category; those bearing pierced designs can be safely attributed to the Pennsylvania region. The large scoops often measure a foot in length. These, as well as apple-butter buckets and paddles, are scooped up by country antique aficionados. The self-supporting Shaker communities made and sold large quantities of apple butter. Their strikingly simple accessories cause a stir whenever they surface at a country auction. American potters profited from potting redware apple butter pots in graduated sizes as well as miniature pots for mamma's little helpers. Apple-butter accessory value guide: bucket, Shaker, circa 1840, $70; kettle, brass, iron bail, 20" diameter, 18" deep, circa 1850, $120; redware bowl, slip decoration, circa 1830, $295; scoop, carved handle, circa 1860, $80; tub, with handle and cover, 9" high, circa 1820, $50.

APPLE-DRYING BASKETS. After apples had been cored and sliced they were dried on the window sill or near the hearth in a tray or basket. Any antique apple-drying basket is almost certain to show signs of apple juice stains. Shallow splint drying receptacles were made in rectangular shapes and in sizes ranging up to four feet in length. Simply by adding a splint handle across the middle section, an apple-drying tray became an apple-drying basket. In Pennsylvania most apple dryers relied on baskets or trays of rye straw. A somewhat rarer apple dryer was known as a "cobweb dryer"; it hung over the hearth slowly rotating due to the heat from beneath. Apple-drying basket value guide: rye straw tray, medium size, Pennsylvania, $75; splint type, rectangular, small size, $40.

4

APPLE-HEAD DOLLS. The primitive dried apple-head dolls represent American folk toys at their finest. They were always crafted with utmost care by early settlers who supposedly copied the idea from their Indian neighbors. A freshly picked apple was crudely carved with facial features and permitted to dry. In the drying process a lifelike expression was achieved, highlighted by some realistic wrinkling. Apples proved ideal for crafting dolls depicting older men and women. The bodies were usually a wire frame, and the clothing was fashioned from dressmaking remnants. More than one homemaker proudly walked away from a community event with a blue ribbon in hand for a handcrafted dried apple-head doll. Apple-head doll value guide: Indian, dressed, circa 1870, $95; Santa Claus, circa 1870, $80.

APPLE PARERS. Since apples were an important part of the daily diet during the 1700s and 1800s, the homemade wooden apple parer consisting of a blade and prongs was always within easy reach. Most primitive parers performed their labor-saving function while perched or screwed onto the table top. A skilled carpenter sometimes attempted a more complicated standing bench model. In 1803 the first American patent for a wooden apple parer was granted. These were quickly relegated to the bottom of the cupboard when fancier cast-iron parers hit hardware emporiums in the mid-1800s. As new improvements were patented, parers capable of paring, coring and slicing the apple appeared in swift succession. The cast-iron parers bearing a maker's name or patent date are preferred. Apple parer value guide: primitive wooden bench model, circa 1780, $180; wooden parer, table top type, circa 1790, $155; "Little Star," cast-iron model, patent 1885, $26; "Enterprise," cast-iron model, circa 1890, $22.

APPLE PICKERS. Farmers regularly scheduled annual apple picking bees every fall when their orchards required harvesting. The event automatically became a community effort as a small band of industrious pickers ventured from farm to farm. Apples hanging on lower branches could swiftly be picked by hand. Those on higher branches necessitated the use of a trusty wooden apple picker. These long wooden rods were fitted with a series of prongs at the top end. The movable prongs grasped the fruit, freed it from the tree and brought it to the ground in record-breaking time. Several variations have been noted, all working on the same principle. These rare primitives are frequently filed under the "what is it" category of country antiques. Apple picker value guide: wooden, primitive type, circa 1835, $125.

APPLIQUÉ RUGS. The attractive appliqué rug, a twin to the appliqué quilt, made its American debut as a homemade floor covering in the early 1800s. Trying to find one is not recommended for the fainthearted as these rugs proved highly perishable. Homespun pieces of fabric were cut out in different shapes and painstakingly stitched to the pieced colored background. Colors were carefully selected in an effort to obtain an interesting overall effect. The applied pieces were further enhanced by fancy needlework using bright yarns worked in various stitches. Considering the detailed handiwork involved in an appliqué rug project, it is surprising anyone had the heart to set foot on one. Appliqué rug value guide: medium size, floral patches against green background, rectangular, circa 1840, fair condition, $325.

ARROW-BACK CHAIRS. The painted arrow-back chair developed in the early 1800s ranks as a second cousin to the reliable Windsor chair. They are easy to recognize whether the flat arrow spindles terminate gracefully at either end or have a sharp arrow cut at the middle section. The later the chair, the fewer the number of arrow splats. By the mid-1800s most country-crafted chairs were being constructed with three large splats. A typical arrow-back chair was painted black, bore a stencil-decorated crest rail, and had gilded lines highlighting leg turnings, arrow splats and stretchers. Due to their scarcity, arrow-back rocking chairs have also attained an air of importance. Scoring a bull's-eye value-wise are the green-painted arrow-back chairs having colorful floral motifs attributed to the chairmakers of Pennsylvania. Arrow-back chair value guide: armchair, New England, plank seat, maple, circa 1830, $175; side chair, painted green, stenciled, Pennsylvania, circa 1840, $275; rocking chair, hickory back, walnut rockers, circa 1860, $200; side chair, arrow stretcher, maple, circa 1870, $130.

B

BAG STAMP MOLDS. These neglected pieces of American folk art frequently suffer the fate of being confused with butter molds. They were used to imprint a farmer's identifying mark on the homespun bags needed to transport grain to the mill. The carved wooden blocks varied in shape from round to rectangular. Some were carved with only the owner's initials; more intricately carved molds combined initials with fascinating patterns. Those incorporating such desirable designs as hearts, eagles, flowers and wheat are assured of fetching substantial returns. Bagging a bag stamp mold can turn any antiquing trip into a triumph. Bag stamp mold value guide: round, wheat and initials, Pennsylvania, circa 1820, $175; Pennsylvania, deep-cut initials, circa 1830, $95; oval, hearts with initials, Pennsylvania, circa 1840, $185.

BAILEY, WILLIAM. This ambitious tinsmith and coppersmith centered in York, Pennsylvania in the late 1700s pursued his profession in several different locations. In an early newspaper advertisement of the 1790s, orders were being secured for such articles of tin and copper as wash kettles, fish kettles, teakettles, saucepans, coffee pots, chocolate pots, boxes, stills in several sizes and various other household goods. The main shop in York was listed, as were branch outlets in Chambersburg, Pennsylvania, and in Frederick, and Hagerstown, Maryland. His ad also stated that he would travel to other communities on a regular basis to secure orders, thereby saving customers the expense and inconvenience of traveling to one of his establishments. Signed specimens of Bailey's work have been recorded. Bailey value guide: copper saucepan, Bailey type, circa 1790, $155.

BALLOT BOXES. Box collectors unite with country antique buffs in casting an affirmative vote for old ballot boxes. Although some were advertised by New England woodworkers in the early 1800s, they apparently were never made in any quantity. Voters in country regions usually cast their ballots in square or slightly oblong dovetailed boxes having a slot in the lid where the paper, wood or ivory ballot was deposited. Never permit an early ballot to slip through your hands as they are treasured by historians. Uncovering one bearing the name of an important political person can fetch substantial returns. Exclusive private clubs and organizations often had custom-designed boxes and covered urns reserved for their distinguished clientele. Ballot box value guide: mahogany, wooden drawer, slot in lid, circa 1830, $165; maple, dovetailed, square shape, slot in lid, circa 1840, $100; pine, original blue paint, 10" square, 20" high, circa 1850, $80.

BANDBOXES. These fragile traveling adjuncts made of pasteboard or thin strips of wood covered with colorful wood block printed papers proved fashionable in the first half of the 19th century. Round or oval bandboxes served as storage receptacles and traveling companions for ladies and gentlemen alike. Hats, hairpieces and bits of frills and finery filled these boxes, which often sold

Banjo clock, Simon Willard style, circa 1825
Both photographs, National Gallery of Art, Washington

Bandbox, log-cabin scene, circa 1840

for a mere twenty-five to fifty cents each. Bandboxes chalked up a considerable amount of mileage journeying about the countryside. The printed designs ran the gamut from romantic, classical and naturalistic motifs to national heroes, famous landmarks and modes of travel. Those made by Hannah Davis and labeled "Warranted Nailed Bandboxes Manufactured by Hannah Davis East Jaffrey N.H." deserve special mention. This energetic Yankee peddler held her own against such bandbox barons as J. F. Barnholt, William Friedman, Thomas Day, Jr., Barnard Andrews and H. Barnes. As the stagecoach rode off into oblivion, it carried the beloved bandbox right along for the ride. Bandbox value guide: George Washington decor, faded, large size, $350; Merchant's Exchange decor, medium size, $300; Hannah Davis box, florals, fair condition, $230; floral decor, pink roses and leaves, medium size, $140.

BANISTER-BACK CHAIRS. The appropriately named banister-back chair has a chair back composed of vertically placed split or round balusters resembling a stair banister. The earliest American-made chairs in this category are the Carver and Brewster styles of the Pilgrim period. Banister-back chairs experienced their major thrust of popularity in the 18th century. They were usually con structed with the flat side of the baluster facing forward, the rounded side to the rear for maximum comfort. Any chair made with the rounded side forward is referred to as a reverse banister. The finest and earliest chairs had elaborate turnings and ornamental crests. They had from three to five banisters, with many furniture makers favoring four. Country chairmakers used local woods such as hickory, pine, beech and maple. The style became more simpli-fied in the 19th century. Earlier banister-back chairs have become increasingly scarce; collector attention heightens on those dating from the late 1800s. Banister-back value guide: armchair, New England, rush seat, pine, circa 1720, $450; side chair, black paint, rush seat, pine, circa 1800, $200; side chair, Queen Anne, maple and cherry, circa 1730, $325; side chair, Pennsylvania, red paint, circa 1870, $190.

BANJO CLOCKS. Simon Willard was only twelve years old when his brother Benjamin opened his original clock shop in the family home at Grafton, Massachusetts in 1765. Simon was to become the most celebrated member of the Willard family of clockmakers. After working at Grafton (1774–1780), he relocated to Roxbury, Massachusetts, where he remained active between 1780 and 1839. Fame tapped on his front door when the mechanically minded Simon produced his "Improved Patent Timepiece" in the late 1700s. This wall clock resembling the shape of a banjo was patented by him in 1802, and widely copied by other clockmakers. Reproductions, rebuilt pieces, fake labeling and other similar pitfalls await the unwary banjo clock buyer. Banjo clock value guide: E. Howard & Co., size No. 5, $750; E. Ingraham & Co., "Treasure" model, 8-day time and strike, $600; New Haven Clock Co. 8-day time and strike, $400; Simon Willard, mahogany case, reverse painted tablet, $3,400.

BAR-BACK SIDE CHAIRS. Economy-minded customers in country regions were enthusiastic about the inexpensive factory-made chairs selling at local furniture houses in the late 19th century. One lightweight style having an open back was reminiscent of earlier Sheraton fancy chairs. It can be recognized by its distinctive bar back, which was composed of an arched flat curved top rail and two matching crossbars placed several inches apart beneath it. The slightly flaring uprights were made with a backward cyma curve at the point where they joined the seat. Most models had elliptically shaped caned seats. Turnings were customarily confined to the front legs and front stretchers. Since this style was favored as a dining chair, it was originally sold in sets of six or twelve. Nowadays it may require attending a few auction sales to accumulate a complete set. Bar-back side chair value guide: black walnut, original cane seat, circa 1880, $100.

BARRELS. When collectors speak of "rolling out the barrel" they prefer an early handmade example. Prior to about 1850 these containers were crafted by the village cooper. After this date they were usually factory produced. A "wet" or "tight" cooper concentrated on containers for storing liquids, usually made of durable oak. Barrels for dry commodities such as flour or sugar were made by the "dry" or "slack" cooper of maple, chestnut, oak, elm or other wood. Coopers reached the shores of America aboard the *Mayflower* and continued arriving in the new country until practically every village had one of its very own. They could make or repair woodenware articles with amazing accuracy. Staved and hooped barrels were made by these craftsmen in large numbers. However, deterioration was inevitable on those designated to hold liquids, so be prepared to barter for any early barrel. Barrel value guide: carved from log, 20″ high, circa 1820, $130; cider, staved and hooped, 4-gallon size, $65.

BASINS. Thanks to the widespread use of the washbasin, furniture designers developed the basin stand or washing stand in the late 18th century. A century later these square, round or rectangular washstands having a hole in the top board to accommodate a washbasin were still found in farmhouses lacking plumbing facilities. The lower shelf held the ewer, while a drawer or drawers were filled with essential toilet articles. There were plain and fancy basins of copper, pewter, glass, pottery, porcelain, ironstone, iron, wood, silver, tin and other materials. Basin buffs battle over the early bone and horn examples, signed pewter specimens, or basins with matching ewers. Agateware basins in various mottled colors splashed on the scene in the latter part of the 19th century and were bargain priced at $3 to $4 each. Basin value guide: pewter, signed "T. Boardman," 13¼″ diameter, $500; brass, engraved motif, 10″ diameter, $85; tin, 10″ diameter, circa 1840, $40.

BATHING VESSELS. Approximately eighty metropolitan areas boasted public water facilities in the United States by the mid-1800s. However, for humble country folk, taking a bath remained a chilling and annoying experience. Bathers shivered in portable bathing vessels of copper, wood, marble, pewter, brass or tin before the built-in tub era. Provincial bathers forsaking privacy for convenience were frequently forced to bathe in the kitchen in portable tubs. Some bathers splashed about in standard round or oval tubs, while others immersed themselves in whimsical hat or slipper forms. The tin-hat tub was amusingly conceived to resemble a wide-brimmed hat. Slipper tubs had the soakers sitting in the heel of the vessel, where they vigorously washed themselves in rapidly cooling water. Portable tubs were being moved about by would-be bathers in homes and public bathing places well into the 1800s. The built-in wooden tubs of oak, cedar or mahogany found in urban homes from the 1830s failed to reach farmhouses for a number of decades. Bathing vessel value guide: tin traveling tub, round, stenciled florals, circa 1850, $225; tin bathtub, 28″ diameter, 14″ high, $110; child's bathtub, circa 1860, $95.

BEAKERS. Country artisans were busy filling orders for these strikingly simple, wide-mouthed drinking vessels in the 18th and 19th centuries. Many ambitious silversmiths and pewterers practiced their trade on a part-time basis while also serving as the town innkeeper, shopkeeper or carpenter. They extracted a meager living by furnishing their rural clientele with simple utilitarian articles. Beakers were crafted for domestic use as well as for church communion services. Many bear a maker's mark, providing a clue to age and origin. However, many country craftsmen working with inferior tools in outlying areas failed to sign their output. The tallest beakers date from the 1700s; a shorter, four-inch-high version won wide acceptance in the early 1800s. Collector interest heightens on marked specimens, those possessing engraved motifs or on rare examples having two handles. Beaker value guide: pewter, American, unmarked, 4″ high, circa 1810, $110; pewter, Samuel Danforth, circa 1790, $475.

BEDPANS. American bedpans made by local tinsmiths and pewterers active in the late 18th and early 19th centuries appear infrequently in the antique marketplace. Their present scarcity results in ever-increasing values on these bedside companions for the incapacitated. The metal models fell from favor in the mid-1800s when economy-minded individuals bypassed them for less expensive pottery bedpans. Yellowware and Rockingham versions were shipped to outlying areas by potters operating in the eastern part of the country. The Rockingham bedpans attributed to the brilliant potters of Bennington, Vermont, are notable acquisitions. Around the turn of the century agateware bedpans sold with amazing regularity due to their modest cost and durability. Bedpan value guide: tin, circa 1840, $20; redware, manganese splotched, circa 1850, $130; yellowware, circa 1860, $22; brownware glaze, circa 1860, $35.

BEDS. The low-ceiling bedrooms found in most country homes of the 18th and 19th centuries necessitated low post beds. They were more widely favored by rural furniture makers than high post beds. Early bedsteads were simply constructed, having plain headboards, posts and side and end rails. Rope beds with holes or knobs along the rails to accommodate the ropes or lacings needed to support the mattress prevailed into the late 1800s in rural areas. Many early beds were constructed by the mortise-and-tenon method. The "under the eaves bed" of the 1700s, available in single and double size, had plain headboards supported by two low head posts slightly higher than the foot posts. A high post bed, known as a "pencil post bed," appeared in the late 1700s; the thin six-sided posts resembling pencils provided this bed with its unique name. A low post bed of the Empire period (1815–1840) usually had a carved headboard and posts of equal height. Another innovation of this period was the well-regarded sleigh bed which bore a resemblance to the front of a horse-drawn cutter or sleigh. The spool bed, often referred to as a Jenny Lind bed, proved popular in the 1850s, coinciding with the Swedish nightingale's American tour. Bed value guide: low post, plain headboard, pine, ¾ size, $225; pencil post, New England, maple, red paint, circa 1810, $850; low post, red paint, carved headboard, acorn finials, maple, circa 1830, $375; spool-turned, ¾ size, cherry and walnut, circa 1850, $375.

BEDSIDE TABLES. A small bedside table or night stand was a staple piece of bedroom furniture from the late 18th century onward. Country woodworkers worked overtime supplying them to local customers crafting them from native woods such as walnut, pine, cherry, maple and poplar. Bedside tables were made with or without one or more drawers. Furniture craftsmen in rural areas offered them in modified versions of the prevailing Hepplewhite and Sheraton styles. There were numerous variations, all certain to draw an admiring glance today from country antique buffs. One of the simplest yet currently popular types is the small drop-leaf style with straight legs and wooden knobs, devoid of any ornamentation. Any bedside table bearing sponged or painted motifs presumably originated in Pennsylvania. Look for signs of superior workmanship such as a shaped skirt, scalloped drawer edge or turned legs. Spool-turned legs suggest a date of production subsequent to 1820. Bedside table value guide: bird's-eye maple, one drawer, Sheraton-style details, circa 1810, $375; black walnut, one drawer, spool-turned, circa 1860, $200.

BEDSTEPS. Bedsteps were an absolute necessity when high bedsteads were fashionable in the 18th and 19th centuries. They resembled a set of steps, or a short step stool, with most examples equipped with rollers for portability. Urban cabinetmakers offered

13

them in open and closed versions, styled to blend with existing furniture forms. Those based on the furniture designs of Thomas Sheraton boasted dual advantages: when the lid and drawers were opened they revealed a storage compartment for a washbowl set or chamber pot. Shoes could also be housed in these handy bedroom standbys. Country examples hastily formed from local woods lacked the finely crafted details found on urban models; however, they served would-be slumberers in a similar manner. Bedstep value guide: mahogany, cupboard section and drawer, circa 1820, $285; mahogany, open-frame type, circa 1830, $200.

BED WRENCHES. The bed wrench, a wooden oddity resembling a large clothespin with a right-angle crossbar, was used to tighten the webbing on early bedsteads. They ranged in size to two feet or more in length. Provincial craftsmen having a way with woods made them in whimsical forms including figural shapes. The bed wrench was a bedroom necessity well into the late 1800s as rope beds were not replaced by slat beds with springs in rural areas until this date. It contributed immeasurably to the comfort of every member of the household. Should you encounter what appears to be a giant clothespin on your next antiquing venture, it may well be a cherished bed wrench. Bed wrench value guide: standard cross-bar type, circa 1820, $40; figural, circa 1840, $100.

BEEHIVE CLOCKS. The clever clockmakers active in Connecticut during the mid-1800s were apparently in the right place at the right time. They never failed to excite the public with their creative timepieces. One popular shelf clock was the beehive or flatiron version, which had a case resembling a beehive or an upright flatiron. It also is known as a "round Gothic." Most clocks had a square tablet and a round wooden dial. They were made in amusing and attractive shapes by many makers, including the Forestville Manufacturing Company, New England Clock Company and C. Jerome, Connecticut clockmakers one and all. Beehive clock value guide: Brewster & Ingraham, rosewood case, eight-day time and strike, circa 1850, $200; Connecticut Clock Company, rosewood, eight-day time and strike, $155.

BEEHIVES. Interior decorators or others imaginative enough to crave the unusual seek early beehives of straw, thatch, wood, rush or glass. A farmer or gardener who wanted to provide a home for bees was instructed to consider the advantages of a straw hive in early farming manuals. According to knowledgeable beekeepers, the inexpensive dome-shaped straw hives best withstood extreme weather conditions, thus guaranteeing an ample supply of honey and wax. To ward off uninvited insects, a farmer encrusted them with a mixture of dung and ash. Settlers from Scotland and northern English provinces called them bee-skeps. While the glass hives afforded a clear view of bees producing honey, few specimens existed in isolated areas where natural substances were primarily utilized. Beehive value guide: straw, fair condition, circa 1880, $75.

BELLOWS. Paul Revere and other less revered craftsmen were known to have made bellows, that object for fanning a fire. The most familiar type was crafted of turned wood and leather with a brass end. By the early 1800s numerous advertisements appeared for carved, painted, stenciled and japanned bellows of curly maple, bird's-eye maple, ash, walnut, mahogany, satinwood and cherry. About 1820 the Philadelphia Bellows Manufactory offered a large stock of "Common Bellows" in various sizes, as well as elegant japanned "Chamber Bellows." The round and rectangular shapes are more available than the heart shapes. Feeding air to the fire in country areas were handmade wooden and cowhide bellows having nailheads and braided leather, or other signs of homespun ornamentation. Bellows value guide: walnut, round, carved motif, circa 1820, $120; ash, undecorated, homemade, circa 1830, $75; leather with brass nailheads, circa 1840, $50.

BELL POTTERY. In the hundred-mile stretch of the Shenandoah Valley south of Pennsylvania, the Bell family of potters worked for a century between 1800 and 1900. Peter Bell was responsible for developing the distinctive glaze and color that distinguishes the sought-after Shenandoah pottery. He was actively pursuing his pottery profession in Hagerstown, Maryland, and Winchester, Virginia, between 1800 and 1845. His eldest son, John, willingly followed in his father's footsteps by establishing a pottery in Waynesboro, Pennsylvania, in the 1830s; John's sons continued operating the pottery until about 1900. Peter's two other sons, Samuel and Solomon, founded a pottery at Strasburg, Virginia, in 1834. Samuel's son was hardly one to break with tradition; he kept the pottery wheel going until 1908. The Bell family toiled long and lovingly over their stoneware and decorated redware, often marking it with the family name and location for easy identification. Bell pottery value guide: pitcher, John Bell, large size, $540; stoneware cooler, applied handles, tulips and birds, $485.

BELLS. Antique bells have certainly taken their toll on collectors. Early bells were handmade by local craftsmen, but from the turn of the 19th century many were factory produced. Practically any bell made specifically for farm use is currently in demand by collectors. Some of the smallest hung about the necks of barnyard animals. Cowbells originated at several New England factories, and those bearing information regarding the maker always command attention. The small turkey bells can be found in Liberty Bell shape, closed sleigh bell shape and open cowbell shape. Most farms had a dinner bell hanging outside the rear door, and an alarm bell at the barn door to signal emergencies. School bells and schoolteacher's bells were used to summon students to study. Other old tinklers now regarded as treasures are Conestoga bells, sleigh bells, store bells, desk bells, fire engine bells and railroad engine bells. Bell value guide: iron farm bell, large size with bracket, $135; brass school bell, 11″ high, 6″ diameter, turned wooden handle, $65; brass cowbell, 5½″ high, $20; cast-iron sheep bell, 4″ high, $17.

BENCHES. What would a farmer's life be like without one or more benches? Impossible! That is why these trusty standbys were made in various styles from the 1600s onward. Very often the farmer took matters into his own hands, fashioning one to his own specifications. Many one-of-a-kind models crafted from native woods fall into this category. Water and wash benches were usually assigned to duty in kitchen areas. Other benches found duty near the hearth, on the porch or in another equally suitable spot. Collectors compete for deacon's benches, milking benches, kneeling benches and any type of tradesmen's bench. Some lacking a specific use remain unnamed, but never unwanted. Plant lovers realize that practically any antique bench can be converted into a pleasing plant stand. Bench value guide: milk bench, original yellow paint, Pennsylvania, circa 1820, $235; porch bench, pine, dovetailed, 4′ long, 16″ wide, original red paint, $150; pine, rectangular top, scalloped base, refinished, 3′ long, 16″ wide, $135.

BENNINGTON. This Vermont town had two well-known potteries active in the mid-19th century. They produced a variety of pottery and porcelain of varying types. Therefore, associating them solely with Rockingham wares is unjust. The original works founded by Captain John Norton in 1793 concentrated its efforts on simple and practical stoneware pieces. The factory eventually operated by his descendants closed in 1894. They utilized a variety of marks, usually incorporating the Norton name. The most common was the "E. & L. P. Norton, Bennington, Vt." mark used primarily between 1861 and 1881. The second factory operated by Christopher Fenton between about 1847 and 1858, produced a diversity of wares including Flint Enamel, Parian, porcelain and Staffordshire-style jugs. Early wares often bear the "Lyman, Fenton & Company" trademark, but in 1853 the name was changed to United States Pottery Company. The firm closed in 1858 due to financial difficulties. Bennington value guide: washbowl and pitcher, Rockingham mottled glaze, $625; stoneware crock, blue floral decor, $175; pitcher, Rockingham mottled glaze, 10½" tall, $130; pie plate, Rockingham mottled glaze, 10½" diameter, $120; bowl, Rockingham glaze, 10" diameter, $70.

BERLIN TINWARE. The town of Berlin, Connecticut, became America's thriving tin center between the late 1700s and middle 1800s. The Pattison family of tinsmiths brought fame in the name of tin to the town of Berlin. Their bags were barely unpacked when Edward, the eldest son, established a tin shop about 1740. After completing a group of utensils, he packed them in baskets and peddled them along the highways and byways. As the demand for his wares increased, several apprentices and paid peddlers were added to the payroll. When the owner died in 1787, the prosperous Pattison Tinware Company was inherited by his sons. They came by their know-how naturally, and the business continued to thrive. Their peddlers were sent into virgin territory as far north as Canada and south below the Mason-Dixon line. Local townspeople referred to the tin shop by the highly descriptive name Bang-All. There was no unemployment problem for the people of Berlin; twelve tin shops were recruiting workers in the early 1800s, offering special incentives and bonuses to skilled workers who could stencil or paint their wares. The japanning and painting of tinware proved popular in the early 1800s, coinciding with the vogue for painted furniture in the Hitchcock style. Berlin tinware value guide: tea caddy, rose motif, aged appearance, $330.

BETTY LAMPS. The crude-oil or grease-burning betty lamp reached the shores of America aboard the *Mayflower*. The earliest iron betty lamps were shallow cups with a spout or indentation for the wick at one end, and a handle or hanging device at the opposite end. Some examples had a link chain or tiny pick for freeing the encrusted wick. Those designed as standing lamps are rarities. This simple cottage lamp of the Colonial period was still shedding a bit of light after dark in rural and frontier areas far into the 19th century. The tin versions met with success due to their light weight and durability. A cover for the bowl or a base for safety were added features found on later models. Prior to the late 17th century these lamps often burned fish oil, which generated a weak light but a strong smell. After this date whale oil became the choice burning fuel as it increased illumination while eliminating the nasty odor. Betty lamps are also referred to as kays, judies or frog lamps. Betty lamp value guide: tin Ispwich, tall, $270; iron, hand wrought on 26″ trammel, $190; copper, iron hanger, 12″, $90.

BIBLE BOXES. Colonial carpenters, working with primitive tools acquired from the local blacksmith, designed small rectangular wooden boxes to hold a Bible or writing materials. The Bible box was placed on a table or chest, where it became a catchall for important family possessions such as jewelry, documents or books. New England craftsmen generally made them of oak with hinged sloping lids. Decoration consisted of carved flowers, foliage and lunettes. In Pennsylvania, where these small boxes or chests were profusely painted, they paraded under various names including gift boxes, treasure boxes and desk boxes. Bible box value guide: oak, floral carving on face and sides, circa 1670, $350; oak, hinged top, carved lunettes, circa 1780, $325; Pennsylvania, slant top, painted tulips and leafy vines, circa 1790, $425; pine, reverse molded cleats at top, New England, circa 1800, $220.

BIRD WHISTLES. The Moravians who settled in Bethlehem, Pennsylvania, in the mid-1700s are credited with introducing these pleasing playthings in their native land centuries earlier. The European prototype of this ceramic wind instrument is known as a Wasserpfeife. The potters of Pennsylvania made these museum-quality bird toys in sufficient numbers to transform any playroom into an aviary. All were brightly painted in eye-catching designs,

Birth certificate, Pennsylvania German, dated 1766

National Gallery of Art, Washington

some incorporating sgraffito or slip methods of decoration. The desired whistle was emitted by filling the toy with water and blowing into the proper opening. Bird whistle value guide: peacock, slip decoration, blue and gray, circa 1790, $650; hen, earthenware, slip decoration, circa 1820, $425.

BIRTH AND BAPTISMAL CERTIFICATES. When settlers arrived in Pennsylvania from Germany they proceeded to keep family records similar to those required by law in their native land. The birth certificate (Geburtsschein) and baptismal certificate (Taufschein) were two such documents, highly embellished with hand-colored lettering and drawings. These Fraktur records were preserved for posterity. A birth certificate contained the names of the parents, mother's maiden name, date, hour and place of birth, plus name of pastor or sponsor. This necessary information was gloriously enhanced with decorative symbols and creative calligraphy. Also included on birth certificates was the appropriate Zodiac symbol. The baptismal certificates were favored by religious sects practicing infant baptism. Earlier hand-drawn manuscripts were superseded in the 19th century by preprinted types, which are slightly less desirable to collectors. Birth and baptismal certificate value guide: birth certificate, Catherine Rudy, Lancaster County, 1812, stars, tulips, angels, framed, $750; baptismal certificate, George Gerhard, 1821, printed border, birds, flowers, hand colored, $375.

BLANKET CHESTS. This forerunner of the hope chest was introduced in America during the 1600s. Blanket chests were simply constructed, having short legs, lids that lifted and one or more small drawers. The Pennsylvania dower chest or blanket chest of pine, maple, walnut, oak or poplar gained favor in the late 1700s. Most were painted with quaint designs incorporating the name or initials of the bride and the wedding date; repainting or refinishing a dower chest lessens its value and desirability. Many fine early dower chests have a movable till inside the top of the chest, for they were frequently made without drawers. A blanket chest of the 1800s often had one or more drawers, or several false drawers. Their country makers favored pine and other soft woods, either grained or painted. The blanket chest fell victim to the Industrial Revolution of the late 1800s, when factory-made specimens far outnumbered their country counterparts. Blanket chest value guide: dower chest, tulip design, original paint, circa 1800, $3,200; curly maple, one drawer, bracket feet, circa 1830, $475; pine, original floral motif, bracket feet, strap hinges, circa 1840, $390; cherry, one drawer, lift top, bracket feet, circa 1840, $350.

BOSTON ROCKERS. New England chairmakers inspired by the Windsor chair developed the famous Boston rocker in the 1830s. A true Boston rocker had a rolling shaped seat curving down in the front and up in the rear to accommodate the body contour. The arms terminated in a downward curve while the legs were set on rockers extending from the rear. Placing it squarely on the Windsor family tree was the high back composed of seven to nine spindles topped by a wide crest rail. This area proved ideal for painted or stenciled decoration consisting of flowers, fruit or rosettes. Often a highly proficient artist attempted a rendering on a crest rail normally reserved for a canvas; he might demonstrate his decorating skills in the form of a landscape, patriotic figure, historical scene, basket of fruit or horn of plenty. Tampering with the original painted or stenciled areas instantly draws a cry of disapproval from art historians. The Boston rocker fell victim to mass production methods in the mid-1800s, when factory-made chairs filled furniture emporiums. Boston rocker value guide: maple, pine seat, stenciled top rail, striping, good condition, $260; maple, pine seat, refinished, no original decor, $165.

BOTTLES. Bottles were a mainstay of many early American glasshouses. The earliest free-blown bottles can be recognized as they lack uniformity, show bubbles or other imperfections and are without mold-seams. Blown-mold bottles were extensively produced in America throughout the 19th century. The novice can recognize those made with two-piece or three-piece molds by examining the mold seams. Some bottles made from wooden molds exhibit imperfections, known as "whittle marks," caused when the hot glass came into contact with the cold mold. All signs of handworkmanship disappeared in the early 1900s when automatic bottling equipment was developed. Some people prefer bartering for old bottles, while others content themselves digging for them. Frequently the diggers uncover finer specimens than the barterers. Bottle value guide: nursing bottle, "Baby's Delight," $50; bitters bottle, Cole Brothers vegetable, aqua, $30; figural bottle, Carrie Nation, clear, $28; medicine bottle, Fenner's Cure, amber, 11″ high, $27.

BOWLS. In the 1800s coopers and turners advertised a diverse selection of wooden bowls designed for items such as cheese, milk, grease, butter, spice, bread and punch, as well as washbowls. The earliest handmade examples carved by the Colonists of ash and maple are practically extinct. These wooden bowls as well as the later lathe-turned bowls were made in many sizes, ranging from several inches up to several feet. The round shapes are more common than the rectangular, hexagonal and oval shapes. The burl specimens always find an eager buyer, as do those crafted by the Shaker communities. A chopping bowl can be recognized by the deep scratches on the inner surface. Everett Moses & Co. of Michigan, and the Levy Wolverton Company of Mississippi, were among the prominent woodenware manufacturers specializing in bowls during the 19th century. Potters of the period did a healthy business in redware, yellowware and Rockingham pottery bowls. Bowl value guide: burl maple, 11″ x 6″, circa 1830, $195; butter, round, 22″ diameter, maple, $125; chopping, oblong, 9″ x 24″, $150; yellowware pottery, 10″ diameter, circa 1840, $50.

BOXES. Plain and fancy wooden boxes proliferated in America during the 1700s and 1800s. The earliest handcrafted boxes were frequently made of oak with covers and bases of pine; they can be recognized by hand-forged nails and inset bottoms secured by pegs. Cut nails with square shanks and heads indicate a date of production subsequent to 1800. Wire nails came into general use about

Left: Utility box, hand-painted, Pennsylvania, 19th century; Right: Brass trivet, high legged type, late 18th century

1880; therefore they suggest a factory-made example. Chip carving achieved by a chisel was fashionable in the late 1700s and early 1800s. Most boxes of this period had carved or painted motifs which blended with contemporary furniture styles. In the first half of the 19th century, when box makers favored pine sometimes combined with maple, birch, hickory or other native woods, the decoration became more elaborate. Able artisans lent their talents to decorating boxes with painted, stenciled or grained effects. After 1850 factory-made boxes supplanted the earlier handmade boxes, quickly making them beloved objects of the past. Box value guide: domed top, floral decor, original paint, 12″ long, circa 1830, $325; Shaker sewing box, Sabathday Lake, oval, $140; pantry box, original yellow paint, 12″ wide, 10″ long, circa 1860, $45; salt box, walnut, diamond shaped, $45; matchbox, handcrafted, animal decor, 6″ high, $35.

BRAIDED RUGS. Since the woefully neglected braided rug has failed to capture the imagination of collectors, it remains an undiscovered antique. This can be attributed to the fact that the braided rug lacks the pictorial quality inherent in the hooked rug. However, these round or oval floor coverings designed from unusable textiles deserve consideration. They were ingeniously crafted by cottage dwellers working under primitive conditions but determined to make their surroundings more livable. These floor-covering keepsakes were made from old clothing, army uniforms and assorted remnants, which were cut in half-inch strips and plaited into a flat braid. The manner in which the light and dark strands were placed side by side added immeasurably to the overall effect. They were warm, durable, comfortable to walk on and fairly easy to make. Who could ask for anything more in a homemade floor covering? Braided rug value guide: oval, blue, gray, green, 10′ long, 8′ wide, circa 1850, $350; round, assorted colors, 8′ diameter, circa 1840, $240.

BRANDING IRONS. The branding iron has left its mark on seekers of Western relics. Stamp irons or running irons with long poker-like handles were pressed into duty for branding livestock. As a general rule the American brands were somewhat less elaborately designed than Mexican examples. To discourage theft, each ranch had its own brand registered at the county seat. The blacksmith always attempted to make these wrought-iron objects tamper-proof. Most were forged in one piece, but occasionally wooden handles were used. Some brands simply utilized letters, or numerals, while others artistically employed hearts, anchors, circles and abstract shapes. Among the more unusual brands are the Lazy S, Hash Knife, Running W, Walking R and Flying O. Branding iron value guide: Lazy Y, $35; heart shape, $25; initials "C.A.," $20.

BRASS. This alloy composed of copper and zinc in varying amounts was an important commodity in Colonial America. Gleaming pieces of brass brought a glow to interiors, whether the object was made domestically or imported from abroad. From the early 1700s, braziers were advertising all manner of brass items shaped from sheets and brazed at the joints. Because they realized that brass was perishable, most workers also offered reliable repair services. Business drifted away from the village brazier in the post-Revolutionary War era when brass foundries sprung up like tulips in spring. These foundries worked overtime supplying brass specialties such as door knockers, furniture mounts, andirons and tons of kitchen and hearthside accessories. Throughout this entire period brass was being imported in enormous quantities; therefore, tracing the origin of an unmarked piece can be troublesome. Brass value guide: mortar and pestle, 5″ high, $80; pot, wrought-iron legs, handle, 16″ high, 10″ diameter, $85; kettle, cast-iron handle, 14″ diameter, $120; door knocker, eagle, $35; cake turner, wrought-iron handle, circa 1840, $50; dipper, iron hook handle, $35.

BRAZIERS. The brazier or brasier is a flat pan typically fitted with wooden handles and iron legs to hold burning coals in the hearth. In the 1700s and early 1800s braziers functioned as chafing dishes for those forced to complete their cooking chores on a wide hearth rather than on the more convenient kitchen stove. Food was placed in these open pans, also known as braising pans, to be warmed or broiled. Silver braziers were quite costly; thus the more moderately priced brass pans became country cooking companions. The copper examples are coveted. General George Washington was known to have tested his culinary skills with a brazier while camping at Valley Forge. Brazier value guide: brass with copper bottom, brass handles, 16″ diameter, 6″ high, circa 1830, $135.

BREAD BASKETS. These utility baskets crafted from narrow strips of hickory and thick spiral twists of rye straw beguile basket buffs. The Palantine German communities scattered throughout Pennsylvania, New Jersey and New York found a multitude of uses for rye straw. After a loaf of bread was shaped and wrapped in a cloth it was placed in an oval or round bread basket to rise. Once the yeast had performed its duty the loaf was removed from the basket by a wooden paddle, known as a peel, and set in a bake oven. The flood of newly manufactured breadmaking products marketed in the late 19th century did not deter the basketmaker from practicing his craft. Bread baskets served double duty around the holiday season when children set them by the fireplace on Christmas Eve awaiting the arrival of Kris Kringle. Bread basket value guide: rye straw, round, 16″ diameter, $90; rye straw, small, oblong, $60.

BREAD BOXES. Early household manuals stated that bread should never be cut until it was at least a day old. Between baking time and cutting time it was stored in a suitable container where it remained fresh, moist and protected from rodents. Bread cupboards of the 1600s were ingeniously designed to resemble small sideboards. They were set on legs and came with two or three cupboard drawers. This form was abandoned upon the introduction of the more practical rectangular bread box with a cover or attached lid. Some country crafted boxes were made by family members and were rarely ornamented, except in the Pennsylvania area. The plain and japanned tinware models graced country pantry areas for generations. Their popularity was threatened when colorful pottery bread boxes reached general stores in the mid-1800s. The delight-fully decorated pottery boxes employing sponged or spattered tech-niques became instant bread box winners. Bread box value guide: spongeware, blue and white, $85; tin, "Bread" painted gold and red on black background, 12″ x 16″, $60.

BREADMAKING ACCESSORIES. Nothing keeps the auction gavel pounding more vigorously than a group of early wooden breadmaking accessories. The turned wooden bowls used in knead-ing dough are constantly rising in value. The bakers of Pennsylvania generally relied on dough trays or boxes having removable lids and slanting tops. The dough was kneaded on the lid and set to rise in the trough portion. Some bread bakers preferred kneading or serv-ing the bread on wooden bread boards, which were available in round, oval or rectangular shapes. Those ornamented with naturalis-tic motifs or religious inscriptions reap highest rewards. For the persistent pursuer there are such fun finds as spoons and paddles once used to stir the ingredients. Dough knives to cut and shape the dough into desired shapes rate as attractive acquisitions. To move the loaves easily in and out of the oven there were long wooden peels, some measuring up to five feet in length. The peel received the seal of approval as a good housekeeping companion, and it was considered a proper gift for a bride-to-be. Breadmaking accessories value guide: bread board, Shaker, circa 1830, $130; dough trough, Pennsylvania, pine with legs, lift top, circa 1840, $260; dough knife, circa 1850, $45; peel, cherry, oven type, 48″ long, $80.

BREECHLOADERS. This type of firearm received its charge at the breech, or rear, of the barrel. One of the initial breechloaders to achieve prominence in America was the type developed by John Hall of Maine in 1811. This flintlock had a section of the breech that lifted up to reveal a chamber permitting a charge to be loaded. The Hall rifle became the first breechloader to be officially adapted as a regulation arm by the United States government. It was also the first one comprised of completely interchangeable parts. A later im-provement, credited to Christian Sharps of Philadelphia, was exten-sively used in the Civil War. Thereafter, the breechloader was widely used by the United States Army with various manufacturers supplying them. Breechloader value guide: Hall patent, U.S. model 1842, $560.

BREWSTER CHAIRS. Never before and never again were turned spindles employed so effectively as on the American-made Brewster chairs of the 1600s. This chair is named for William Brewster, an elder of the Pilgrim colony. It has rows of turned spindles on the back, under the arms and below the seat. Those found on the back and under the arms are generally arranged in tiers. Any chair having turned spindles below the seat can be identified as a Brewster-type chair. The earliest examples have heavily turned posts surmounted by ball finials. Chairs after 1700 usually had simpler turnings. These stationary armchairs were crafted by their New England makers from a combination of woods, including ash, hickory, maple and elm. Brewster chair value guide: hickory and ash, turned spindles, New England, circa 1700, fair condition, $2,500; Brewster-type armchair, New England, circa 1850, $525.

BRIDE'S BOXES. Gaily painted splint or reed boxes decorated with flowers, figures and verses were traditionally presented to brides throughout Europe centuries ago. Because many originated in the woodworking center of Berchtesgaden, Germany, they became known as Berchtesgaden boxes. Female settlers brought their sentimental oval bride's boxes with them to the shores of America, where the custom persisted. They were duplicated by American artisans with such accuracy that distinguishing one from its European counterpart can pose a problem. Documentation is easier if the box bears typical Pennsylvania motifs such as hearts, birds, tulips and geometric designs. A bride's box should never be altered in any manner if its antique value is to be preserved. Bride's box value guide: reed box, oval, figures and hearts, German verse, circa 1820, $475; splint box, flowers and figures, blue ground, circa 1830, $450.

BROOMS. The early settlers swept their floors with so-called Indian brooms fashioned from birch saplings. In the 1700s the broom business prospered in America, for broom corn was being grown in sufficient quantities to meet the ever-increasing demand. Itinerant peddlers earned their living by peddling brooms door-to-door. The Shakers entered the bustling broom business in the early 19th century when they were added to their list of available articles. Johnathan Constable, Jacob Walters, William Hall and Noah Urion were among the makers sweeping in profits from broom sales in the 1800s. The Highland Broom Company of Massachusetts and McLoughlin

& Diffendorfer of Pennsylvania competed for sales in the latter part of the century. Broom value guide: birch, peeled splint, circa 1800, $85; Shaker, circa 1840, $60; hearth broom, oak handle, circa 1870, $25.

BUCKET BENCHES. Provincial furniture makers residing in Pennsylvania made this kitchen piece from the 1700s onward. The bucket bench or water bench was definitely designed to ease back-breaking chores encountered daily by a busy homemaker. It held buckets of water, extra buckets, pails and dippers at a convenient height and within easy reach. The earliest primitive models were crudely composed of two or three shelves attached to upright supports. This form was superseded by a more conventional dresser-type arrangement having an open counter with a cupboard base to store extra buckets and other household necessities. Above the counter top were drawers for utensils and soaps. Since bucket benches were usually made of pine or maple, any constructed of cherry or walnut rate as rarities. Bucket bench value guide: Pennsylvania, boot jack ends, red paint, pine, circa 1830, $475; Pennsylvania, cupboard type, two shelves above counter top, walnut, circa 1850, $600; Pennsylvania primitive, three shelves, maple, circa 1790, $245.

BUCKETS. There were many village coopers operating in outlying areas by the early 1800s. Wooden buckets constructed with upright staves bound together with hoops became a staple item with these woodworkers. The handles were attached to the body of the piece by means of wooden pegs. Those hooped with narrow strips of wood are the earliest. When the hoops are secured with machine-

Maple sugar bucket, 19th century
National Gallery of Art, Washington

made nails, a date of production subsequent to the 1820s is indicated. Later iron bindings were generally employed, followed by copper staples. Look for signs of tool marks found only on the hand-made specimens. Dating one of these containers can be puzzling as they were subjected to vigorous daily abuse. By the mid-1800s such woodenware manufacturers as Gideon Cox of Philadelphia, Pennsylvania, and Henry Christhilf of Baltimore, Maryland, were instrumental in relegating "the Ole Oak'en Bucket" to national prominence. The men who manufactured metalwares joined the bucket brigade with a long list of buckets for various uses throughout the same period. Bucket value guide: brass, iron bail, 16" diameter, $75; copper, iron bail, 11" diameter, $60; wooden sap bucket, staved metal hoops, 10½" high, $30.

BUGGY SEATS. Have you tried in vain to acquire an early wagon seat? Why not consider a buggy seat as a suitable substitute? Unlike the wagon seat, the buggy seat was usually built right into the vehicle. Restoring one requires only a minimum of work by a handyman. After being reupholstered and mounted on legs they can chalk up additional mileage as country-type love seats. The seats from antique sleighs can be rescued from obscurity in exactly the same manner. Buggy seat value guide: restored and upholstered, circa 1830, $265.

BUILT-IN CUPBOARDS. The hand of the architect is truly in evidence on the fine built-in cupboards found in American homes of yesteryear. They were made to complement the paneling or other architectural features found in a particular residence. Since they were built into a side wall or corner as a permanent part of the structure, they were not movable. These one-part cupboards were made with solid or glazed doors hung with H-shaped, rat-tail or plain butt hinges. Since the piece rested directly on the floor it was made without feet or molded base. Early cupboards had diagonal fronts and molded cornices. Handwrought nails are an indication of an early example. Pine was particularly popular, often painted in a color to blend with existing woodwork. There were countless variations with many fine examples made from mahogany, cherry, maple or walnut. Occasionally a built-in cupboard is freed from its imprisonment and sold separately. Built-in cupboard value guide: corner type, diagonal front, open-front scalloped-edged top frame, three shelves, single solid door lower part, pine, circa 1760, $775; pine, open front, four shelves, two-door cupboard lower section, painted white, H-shaped hinges, 72″ high, circa 1830, $650.

BULB JARS. More than one casual browser has cast an inquisitive eye in the direction of the truly unique bulb jar. This jar, having a series of round openings over the body portion, was used in planting onion or crocus bulbs. As they sprouted from every opening they brought a needed touch of spring indoors on the coldest winter day. The bulb jar, or bulb vase, was always placed in a prominent position for maximum enjoyment. They were made by the potters of Pennsylvania, who decorated them with eye-catching peasant-type designs, usually brightly colored. The European prototype was the Swiss bolle-kessel, a metal pot hung from the ceiling on chains. Bulb jar value guide: red clay, yellow swirls, circa 1850, $165.

BULTOS. A bulto is a religious figure carved of wood treated to a base covering of gesso and painted. Santeros working in the southwestern section of the country crafted them from the mid-17th century onward. They were carved of cottonwood roots or pine by their anonymous makers. When carved of several parts, the bulto was pegged together and covered with gesso. If the creator wanted to suggest a draped effect, he usually dipped the fabric in wet gesso and sculptured it into realistic folds. Because most of the later figures were covered with fabric, the santero finished them hastily, reserving his major carving effort for the visible head and hands. Bulto value guide: crudely carved figure dressed in robe, small size, circa 1880, $215.

BUREAU BOXES. Handcrafted wooden bureau boxes vied for their share of crowded bureau top space in the 18th and 19th centuries. Plain and decorated boxes, usually having hinged lids, appeared in round, rectangular and oval shapes. Those originating in Pennsylvania were gaily painted with typical motifs, including morning glories, hearts and tulips. Some had the overall sponged or spatterware effect utilized on earthenwares associated with the region in the early 1800s. Regardless of origin, most artisans limited their major decorating thrust to the lid of the bureau box, often sponging or painting the remainder of the piece in a solid color. Commercially made collar and trinket boxes from pioneer manufacturers such as Aaron Dennison adorned bureau tops of the mid-1800s. Cardboard advertising boxes issued by numerous firms in the latter part of the century appeal to those addicted to American advertising articles. Bureau box value guide: Shaker, round box, original paint, circa 1860, $130; Pennsylvania, painted florals, sponged technique, blue, $110; snowflake collar box, circa 1890, $17.

BUREAU DESKS. The bureau desk made its American debut in the early 18th century and has never been out of production to the present day. Early types were typically crafted with three or four drawers, as the piece resembled a chest of drawers. They had slant tops which opened to reveal an inner compartment. In each succeeding period throughout the 18th century there were minor changes in the shape of the front, feet, handles and other details, as furniture makers endeavored to copy contemporary styles. Most makers showed their greatest versatility in the arrangement of the interior compartment: early desks had variously designed small and secret drawers, which appeal tremendously to collectors. As country versions developed, regional characteristics manifested themselves in bureau desks. Bureau desk value guide: Chippendale, slant front, curly maple, circa 1770, $2,300; Hepplewhite, slant front, French feet, birch, circa 1800, $1,200; maple, eight pigeonholes, four small drawers within compartment, four graduated drawers, circa 1840, $560.

BUTCHER BLOCKS. The butcher block once confined to the butchering shed is a real heavyweight in the country antiques field. Anyone who disputes that claim obviously has not tried lifting or finding one! They were little more than a slice of wood from a nearby tree mounted on legs. Based on current-day values, perhaps a choice cut would be a better definition. They were always left in their original condition by their owners of yesteryear. A scarred top surface apparently does not discourage the avowed butcher block seeker. When converted into tables they generate considerable conversation. Butcher block value guide: 30" wide, 26" high, 48" long, circa 1870, $265.

BUTLER TINWARE. The enterprising Butler family of tinsmiths and decorators served up a generous quota of collectible American tinware. Aaron Butler established his tin shop in Greenville, New York, in 1824. Most of his eleven children participated in the thriving tin business in one capacity or another. The Butler girls, particularly Anne and Minerva, became proficient at painting tin. They often signed their work with full names or initials. Attribution of an unsigned piece is possible due to their unique painting style. Larger pieces were brightly decorated with full-blown roses, tulips and other flowers, combined with cross-hatching, zigzag lines or similar artistic additions. The same designs were repeated, but simplified, on smaller items to make them commercially profitable. The bustling Butler tin shop closed in 1859 due to the illness of its founder. Butler tinware value guide: deed box, floral motif, signed "A. B.," $450; scoop, flowers, unsigned, $75.

BUTTER BOXES. The fine workmanship inherent in early butter boxes enables them to be listed among the better boxes by collectors. Although some oval examples exist, most were round, generally ranging between twelve and twenty-four inches in diameter. There were stave-made containers and others of solid winding construction. The staved boxes usually had odorless pine staves, bottom and cover. The earliest ones were secured with hoops of ash, oak or hickory. The staved containers were preferred as they allowed for the expansion and contraction of the moisture laden contents. The lapped box with either a joint of finger shaped laps, or a vertical seam was usually made of oak or ash with a bottom and cover of pine. Butter box value guide: pine, pine bottom and cover, round, 16" diameter, circa 1845, $80.

BUTTERFLY TABLES. The illustrious furniture makers of New England introduced this small drop-leaf table to the American public about 1700. The name is derived from the style of the table, which has one or more swinging solid brackets supporting the leaf. The brackets resembled butterfly wings, thus the name butterfly table. More than one bracket makes a butterfly table even more valuable. Although the style is usually assigned to American furniture makers, it was actually based on an earlier table popular in England during the Gothic-Tudor period (1485–1558). American-made tables typically have splayed legs, brackets extending from the top of the stretchers and a small drawer. Beautifully constructed butterfly tables of maple, cherry and assorted woods are cherished

31

by connoisseurs of country antiques. Butterfly table value guide: New England, one bracket, one drawer, maple, circa 1750, $1,800; American, cherry and maple, one bracket, circa 1760, $2,000.

BUTTER-MAKING COLLECTIBLES. All of the farm accessories once used in making butter are coveted by collectors. This includes the long handled scoops used in removing the butter from the churn. Shaker hands made the plain ones, while fancier examples originated in Pennsylvania. A semicircular butter paddle with a flat handle worked the butter once it had been placed in a tray or butter bowl. It was employed to remove the water from the butter working it into the proper consistency. One having a butter print at the top, or shaped like an artist's palette, earns the nod value-wise. Two round paddles known as Scotch hands rolled the butter into balls for table use. For packing butter into a butter tub, a small object resembling a potato masher, known as a tamp, was utilized. A butter spade or spatula removed the butter from the tub at the appropriate time. Butter prints and molds capable of making the butter look better are among the best in butter-making collectibles. Butter-making collectibles value guide: butter bowl, original red stain, large size, $75; butter ladle, tiger maple, 11″ long, $50; butter paddle, carved, yellow paint, 12″ long, circa 1830, $45; butter scoop, handcrafted, tiger maple, circa 1840, $40.

BUTTER MOLDS. The lowly butter mold, long neglected by serious collectors, currently delights devotees of American folk art. A century or more ago when practically every farmhouse churned its own butter, these carved molds in various sizes, shapes and patterns were an absolute necessity. They imprinted attractive and identifying designs on butter. There were cup-or-box shaped molds with plunger handles and collapsible box molds. On the plunger type the selected design was carved on the plunger face. New England carvers showed a preference for animals and naturalistic motifs. Regional forms dominated those originating in the Pennsylvania area where tulips, cows, crescents, pineapples and sheaves of wheat were among the distinctive designs. That symbol of patriotism, the eagle, landed squarely on butter as a decorative accent during the Federal period (1783–1815). Molds were carved from locally available woods such as poplar, pine, walnut or cherry. The lathe-turned disc made with or without a handle, known as a butter

Butter mold, tulip motif, circa 1830
National Gallery of Art, Washington

print, was a household favorite for imprinting a motif on a block of butter. Variations occur as some were cut in square or rectangular shapes. Butter mold value guide: eagle, Pennsylvania, circa 1810, $175; cow, circa 1840, $125; swan, oval, circa 1835, $70; heart, round, circa 1850, $65.

BUTTON RUGS. Rugmaking was truly a folk art born out of necessity, as commercially made carpets were a rarity in rural communities well into the 1800s. In outlying areas old stockings, worn-out blankets and clothing, plus assorted rags and remnants were recycled into floor coverings by thrifty homemakers. A homemade button rug of the early 1800s can be distinguished from other rag family rugs by the concentric small button-size scraps covering the background. On some rugs the background was visible between the cloth buttons, while on other specimens this area was filled in with sewn wool. Obviously, the humble button rug was a step in the right direction as it inspired amateur rugmakers to achieve even greater heights of creativity with the later appliquéd and patched rugs. Button rug value guide: small size, completely covered background, circa 1820, $225.

C

CABBAGE CUTTERS. When the dinner menu called for sauerkraut or cole slaw, a busy homemaker started searching for her oblong wooden cabbage cutter. The earliest cutters were quite sim-

33

ple, having one or more blades and a frame usually made of cherry. Some cutters came equipped with a boxlike arrangement on the frame for holding a head of cabbage. They were used in preparing sauerkraut. Commercially manufactured cutters operating on the same principle as the earlier wooden cutters were widely advertised in the late 1800s. They retailed from $1.25 to $12.50, depending on size and operating procedure. Two of the foremost firms counting cabbage from cabbage cutters around the turn of the century were Henry Disston & Sons and the T. & D. Manufacturing Company. Cabbage cutter value guide: wooden, heart design, Pennsylvania, circa 1840, $65; triple cutter, tulipwood, 28" x 10", circa 1840, $35; wooden, adjustable model, Disston & Sons, circa 1900, $25.

CALENDAR CLOCKS. As time marches on, so do collectors in search of calendar clocks. The term calendar clock identifies any timepiece having attachments for indicating days, months or years. Thus the calendar dials and indicators were always important features. Following the Civil War, groups of salesmen traveled about the countryside selling these clocks from town to town. Nowadays, not only the clocks but also the advertising pamphlets they distributed are of interest to antiquers. American firms marketed them in a variety of sizes and shapes. Among the foremost makers were the Ithaca Calendar Clock Company, Waterbury Clock Company and Seth Thomas. Doesn't that sound like a Who's Who in Clockmaking? Calendar clock value guide: Waterbury Clock Company, shelf type, double dial, walnut, $650; Ithaca Calendar Clock Company, 2 dial, H. B. Horton patent, 1866, $600; farmer's model, double dial, $440.

CAMPHENE LAMPS. The various kinds of illuminating fuel developed in the 1800s brought about necessary changes in lamp styles. Lighting by candlelight flickered into the past when kerosene and camphene came on the scene. Purified oil of turpentine and alcohol were blended to create the burning fluid known as camphene. It was perfected in the 1830s. Camphene achieved a bright flame but necessitated extreme caution on the part of the user, as it was highly explosive. Camphene lamps of glass, pewter, tin, britannia and other materials lighted the way in the mid-1800s. The tall wicks on these small lamps pointed away from each other. Many had metal caps connected by a small chain. Camphene lamp value

Candlebox, floral motif, Pennsylvania,
circa 1800

National Gallery of Art, Washington

guide: pewter, American, circa 1835, $245; brass, handled, American, circa 1840, $175; tin, circa 1840, $95.

CANDLE BOXES. Candles, a costly necessity in the 1700s and early 1800s, were carefully stored in narrow wooden boxes with sliding lids. The rectangular boxes, often of pine, varied in size, holding from several to several dozen candles. Ornamental candle boxes originated in Pennsylvania, where artisans carved or painted them in charming designs associated with the region. A beautifully painted candle box was frequently converted into a trinket box by the lady of the house. A box bearing the name of the maker or decorator is particularly salable. Sturdy Shaker candle boxes constructed with wooden pegs or dovetails were completely devoid of ornamentation. Many families stored a small supply of candles for immediate use in a tin candle box that usually hung near the hearth. These functional cylinders were always quite plain except for some occasional beading. Candle box value guide: pine dovetailed, sliding lid, circa 1830, $85; Pennsylvania, pine, floral decor, red paint, circa 1850, $165; tin, cylindrical, 14" tall, $140.

CANDLE EXTINGUISHERS. The sole responsibility of the candle extinguisher was to put out the candle flame. Thus it differed from the candle snuffer, which trimmed and cut the wick. This cone-shaped utensil had a long stem with a small ring handle at the opposite end. The ring handle enabled the user to reach a candle burning in a chandelier or a candle sconce. They were made of tin, pewter, iron, steel or silver. Sometimes an extinguisher was attached to a chamber stick or candle holder by means of a small chain. Even a casual browser can accumulate a representative collection of small candle extinguishers without exceeding the family budget. Candle extinguisher value guide: iron, small cone, ring handle, 7½″ long, $30; tin, small cone, long handle, $25.

CANDLEHOLDERS. The American-made candlestick or candleholder, whether of metal, pottery, porcelain, wood, horn or stone, tended to follow English styles. Many were spiked to hold the candle, but the type having a socket or nozzle into which the candle was inserted proved most popular. Some had ejector rods, or a slot for pushing the candle from the socket. A special type for holding small candles was known as a taperstick. The metal models made in various baluster forms had square, rectangular, round or octagonal bases. The balusters became somewhat modified on later examples. Early candleholders had the grease tray midway up the stem, but by the mid-1700s it reached the socket lip. By the mid-19th century, low-cost pottery and pressed glass candlesticks were vying for customer consideration. Candleholder value guide: brass, pushup, octagonal base, 10″ high, circa 1830, $85; brass candlesticks, square bases with pushup, 7″ high, pair, $60; tin, tole, saucer type with pushup, 6″ high, circa 1840, $40; tin, plain, pushup, 8″ high, $20.

CANDLE MOLDS. The tin or pewter candle mold lightened the long and arduous task of dipping candles by hand. These molds were originally housed in wooden frames. A mold could make anywhere from a single candle to eight dozen in a fraction of the time previously spent on hand dipping. The molds varied in height, with most models designated for home use making two, four, six, eight or twelve candles. The single molds were usually arranged in two straight lines. Circular molds are extremely scarce. Models capable of making candles by the dozens were designed for commercial purposes. Candle mold value guide: two tube, tin, $55; six tube, side handle, tin, $60; twenty-four tube, tin, $80; sixteen tube, pewter, pine frame, $360.

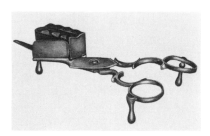

Candle snuffer, trivet base
National Gallery of Art, Washington

CANDLE SNUFFERS. The candle snuffer served an entirely different function than the candle extinguisher. It was used to clip off the burnt wick, thereby creating a brighter flame. Candle snuffers were in general use prior to the development of the hard candle, which was consumed by the fire of the candle itself. They were made of silver, gold, tin, iron or polished steel. Sometimes they were purchased in a design to match the candlesticks. These small wick trimmers had scissorlike blades with a snuff pan or box for catching the snuff on the top of the blade. After 1750 most versions rested on three small feet, and many came with their very own matching trays. Candle snuffer value guide: tin, with tray, tole, leaves and vines, circa 1850, $75; brass, scissors snuffer, pear-shaped tray, circa 1820, $55; wrought iron, circa 1790, $35; brass, scissors type, 4½" high, $25.

CANDLESTANDS. The accound record of a country cabinet-maker dated 1800 lists a "candle stan" for the grand sum of $1.50. The candlestand evolved in the early 18th century as a small table simply constructed, of a size suitable for holding a candle or a candle frame. Because the form remained virtually unchanged from its inception, accurately dating a country candlestand can pose a problem. The contoured foot heavily favored by furniture makers of the 1700s was gradually replaced by the flat foot in the 1800s. Tripod and screw-type candlestands, both innovations of the 1700s, were still being made by country woodworkers a century later. The "Weaver's Stand" candlestand, characterized by its T-bar foot, also experienced enduring popularity. A version of the formal Chippendale tilt-top candlestand remained fashionable in country communities long after it faded from favor in urban areas. When electricity replaced candlelight, these functional tables continued to grace interiors, and reproductions abound. Candlestand value guide: cherry, rectangular top, splayed legs, New England, circa 1790, $290; Hepplewhite style, cherry, New England, circa 1810, $285; Federal style, maple and cherry, tripod type, circa 1815, $280; walnut, S-shaped legs, hexagonal top, circa 1860, $230.

CANE-BACK ROCKERS. A rectangular or elliptical cane-seat rocker was often included as part of a cottage bedroom set by furniture factories of the late 1800s. Sometimes the caned panel was highlighted with carved flowers, fruit or foliage motifs. They usually had turned front legs and plain rear ones. The stretchers were plain except for the front one. When made of maple or birch they were usually painted or grained to match other cottage bedroom pieces. Those of black walnut and cherry usually retained a natural finish. Because the caned back proved fragile, it has often been replaced by either new caning or upholstery. Always strive to re-cane such a rocker when presented with a choice, as this retains its original appearance. Cane-back rocker value guide: walnut, original seat, circa 1880, $140.

CANE-SEAT SIDE CHAIRS. Scattered throughout farmhouses of the mid-1800s were simply constructed cane-seat side chairs. They were usually made with a single splat midway between the top rail and the seat. Such chairs could be found in almost any room of the house, often in matching sets of two, four or six. A scroll-cut finger opening frequently provided the sole decorative accent on the top rail. For maximum comfort the top rails were slightly concave, mortised into cyma-curved uprights. The front legs, usually turned in the manner of Hitchcock chairs, were gener-ally braced by stretchers. On most surviving specimens the seat has been recaned or is in need of recaning; this does not detract from the salability of a cane-seat side chair. Cane-seat side chair value guide: maple, replaced cane seat, circa 1870, $70.

CANNONBALL BEDS. Any bed possessing four turned posts each topped with a ball finial can be correctly classified as a can-nonball bed. The style won wide acceptance in rural communities primarily between 1820 and 1870. They were fashioned from local woods by country woodworkers, the form varying slightly according to region. The ever-present ball finials provide the distinguishing feature. A cannonball bed can have a matching headboard and footboard, a low footboard or a blanket rail at the end of the bed. The cannonball bedposts generally appear on low post beds, a type favored by country cabinetmakers. Cannonball bed value guide: cherry, Tennessee, circa 1830, $425; tiger maple, low post, circa 1840, $425; maple, twin size, circa 1845, $330; tiger maple, double width, circa 1850, $460.

CANNON STOVES. The free-standing upright stoves produced by New York and Pennsylvania iron foundries in the 18th century were similar to a type known on the European continent earlier. These cylinder stoves, which resembled the barrel of a cannon, were constructed so that the pipe fitted into the chimney flue. It was a familiar and welcome sight on a cold winter's day to find a cannon stove dispensing heat in a meetinghouse, church or public building. They were made in several different sections with the lowest one housing the grate and door. Cannon stoves were cast at the Elizabeth Furnace of Manheim, Pennsylvania, which was operated by that illustrious iron-master and self-professed Baron, Henry William Stiegel. Extremely rare.

CANTEENS. Collectors go marching off in search of the small wooden kegs or casks carried by soldiers in major and minor historical military conflicts. Although canteens did duty in the Revolutionary War, the War of 1812 and the Civil War, they are far from plentiful. Most canteens were round and fitted with bung holes by which they were filled as well as emptied. Often a leather strap was fastened near the bung hole for carrying. Most examples held three pints of liquid, but some larger canteens held even more, posing a weighty problem for the fatigued soldier. A skirmish is likely to develop over a dated or initialed canteen. These flasks for holding water or other beverage were also used by field workers or people temporarily deprived of a handy supply of water. Canteen value guide: handcrafted from log, original red paint, circa 1770, $110.

CAPTAIN'S CHAIRS. This 19th-century version of the 18th-century low-back Windsor ranked as a winner from its inception. Due to its unending popularity, it is still in production presently. The finely turned spindles on these chairs were enclosed by a horseshoe-shaped seat from a single block of wood. Legs were raked similarly to other early Windsor chairs, and were braced by either a single or double stretcher. In the late 1800s the captain's chair went commercial when scores of factories manufactured them for the masses. These chairs had wider backs and thicker spindles, but still generate plenty of excitement at local house sales. Captain's chair value guide: pine, circa 1870, refinished, $145.

CARPET BEATERS. In the closing decades of the 19th century, general stores featured a complete line of intricately designed wirework and rattan carpet beaters. One of the leading factories engaged in marketing wirework carpet beaters was Woods, Sherwood & Company of Massachusetts. Some wirework beaters had wooden handles. The buyer of such a carpet beater retailing for a mere twenty-five cents received full assurance from the manufacturer that the handle would remain intact indefinitely. Fancy rattan carpet beaters designed to reflect exotic Oriental influences appealed to restless homemakers who romanticized about exotic faraway places in the 1880s and 1890s. Carpet beater value guide: rattan, circa 1880, $22; elaborate wirework design, circa 1885, $25; "The Niagara Beater," heavy steel spring wire, $18.

CARVER CHAIRS. This chair was named to honor the Pilgrim Governor John Carver, who supposedly brought a chair of this type with him to America on the *Mayflower.* Carver-type chairs were made by numerous furniture makers centered in the New England area during the 1600s. The makers favored available woods such as maple, beech, ash and elm. They typically had triumphantly turned posts and spindles; the earliest armchairs were more massively turned than those crafted at a later date. The finest examples of these stick-type chairs had large turned finials on the back posts. The chair backs were composed of a single row of vertically placed spindles, set between crossed rails. Rush seats were preferred by many makers, although splint and solid planks also proved popular.

Left: Rabbit cast-iron lawn ornament, 19th century; Right: Chalkware angel ornament, 19th century

Both photographs, National Gallery of Art, Washington

Many Carver-type chairs presently rest securely within the confines of America's foremost museums. Carver chair value guide: armchair, turned spindles, curly maple, circa 1790, $4,500.

CAST IRON. Unlike wrought iron, which was forged by the blacksmith, cast iron was cast in a mold at the iron furnace. It had a high percentage of carbon, making it quite hard and brittle. Iron manufacturing became a major industry in the 19th century when cast-iron factories started springing up in major metropolitan areas. These foundries produced cast-iron creations suitable for interior as well as exterior use. Among the household items of growing importance in America during this era were such collectibles as umbrella stands, footscrapers, matchboxes, hatracks, and fireplace and kitchen equipment. Cast-iron furnishings suddenly came into vogue for either indoors or outdoors. Finer residences were treated to iron railings, fences, balconies, grillwork and other architectual attrac tions. Cast iron value guide: bootjack, beetle, $22; calf weaner, $16; door knocker, eagle, $24; kettle, gypsy, 3 legs, 16" diameter, $65; mortar and pestle, 8" high, $50.

CHAIR-TABLES. Dual-purpose furniture met with instant acceptance in Colonial America. As early as the 1630s joiners were busy making chair-tables, with pegged mortise-and-tenon joints. It served as a chair when the top was raised and as a table when it was lowered. In a chair position it could be placed against the wall or in a position where the raised top protected the user from chilly drafts. Chair tables of the 1600s were heavier and had square, round or oblong tops. A century later they were more humbly constructed, usually of pine with round tops and bases of maple or other hardwood. The demand for chair-tables far exceeds the supply, as present-day apartment dwellers compete for existing examples. Chair-table value guide: cleated top, New England, oak, circa 1670, $4,000; oval top, oak, New York, circa 1700, $2,200; round top, pine and maple, circa 1840, $850.

CHALKWARE. Charming chalkware mantel ornaments made in imitation of costly pottery and porcelain figures were in vogue in country areas following the Revolutionary War. Originally they were imported from Europe, but throughout the 19th century chalkware was commercially made in this country. The subject matter was limitless, the handpainted colors bright and gay; no one could resist it. The name chalkware evolved from its resemblance to chalk. Peddlers sold it in many areas and obviously found tremendous customer acceptance among the Pennsylvania Germans. So many pieces of chalkware were sold in this region that it is often erroneously referred to as Pennsylvania folk art. The earliest pieces were colored with oil paints; watercolors were utilized later. Many pieces were initially sold in pairs, but currently collectors appreciate finding even single subjects in good condition. Chalkware value guide: Indian statue, ceremonial dress, 22″ tall, $140; rabbit, sitting, circa 1860, $120; dog, seated, red, yellow and green paint, 9″ tall, $100; sheep, soft colors, 9″ tall, $100.

CHAMBERSTICKS. This type of short candlestick had a saucer-like base, or a shallow dish base. This large base was regarded as a safety factor since it not only caught the hot wax drippings but also prevented the candleholder from tipping over. Chambersticks of brass, pewter, silver, tin and pottery were lighting the way to bedchambers principally in the late 1700s and early 1800s. They remained standbys in country regions long after more modern conveniences had caused them to become outmoded in urban areas. Their small handles made them quite portable. Most had conical extinguishers attached by a chain, and occasionally matching snuffers. Chamberstick value guide: redware, J. Medinger, orange glaze, brown splash decor, $310; pewter, pushup type, saucer base, handle, unmarked, 4½″ high, $80; brass, square base, 4″ high, $70; tin, rectangular base, pushup type, japanned, $45.

CHANDELIERS. The wood, glass and brass chandeliers mentioned in Thomas Chippendale's *The Gentleman and Cabinetmaker's Directory of 1762* were most assuredly designated for proper city dwellers. Who else could afford these sumptuous lighting fixtures? Surely not the common folk in rural areas who could scarcely secure sufficient funds for a supply of candles. Those fortunate enough to own a simply made iron, wood or tinplate chandelier with a central cylinder and four arms for the candles were few and far between. Most of these locally crafted pieces hung in churches, meetinghouses or taverns. The painted wooden versions are extremely scarce. Some deluxe models had two dozen or more arms for single candles. The striking Spanish influence is reflected in the pierced tin chandeliers originating in the

Tin chandelier, six-arm type, 18th century

National Gallery of Art, Washington

Southwest. The arms were intricately twisted by able artisans who proceeded to ornament these tin lighting fixtures with tin fins, birds and flowers for a visually impressive reminder of America's Western heritage. Chandelier value guide: tin, hanging, six-branch type, $530; maple, intricately turned, four-branch type, circa 1820, $450.

CHEESE BASKETS. During the hot summer months when cheesemaking activities intensified, the neglected cheese basket was rescued from hibernation. These woven splint baskets of hickory or ash were essential in the days of home cheesemaking. Once the cheese was ready to be cured or seasoned, it was stored in a round cheese basket usually crafted with open hexagonal weaving. Some baskets with straight or tapering sides measured a full two feet or more in diameter. Their makers reinforced the tops with bound hoops. The Shakers, who excelled in basket making, found themselves inundated with orders for cheese baskets in the mid-1800s. Cheese basket value guide: ash, drying basket, $70; Shaker type, circa 1850, $65.

CHEESE BOXES. When cheese was ready to be stored or sold at market, it was packed in a shallow circular wooden box. Crafted in various sizes with tight overlapping tops, these boxes were customarily made of ash, hickory or maple. Large handmade nails distinguish a handcrafted box from a later factory-made specimen. Copper nails, machine-made nails or wire nails suggest a later date of production. Although the handcrafted and Shaker-made boxes rate best with box buffs, their scarcity has caused attention to focus on manufactured examples. Factory-made cheese boxes were often made of quartered oak and painted in a solid color. Cheese was

43

stored with ease in boxes provided by such woodworking firms as J. O. Miller of Ohio, Johnson & Graves of Pennsylvania and Layman Benedict of Connecticut. Cheese box value guide: hickory, round, small size, original red stain, $40; maple, round, large size, red stain, $55.

CHEESE DRAINERS. Any representative collection of early cheesemaking implements would be incomplete without one or more wooden cheese drainers. The raw curd was placed in this type of drainer during coagulation, permitting the whey to drain off. Some of the most primitive models were little more than boxes covered with crudely cut holes on the sides and bottom. Eventually a standard form evolved when rod-constructed square and circular boxes bore turnings reminiscent of Windsor chairs. The cheese drainer was covered with a piece of cheesecloth on the bottom, which acted as a strainer through which the whey passed. The drainer rested on a rack, called a cheese ladder, which was set on a tub. Sometimes the cheese drainer was combined with the cheese ladder as a single piece. The curd was now ready to be processed further in a cheese press, which drained it completely of whey. The first "self-acting" cheese press was developed by the Shakers. Cheese drainer value guide: wood, pine, round sticks with attached ladder, refinished, $145.

CHERRY STONERS. In the 1800s the United States Patent Office was besieged with new inventions for labor-saving kitchen

Below: Cherry stoner, cast iron, 19th-century; Right: Pennsylvania decorated chest-of-drawers

Both photographs, National Gallery of Art, Washington

gadgets. Many were issued in relation to improvements in the field of cast-iron cherry stoners. Each new patent promised to remove the seed from the cherry with a minimum of disfiguring or cutting. There were crank-handled and spring-driven models equipped with regulating devices. The Enterprise Manufacturing Company of Philadelphia, a leader in kitchen accessories, offered three models in a 1900 catalogue, retailing between seventy-five cents and a dollar and a half. Any cherry stoner bearing a firm name or patent date is particularly cherished. Cherry stoner value guide: Enterprise, cast iron, circa 1893, $25; "New Standard" model, circa 1870, $20; Rollman Manufacturing Co., spring-driven model, circa 1900, $25.

CHEST-ON-FRAME. This 17th-century innovation resulted in lifting the storage chest off the floor, which brought it up to a more convenient height. Many early chest-on-frames made by New England cabinetmakers displaying Jacobean influences were made in one piece. Eventually this was superseded by the two-section form. Some survival pieces reflecting William and Mary and Queen Anne styles were fabricated by country crafters working with limited tools and training. During the Queen Anne period (1720–1750) the upper case piece usually had four or five drawers of graduated size, the top one being the smallest. The frame section had curving cabriole legs terminating in Dutch or drake feet. Later, during the Chippendale period (1750–1780), the supporting frame had a bolder, wider skirt and shorter cabriole legs terminating in claw-and-ball feet. Chest-on-frame value guide: Queen Anne country style, maple, five drawers, cabriole legs, Dutch feet, circa 1750, $2,800.

CHESTS-OF-DRAWERS. The chest of drawers superseded the rectangular boxlike frame as a storage receptacle in America during the William and Mary period. The earliest chests of drawers were of stile and rail construction. Most were approximately table high with three or four drawers. The backboards were roughly planed and often show saw marks. Those crafted prior to 1850 were cut with a straight saw and exhibit a houndstooth pattern. A circular saw mark denotes a date of production subsequent to 1850. Early chests had one or two backboards of varying width and thickness. Those dating from the 1800s were fabricated with three or four backboards of equal size. The wider and thicker the backboards, the earlier the chest. A plywood back suggests a date of production after 1900.

45

Country versions always exhibited traces of the currently prevailing furniture style. Grained or painted soft woods were favored by 19th century cabinetmakers. Chests from this period were usually fitted with casters or wheels for portability. Chest-of-drawer value guide: Chippendale country style, maple, New England, circa 1780, $1,400; Shenandoah Valley style, walnut, 4-drawers, French bracket feet, 40″ wide, 39″ tall, circa 1810, $1,350; Federal style, pine, 5 drawers, circa 1810, $875; pine, 4-drawers, bracket feet, grained, circa 1870, $245.

CHILDREN'S FURNITURE. American furniture makers have been addressing themselves to the needs of minor family members since the Pilgrim period. The 17th-century craftsmen designed diminutive Pilgrim style slat-back chairs, Carver chairs, Brewster chairs, chests, tables and stools. The pieces they crafted were usually custom made, accounting in part for their present scarcity. Cabinetmakers of the 18th century advertised many articles made expressly for children, including Banister-back, wing and Windsor chairs. Any piece of Windsor furniture made for a child is a rarity, particularly highchairs and rocking chairs. In every period there was an attempt to fabricate furnishings for youngsters which would blend with existing styles. When Hitchcock chairs, Boston rockers and fancy chairs gained prominence in the first part of the 19th century, they were all made in smaller versions. There were also bentwood and wicker pieces, plus numerous potty chairs and highchairs of every description. Children's furniture value guide: Windsor highchair, firehouse style, $130; potty chair, walnut, lift cover, graniteware pot, $85; ladder-back child's chair, circa 1850, oak, $85; bentwood highchair, $60.

CHIPPENDALE CHAIRS. The Chippendale style, which had its origins in England during the 1730s and 1740s, first made its mark in America about 1750. Although formal furniture makers abandoned the style by the 1780s, rural craftsmen clung to the Chippendale forms indefinitely. It was a blending of three style influences: Gothic, French rococo and Chinese. Thomas Chippendale would have been duly impressed by the country translations of his furniture forms. Workers endeavored to imitate the cabriole legs with claw-and-ball feet, or straight legs, and the rounded or cupid's bow top rail, but all carving disappeared in the transition from town to country. There was a charming naïveté in their country construction of regional woods with rush rather than upholstered seats. Chippendale chair value guide: corner chair, mahogany, rush seat, open splat back, circa 1760, $375; cherry, pierced splat, rush seat, cabriole legs, circa 1770, $350.

CHIPPENDALE CHESTS OF DRAWERS. The straight-front chest of drawers inspired by the designs of Thomas Chippendale won everlasting popularity in country regions. It was crafted with minor variations well into the early 19th century. These chests usually had three or four drawers of graduated size, and were usually made of mahogany, walnut, maple or cherry. The drawer fronts with overlapping edges were usually fitted with keyholes. Many had willow plates with bail handles, or rosette-and-bail handles. They were usually supported by low and curved bracket feet. Slight traces of Gothic, French and Chinese influences appeared on some models. While formal furniture makers busied themselves with serpentine and bow front chests, most country craftsmen confined their efforts to the straight-front form. Chippendale chest of drawers value guide: cherry, four drawers, ogee feet, ball and bail brasses, 40" wide, 41" high, circa 1780, $1,100; maple, six graduated drawers, bracket feet, large size, $1,250.

CHIPPENDALE DESKS. The straight-front bureau desk of the Chippendale period (1750–1780) was fabricated in various sections of the country principally of curly maple, maple, cherry, mahogany and walnut. Some desks adhering only slightly to the details found on formal models were made in rural areas. The more elaborate serpentine-front bureau desk combining elegant decorative features was always the work of a skilled cabinetmaker. Among the distinguishing characteristics found on Chippendale-style slant-top desks were incised fan and sunburst carving, elaborate interior compartments, reeding, bracket feet and small drawers beneath the pigeonholes. The hardware consisted of brass willow plates, or rosette-type bail handles. Secret compartments and hidden drawers found on 18th-century desks had vanished by the 19th century. Chippendale-style desks in modified variations originated in country workshops. Chippendale desk value guide: curly maple, slant front, four graduated drawers, claw-and-ball feet, 38" wide, 43" high, circa 1780, $2,600.

CHIPPENDALE TRAYS. The curvaceous tin Chippendale trays originated in England during the Chippendale period (1750–1780). For generations thereafter these show pieces were assured of drawing gasps of admiration while adorning sideboards, dressers or walls. Since Chippendale trays were extensively exported from England to country areas, every acquisition cannot be designated as a piece of American country tinware. This style tray with its scalloped edge and sharp points was also known as a Gothic or Piecrust tray. It differed from the scalloped-edge Queen Anne tray, which had rounded points. Collectors compete for Chippendale trays displaying original handpainted or stenciled decoration. Those possessing Oriental motifs are breathtakingly beautiful. Many artists drew inspiration from Nature's wonderland, executing renditions of flowers, fruits, birds and garden greenery. Chippendale tray value guide: Oriental scene, original decor, fair condition, large size, $185; tole, fruit and flowers on black background, original decor, slightly worn, medium size, $125.

CHURNS. American farmers used churns of wood, pottery, copper, tin, stoneware and other materials to facilitate converting cream into butter. The earliest and best-known churns were the round, rectangular or barrel-shaped models, usually made of oak or cedar. These churns were manually operated by the energetic motion of the paddle. Rocking, swinging and crank-driven churns were introduced in the 1880s to ease this back-breaking chore. Copper churns were always expensive; therefore, they are rare finds. Stoneware churns, delightfully decorated with cobalt blue folk motifs, rarely go unnoticed by seasoned antiquers. Flea markets and country estate auction sales are super hunting grounds for those who yearn for an antique churn. Churn value guide: wooden hoops, wooden dasher, original top, painted green, circa 1820, $155; wooden cylinder type, three-gallon size, circa 1860, $80; metal, wood dasher, circa 1870, $60; stoneware, dasher type, cobalt blue decor, "White & Sons, Utica, N.Y.," $200.

CLAM BASKETS. Basket seekers would forego clams on the half-shell in lieu of a 19th-century clam basket. The square-shaped splint clam baskets generally had handles of hickory, usually nailed to the rim with tin supports. Hand-cut nails found on earlier specimens were replaced on later factory-made examples by machine-cut nails or wire nails. Sand-dwelling clams were gathered in containers made by The Select Basket Factory of Pound Ridge, New York; Robert B. Bradley Co. of New Haven, Connecticut; and Joseph Coddler of Danielson, Connecticut, among others. Clam basket value guide: splint, circa 1850, $50.

CLAY PIPES. Clay pipes were introduced to early American settlers by their Indian neighbors. A number of clay pipes were simply molded, although some had figural bowls. Those of 16th-century origin had small bowls, while later examples increased in size as tobacco became more plentiful. They were made from low-cost clays such as yellowware, stoneware, brownware and redware, often with stems of reed or willow. Moravian settlements in Pennsylvania and Shaker communities of New York State prospered from pipe-making activities in the 19th century. Those molded to represent political candidates, including Henry Clay, James Buchanan and Abraham Lincoln, win a vote of confidence based on their historical significance. Clay pipe value guide: wooden stem, 8" long, $15; Henry Clay figural head, $23.

CLOTHES DRYERS. When inclement weather conditions prevailed, wet clothes could be found drying indoors by the open hearth. A long clothes-drying bar which swung out in front of the hearth was known as a clothes bar, clothes crane or drying crane. A simply constructed wooden frame called an "airing horse" or "dripping horse" was another step on the tedious road to automatic dryers. Some clothes horses were of the folding type. In the late 1800s many clothes dryers consisted of a series of folding arms supported by a central frame. They were light, portable and folded easily for storing. A convenient folding umbrella-type clothes rack with sixteen hardwood arms weighing a mere five pounds sold for just ninety-eight cents in the 1890s. Clothes dryer value guide: folding-arm type, circa 1870, $55.

CLOTHESPINS. Collectors hung up on early clothespins prefer the sturdy hand-carved types of birch and pine. They often measure six inches or more in length. Since the clothes were heavier and the clotheslines thicker in the days of the early settlers, these crudely fashioned clothespins were subjected to vigorous usage. Those whittled in figural or naturalistic designs rate as rare finds. Lathe-turned clothespins superseded the earlier types in the mid-1800s. Many originated at the woodworking centers scattered throughout New England. A Van-Heusen Charles Company catalogue of the 1890s lists first-class clothespins bargain priced at eighteen cents per gross. Hand-carved whalebone clothespins crafted by seafaring men on long voyages for a wife or sweetheart delight fanciers of American folk art. Clothespin value guide: figural, circa 1830, $55; whalebone, circa 1850, $95; birch, 6" length, $10.

CLOTHES POUNDERS. The wooden clothes pounder is an oddity based on the principle of the modern-day suction-type plunger. These washday standbys were typically made with long handles set into round or square bases. To produce suction, their makers hollowed out the bases or drilled them with a series of small holes. Therefore, once the clothes had been placed in water, the clothes pounder performed its plungerlike action. As a general rule, most pounders were made of maple. One patented model was capable of dispersing soap suds through openings in the base. Collecting early clothes pounders can be infinitely more enjoyable than operating one. Clothes pounder value guide: maple, hollowed-out base, circa 1800, $90.

CLOTHES WRINGERS. When crank-handled clothes wringers reached general stores in the 19th century, a major step toward combating the Monday morning blahs was scored. The wringers with wooden rollers were the earliest. They were eventually superseded by wringers with rubber rollers. The models bearing a horseshoe trademark enclosing the initials A. W. Co. can be attributed to that industry giant, The American Wringer Company of New York City. Clothes wringer collectors will start some excessive hand wringing if the auctioneer offers a name model such as a Household, Superior, Novelty, Protection, Daisy, Vim or Conqueror. These washday favorites crank up considerable conversation as eye-catching wall decor. Clothes wringer value guide: American Wringer Company, Daisy model, $25; Relief model, complete, $30.

COBBLER'S BENCHES. These tradesmen's benches are desirable acquisitions for those striving to create a country atmosphere. Since the shoemaker earned his livelihood at the cobbler's bench, most remaining examples show signs of physical abuse.

These benches rate as true one-of-a-kind pieces and were usually constructed by their owners. A typical bench had a seat, drawers, bins and tool compartment. Some were simply made, although larger shops had stand-up, sit-down benches. Although the cobbler's bench serves no functional purpose, it warrants the interest of most country antique buffs. Surviving specimens are at a premium and fetch sizable returns. Cobbler's bench value guide: pine, primitive type, one drawer, rough condition, circa 1840, $330; pine, leather seat, three drawers, refinished, circa 1860, $600; pine, original hard leather seat, small type, circa 1870, $360.

COFFEE BEAN ROASTERS. Once able tinsmiths fashioned box-like or cylindrical coffee bean roasters in America in the 1700s, coffee drinkers multiplied at a rapid rate. Primitive roasting methods simply failed to capture the full-bodied flavor needed to create a satisfying brew. Coffee beans could often be found roasting by the hearth in round covered containers with tight lids. The cylindrical type evolved into a rather standard form having a long handle and sliding doors. The beans were rotated about in the cylindrical head with utmost care, as the amount of roasting time determined the flavor. When coal stoves were introduced, specially made coffee bean roasters of a size to fit into the stove top openings housed roasting beans. Coffee bean roaster value guide: tin, round, long handle, $95.

COFFEE MILLS. Once the coffee beans had been roasted, they were ground in a coffee grinder or mill. The plate-iron coffee mill

Coffee mill, store type, late 19th century

National Gallery of Art, Washington

operating somewhat like a spice grinder was in use in the early 1700s. The ground coffee was caught in a dish, but by the mid-1700s a drawer had been added. Others were made of steel or brass, often set on a wooden box having a drawer below. Frequently the cases lent themselves to japanned, painted or gilded designs. The United States Patent Office was inundated with improvements and patents for home coffee mills in the 19th century. There were newly improved table and wall models of cast iron and wood. The familiar wooden boxlike grinder with a metal hopper or cover was widely distributed. Larger table models for in-store use were made by such industry stalwarts as Enterprise Manufacturing of Philadelphia. Coffee mill value guide: counter model, two wheel, "Enterprise No. 12," eagle finial, $450; "Enterprise" No. 1, working condition, $150; lap type, tin, "Universal No. 110" model, $30; lap type, wooden pine base, brass hopper, $25.

COFFEEPOTS. America's first coffee house was established in Boston in the late 1600s, followed in rather close pursuit by the first American-made silver coffeepot. Straight-sided pots introduced in the early 1700s were supplanted by "single and double belly'd" pots advertised as the century progressed. By the 1800s fat round coffeepots were gracing country tabletops. The scarcity of pewter coffeepots experienced in the 1700s was corrected in the first half of the 1800s during the so-called "coffeepot era." Many pewter serving pots of the period followed the "Lighthouse" shape favored by rural tinsmiths, who left us a rich legacy of distinguished handiwork in

Pewter coffeepot, conical, ribbed, domed lid
National Gallery of Art, Washington

52

their coffeepots. Painted, punched and wriggle designs dominated their output. A wrigglework pot was sometimes stamped with the name of the maker near the handle. The bidding perks up instantly whenever a signed silver, pewter or tin coffeepot hits the auction block. Coffeepot value guide: tin, straight spout, original decor, leaves and flowers, bright colors, original, $950; tin, goose-neck spout, original floral motif, slightly worn, $350; pewter, Boardman, acorn finial, circa 1830, $460; pewter, Ward & Co., $165.

COFFIN TRAYS. These octagonal trays with narrow edges and cut corners resembled early pine coffins; thus they were nicknamed coffin trays. American tinsmiths served up a generous quota of coffin trays in the early 1800s. The size of the tin sheets imported from England dictated the size of the articles. These sheets, which arrived in Boston destined for the New England tin centers, measured 10″ x 14″. Coffin trays appeared in half-sheet, one-sheet and two-sheet sizes. A middle seam is visible on larger examples, indicating that two sheets were seamed together. Coffin trays were often made in graduated sizes, and all were decorated by the swift stroke of the artist's brush. The pleasing motifs had a homespun style inherent in 19th century country tinware. Coffin tray value guide: stenciled birds, fruit and leaves, black background, original decor, slightly worn, $150.

COIN SILVER. During the 18th century many coins were melted down to produce silver objects. The Colonists thought it safer to melt their coins and have them fashioned into a piece of silver, thereby reducing the risk of theft. The so-called coin silver popular in America during the early 1800s was totally different. It obtained its name because it had the same silver content as coins from the United States mint. Any one of the following markings may be found on American coin silver: "Coin," "Pure coin," "C," "D," "Dollar," "Standard" or "Premium." This mark indicated that the piece had 900 parts of pure silver out of 1,000. Most makers also included their name or initials within a selected shape. The word "Sterling" did not come into general use until about 1860. Coin silver value guide: water pitcher, John Targee, circa 1820, $425; cream ladle, Smith & Chamberlain, circa 1835, $55; teaspoon, fiddle-tip handle, Lincoln & Reed, circa 1845, $26; butter knife, C. Harvey, circa 1850, $25; sugar tongs, Edward Watson, $50.

COLT REVOLVERS. In 1830 Samuel Colt, a mere lad of sixteen, began tinkering with a new firearm design. After returning to the United States from a tour of sea duty, he proceeded to have his work patented in England and France in 1835. The American patent quickly followed in 1836. His achievement made the pepperbox obsolete. Colt's model with its automatically revolving cylinder when the hammer was cocked became America's original repeating gun. Despite the revolutionary concept of this firearm, his first factory located in Paterson, New Jersey, was a financial disaster. But the so-called "Colt Patterson's" originating at this plant are sure-fire sellers nowadays. Thanks to improvements suggested by Captain Sam Walker, Colt began manufacturing the "Walker Colts" with enormous success. Later his 1851 Navy revolver and 44-caliber revolver proved to be a shot in the arm financially for this famous inventor of firearms. Colt revolver value guide: Colt, 1849, pocket, 31-caliber, $700; Colt, 1862 belt model, $500.

COLUMN STOVES. These stunning cast-iron parlor stoves are characterized by two or four columns topped by a horizontal member. The two-column model, introduced in 1842, was followed in hot pursuit by the four-column version. Foundry catalogues of the 1840s and 1850s listed many fancy yet functional column stoves under various trade names such as Lyre Stove or Dolphin Stove. A two-column stove made by Low and Leake of Albany, New York, topped with a spread eagle, is truly a piece of Americana. A four-column Dolphin Stove made by Johnson, Greer and Cox is another cast-iron confection in this category. The earliest stoves had stovepipe funnels, replaced on later models by ornate cast patterns. Column stove value guide: Lyre model, circa 1850, $1,400.

COMB-BACK WINDSOR CHAIRS. From about 1760 to 1860 Windsor chairs were wooing and winning customers in many sections of the country. George Washington did his best to make the American Windsor chair better known when he purchased thirty of them for Mount Vernon. The comb-back introduced in the mid-1700s was a variation of the low-back chair with the spindles extending through the arm to the curved thin comb, or cupid's bow top. Most comb-backs were made with seven or nine spindles, the nine-spindle back being particularly prized. Some makers braced the back with two additional spindles for added support. They

Comb-back Windsor chair, 18th century

National Gallery of Art, Washington

went from the seat to the top. Following the Revolutionary War, the Windsor chair ranked as the most popular piece of furniture marketed in America. Therefore it is not surprising that a comb-back Windsor rocking chair was also made. Comb-back Windsor value guide: side chair, cupid's bow crest, saddle seat, turned legs, seven spindles, original finish, circa 1790, $565; armchair, seven-spindle back, saddle seat, turned legs, New England, circa 1800, $625.

COMMODES. Many collectors use the words "commode" and "washstand" interchangeably, while others prefer to differentiate between the two. A commode is a case piece with a closet or cupboard beneath the drawer, while a washstand is a stand with an open area beneath the drawer. The commode designed to hold a washstand set had a gallery piece or towel bar ends above the top section and one or more drawers under the top above the cupboard area. In the preplumbing era the commode was an essential piece of bedroom furniture. Early ones were fabricated by country cabinetmakers, but by the mid-19th century commodes were primarily produced by furniture factories. A style having a marble top, often with a matching marble gallery, proved enormously popular. Another version had a lift top with a cupboard door beneath. Commode value guide: pine, painted, cottage type, florals, splashboard, circa 1850, $235; lift top, pine, circa 1860, $170; pine, medium size, towel bar ends, circa 1860, $185.

CONESTOGA BELLS. The famous Conestoga bells are dearly prized by collectors due to their association with the westward movement in the mid-19th century. The historic six-horse bell teams used in hauling freight and families westward in the "prairie schooner" wagons were of the Conestoga type. Each team was equipped with a complete set of bells attached to a wrought-iron frame fastened to the bridle. These bell arches had five bells each for the lead horses, four for the middle ones and three for the two rear ones. Conestoga bells made the sounds that won the West, therefore collectors deem them best. Conestoga bells value guide: single arch, three bells, $205.

CONNECTICUT VALLEY SUNFLOWER CHESTS. Admittedly this is not the type of item one is likely to encounter in the marketplace, but a knowledge of this style chest can be beneficial due to its influence on other styles. While it is assumed that most surviving specimens are safely confined to museum or private collections, the possibility exists that one may appear unexpectedly in some neglected spot. These handsome chests were a specialty of cabinetmakers active in the Connecticut area between the late 1600s and early 1700s. There are several acceptable names for such chests, including "Hartford Chests," "Sunflower Chests," or "Connecticut Sunflower Chests." Peter Blin and Nicholas Disbrowe were two of the noted cabinetmakers instrumental in furthering this distinct decorative treatment. Most chests in this style were made of oak with pine tops and had two drawers below the chest area. The unique carving of stylized sunflowers and tulips on the front panels, combined with split spindles, ebonized bosses and other Jacobean themes made these chests unmistakable. Extremely rare.

COOKIE CUTTERS. Household cookie cutter inventories experienced a decided upsurge about 1800, when itinerant tinsmiths converted leftover tin scraps into cleverly designed cookie cutters. The earlier cutters were cruder, heavier and thicker. Their makers employed the soft soldering technique. Therefore, a shinier solder denotes a later specimen. Those having the cutting edge soldered by an almost invisible line are of more recent vintage. The deeper the cutting edge, the earlier the cookie cutter. Air vents stamped or punched into the backing are a sign of superior workmanship. The patterns range from pleasing to puzzling, with collector preference centering on those possessing Pennsylvania motifs. These holiday treat makers from Christmases past currently keep collectors happy 365 days a year. Cookie cutter value guide: Kris Kringle, $48; running horse, $30; tulip, $25; chicken, $15.

COOKIE PRINTS. Cookie prints are pursued by people fascinated by American folk art finds. These flat circular wooden discs were carved on one or both sides with eye-tempting motifs. Since cookies are synonymous with the Pennsylvania German communities, regional motifs manifest themselves in these folk art finds. Cookie munchers devoured the output with such gusto that they probably never noticed the bird, flower, fruit or animal prints. The oblong wooden blocks containing different sections known as gingerbread blocks or cake boards had a single pattern or a related pattern carved on each divided square. Cookie print value guide: cow, $40; bird, $30.

COPPER. Fine pieces of antique copper continue to be traffic stoppers at antique shops and shows. Coppersmiths were advertising their wares in newspapers of the early 1700s. They offered bedwarmers, weather vanes, coal hods, teakettles, stills, funnels, footwarmers and piles of pots and pans. Early pieces can be identified by seams, hand-riveted handles, hammer marks and dovetailed joints. Marked specimens warrant higher returns, as some workers marked their output with a name or address. Throughout the 19th century a potential buyer had the choice of either copper or brass utensils; both were made in similar sizes and shapes. Since raw copper is red in color, a highly polished object often shows a warm golden pink patina. Those possessing a green coating, known as verdigris, can be brought back to their original finish with a fine-grade commercial polish. Copper value guide: teakettle, gooseneck, dovetailed, $270; coffeepot, pewter trim, burnished, $80; hot water bottle, $65; funnel, burnished, gallon, $35.

CORNER CHAIRS. Innovative furniture designers of the Queen Anne period (1720–1750) introduced the decidedly different corner chair or roundabout chair. Formal furniture makers endeavored to corner the market on this group of chairs specifically designed to fit into a corner, but country carpenters quickly copied the idea. These unique armchairs have four legs, one at either side, and another at the front and back. The seat shapes vary from round to rectangular, while the chair backs are so low they only reach the armrests. The country-made versions were simpler adaptations of the formal styles. Woodworkers preferred such woods as maple, ash, hickory or other native woods; most examples have rush seats. Corner chairs succumbed to the rage for painted furniture in the early 1800s, when painted specimens emerged from country workshops. Corner chair value guide: Chippendale style, cherry, New York, circa 1780, $625; cherry, New England, rush seat, circa 1790, $475; maple, red paint, New England, circa 1810, $365; hickory, painted yellow and red, Southwest, circa 1870, $220.

CORNER CUPBOARDS. The space-saving three-sided corner cupboard was especially designed to fit into a corner. There were one-part built-in cupboards and two-part movable cupboards made by numerous American craftsmen with minor variations. Dating a corner cupboard can be baffling as similar styles remained fashionable for extended periods of time. When cupboards show influences derived from Hepplewhite or Sheraton styles, they may be dated with more accuracy. The majority of corner cupboards, except for the built-in types, were movable, so they could be placed in one corner or another as desired. Early examples had solid wooden doors. By the mid-1700s, paneled doors became fashionable. In the late 1700s, glass panes were quite small, becoming larger in the early 1800s. Molding and trim were less elaborate on early 19th-century cupboards. The lower section usually had one or two doors enclosing a cabinet with shelves. Those crafted from finer woods graced dining areas, while the plainer pine versions became kitchen staples. Corner cupboard value guide: pine, graining, two-door upper section, two-door base, raised panel doors, circa 1840, 7′ tall, $750; pine, two-piece top section, twelve-pane glass door, lower section raised panel door, original red finish, 7′ 4″ tall, circa 1820, $1,050.

CORNHUSK DOLLS. Toy collectors may find themselves competing with museum curators for cornhusk dolls, now acclaimed an integral part of American folk art. This age-old craft flourished in country areas where youngsters were unacquainted with the fancy imported dolls found in metropolitan toy emporiums. Homemade cornhusk or corncob dolls were ingeniously designed with the husks forming head, limbs and often clothes. The body of the doll was made from a corncob and the hair fashioned from corn silk, both combined with equal amounts of imagination. A crudely painted face, plus some scraps of clothing and, presto, another folk toy. Cornhusk dolls were shown at fairs and exhibitions throughout the 19th century. Many visitors to the New Orleans International Exhibition of 1884 returned home determined to duplicate the dolls they had viewed in utter amazement. Cornhusk doll value guide: mother with child, dressed, circa 1870, $90; peasant, dressed, circa 1880, $70.

COTTAGE BEDROOM SETS. As cottage furniture styles hit the hinterlands, the so-called cottage bedroom set became the mainstay in the late 1800s. Some were modified adaptations of Rococo Revival styles, while others displayed spool turnings. Their makers often painted them in various shades, including blue, white, gray, drab or a soft lilac. The hard, durable surface resembling enamel was enlivened on the finer sets with flowers, fruit or other suitable designs. Sometimes sleigh beds were featured in factory illustrations, along with other matching bedroom pieces including a bureau, washstand, side chair, wardrobe, table and towel rack. The number of matching pieces varied from maker to maker. Between the 1840s and 1880s painted cottage bedroom sets were offered with or without gilt lines and marble tops. Any set having its original paint intact wins collector endorsement. Cottage bedroom set value guide: pine, painted floral motif, original, seven-piece set, $1,250.

COTTAGE CHEESE COLANDERS. A mild type of cottage cheese called schmierkase was a staple item on country menus in Pennsylvania German areas. Local tinsmiths and housewives combined their sizable talents attempting to make the product as attractive as it was mouth-watering. Pierced tin colanders in which the cheese was drained appeared in heart, round, diamond and square shapes. As the cheese solidified it retained the shape and pattern of the mold. The all-over pierced designs executed with infinite care are lasting mementos of American folk art. Early examples pierced with old square-cut nails are heavier than the later specimens. Colanders were frequently footed. They were made with and without lids, with most types having a tab or wire handle for hanging. The tulip cottage cheese mold with a handled cover springs up infrequently on the antique path. Cottage cheese colander value guide: round shape, pierced pattern, circa 1840, $95; tin, pierced heart shape, Pennsylvania, 1840, $125.

COTTAGE CHESTS OF DRAWERS. Cottage furniture factories shipped these chests into outlying areas usually as a piece in a set of bedroom furniture. Quite often they were made from pine combined with other softwoods. Some had rounded front corners, rounded edges, plain or serpentined ends and a gallery piece. Most chests held four full-width drawers in the straight-front carcase. Factories offered them with more tiers of drawers, serpentined fronts, recessed tops, marble tops and spool-turned details. However, most examples had fruit- and foliage-carved handles, or mushroom-turned wooden knobs, along with inset iron keyholes. They were painted or grained, with some versions delightfully decorated with enchanting fruit, floral or landscape motifs. All styles bore one thing in common: they were fitted with casters. Cottage chest of drawers value guide: pine, grained, flower and leaf medallions on drawer fronts, circa 1860, $275; pine, painted red, five graduated drawers, mushroom-turned wooden knobs, circa 1870, $225.

COTTAGE CLOCKS. About 1845 a revolutionary change occurred in clockmaking. The coiled spring was being marketed throughout New England, selling for seventy-five cents or less. The use of coiled springs for power brought about the development of a smaller clock case. These small shelf clocks in various styles having brass movements were produced in ever-increasing numbers by Connecticut clockmakers from about 1850 to 1890. They were made in various sizes and shapes and are collectively referred to as Cottage clocks. Several of the larger factories were making them at the rate of 100,000 per year in the late 1850s. As prices become prohibitive on earlier clocks, collectors are taking a second look at Cottage clocks. Cottage clock value guide: New England Clock Co., eight-day time and strike, $165; Seth Thomas, eight-day time and strike, $175.

COTTAGE FURNITURE. This mass-produced type of factory-made furniture was popular in the Victorian period when it was featured in *Godey's Lady's Book.* Sara Josepha Hale, the distinguished editor, was influential in promoting cottage furniture. A

60

Cottage Furniture Department was instituted as a regular feature in this periodical in 1849, consisting of line drawings of cottage furniture. This type of simple utilitarian furniture was manufactured by many factories in modified rococo styles, or with spool turnings. Through the latter part of the 19th century, furniture catalogues featured cottage bedroom sets, tables, chairs, sofas and other items at affordable prices. Many pieces were painted, and those still possessing original decorations are desirable. The so-called cottage furniture became a category of country furniture. Among the factories flourishing from production of this furniture were Hennessey's of Boston, Gillies & Byrne of New York and J. W. Mason of New York. Cottage furniture value guide: bed, spool-turned, maple and pine, ¾ size, circa 1850, $375; rocking chair, cane seat, painted florals, circa 1850, $135; side chair, pine, painted with floral decor, original, $100.

COTTAGE MIRRORS. Frame manufacturers pleased their cottage furniture customers with matching cottage mirrors in the 19th century. These simply constructed mirrors could be found wherever a mirror was needed throughout the home. Many were painted to blend with existing cottage bedroom furnishings. Therefore, they are frequently found with one or more coats of paint hiding their original finish. They were typically made with a convex simply molded rectangular frame surrounding the mirror panels. Sizes varied according to the maker, with some larger models measuring 32" tall and 26" wide. The finest specimens were made of rosewood, walnut or mahogany, although some factories utilized pine, painting it to resemble a darker wood. Cottage mirror value guide: pine, painted white, 22" tall, 18" wide, circa 1870, $70.

COTTAGE TYPE EXTENSION TABLES. Following a successful exhibition of Cottage furniture at the New York Crystal Exhibition of 1853, many American furniture factories advertised extension tables. Despite the numerous variations, most dining tables had four or six leaves. Earlier examples dating from the 1840s were often made by skilled cabinetmakers. One of the earliest types was the pedestal table with a circular or rectangular top supported by a column having projecting cyma-curved castered feet. Later circular and rectangular tables with turned legs were made by factories from assorted hardwoods, including black walnut, rosewood and ma-

61

hogany. Some were stained while others had a natural finish. A buyer should always remember to inquire about the leaves, as they have often been misplaced. Cottage type extension table value guide: black walnut, circular top, 48" diameter, turned legs, two leaves, circa 1880, $235.

COUNTINGHOUSE DESKS. In *Familiar Rhymes from Mother Goose*, dated 1888, the countinghouse desk is pictured amidst considerable clutter. This was the fate it suffered at its height of popularity, when it was often called a storekeeper's desk. A desk of this type was often custom designed by the country cabinetmaker for a local establishment, varying in accordance with the needs of the owner. It was typically made with a full-width slant-top writing surface across the front and a flat-top back area boasting a varying number of pigeonholes. Small drawers were often included beneath the slant top and down either side of these abnormally high pieces. Their height necessitated the user to sit on a high stool rather than a seat while probing through piles of paperwork. Countinghouse desk value guide: pine and maple, New England, circa 1820, $525.

COUNTRY STORE COLLECTIBLES. Practically every fixture and colorful container once used or sold in an old-fashioned country store has become a sought-after collectible. There are thousands of collectors willing to part with money at the sight of a store cabinet, bin, ceiling fan, counter, tobacco cutter, coffee grinder, sign, scale, sack, pail or other in-store item. Those having interesting advertising information regarding a product are treasured. The Clark's O.N.T., Willimatic, or J. P. Coats spool thread cabinets are extremely salable, as are the Peerless or Diamond Dyes cabinets. All the fancy packages and containers which once lined a country store shelf are on view every weekend year-round at local flea markets. With a bit of luck and adequate financing, it is possible to re-create your own country store—exactly what many people are doing. Country store collectibles value guide: cabinet, tin, Diamond Dyes, children with balloon decor, $250; tin bin, roll top, "Co. Yel. Meal," original red decor, $210; ceiling fan, wooden blades, $125; cabinet, Clark's O.N.T. spool thread, two drawers, $150.

COURT CUPBOARDS. The impressive court cupboard ranks as one of the most important forms made in America during the 17th century. This low rectangular cupboard possessing Jacobean details had an open shelf below or above the storage area. Decoration consisted of low-relief carved panels and applied ornamentation in the form of ebonized bosses, split spindles and ovals. Those originating in New England were usually made of oak with pine shelves. Southern craftsmen showed a preference for southern yellow pine as the secondary wood. This piece provided a storage or display area for family treasures or household goods. Only the wealthiest families could afford a court cupboard, contributing to their present scarcity. Thomas Dennis, the English-born carver and joiner working in New England in the 1600s, excelled in crafting these cupboards. Extremely rare.

COURTING MIRRORS. Since these elegant mirrors were frequently presented by suitors to young maidens, they are appropriately named courting mirrors. The earliest examples were imported from China and Northern European countries in the 18th century. The Oriental versions were usually made of camphorwood. These small-size mirrors can be recognized by the delicately handpainted glass bands enclosed by beaded moldings along the outer and inner edge. A treasured courting mirror was generally encased in a protective box, with the lid removed, and hung on the wall. American woodworkers imitated the imported courting mirrors, creating them from such woods as maple, pine and cherry. The coveted courting mirror has entered the "now you see them, now you don't" category. Courting mirror value guide: Oriental, camphorwood, painted panels, original box, $650; American, painted panels, circa 1830, $475.

COVERLETS. Some coverlets were made by homemakers, others by professional weavers. There were several different techniques employed by their makers, notably the double woven, overshot, or summer and winter weave. Because of the small size of the loom, they were woven in two or more strips and sewn together when completed. Early types were woven from homespun and home-dyed yarns. Most were woven in two or three colors, such as blue and white, green and white or red and white. Geometric patterns were favored for American coverlets, many based on traditional European designs. Many had geographical or historical names, including Tennessee Flower, London Beauty, Indian Wars and Federal City. True Lover's Vine, Wheel of Fortune, Rose in the Bush and Young

Coverlet, patriotic motif, dated 1842

National Gallery of Art, Washington

Man's Delight were among the more romantic-sounding names. About 1820 the flowered coverlets, sometimes referred to as Jacquard coverlets, supplanted earlier types. Coverlet value guide: geometric pattern, overshot, red, white and blue, circa 1830, $275; peacocks and flowers, with floral border, blue, green and white, full size, circa 1840, $300.

COWBELLS. The earliest small cowbells were often the work of the village blacksmith, but by the 19th century they were being commercially produced. According to legend, cows are so enamored of sweet-sounding bells that they respond by delivering more milk. Whether this spurred additional bell business is debatable, but many New England firms were busy making sheet metal cowbells in various sizes with metal or bone clappers. Any Holstein bell made by the Blum Manufacturing Company bearing its original paper label is a fortunate find, as is any other labeled cowbell. The famous Bevin Brothers of East Hampton, Connecticut, began marketing their long-distance and Kentucky cowbells in the 1830s. Many cowbells of New England origin had a riveted vertical side and were made of sheet metal plated in brass. Cowbell value guide: brass with leather strap, 4½″ tall, $20; iron, 5″ tall, $15.

COWBOY COLLECTIBLES. The romance of the Old West lures collectors to accumulate cowboy equipment and gear. Interest continues to mount on items in this category, particularly on items of late 19th-century origin. Among the brisk-selling articles are cowboy shirts, bandanas, hats, gauntlets, holsters, belts, chaps, overalls, spurs and other regalia. Horse trappings and other accessories of ranch life or cattle tending are among the fun finds encountered along the flea market trail. Often the blacksmith, leathersmith and silversmith combined their efforts to craft elaborate and expensive accouterments. To a cowboy such gear was considered a status symbol; many prided themselves on their personal attire. Some of the items that won the West and currently win the hearts of collectors are saddles, saddlebags, bridles, bits, spurs, rawhide bottles, stirrups and reins. Cowboy collectibles value guide: bandana, colorful, circa 1870, $50; iron bit and mouthbar, silver overlay decor, circa 1880, $170; spurs, decorated leather straps, $145.

COW CREAMERS. Considerable controversy surrounds the Rockingham cow creamer, which was a familiar sight on 19th-century tabletops. Practically every find in this category is automatically attributed to the potters of Bennington, Vermont. But, alas, dozens of other American and English potters produced them in similar sizes and shapes. Unfortunately, they were rarely marked in any manner. Long after the close of the United States Pottery Company of Bennington in 1858, cow creamers were still shipped into the area from potters near and far. A true Bennington cow creamer has well-defined nostrils, delicately molded eyes, shallow ribs and a plump, almost bloated body. Should a cow creamer meet these specifications, perhaps it was indeed Bennington born. Cow creamer value guide: Bennington, brown glaze, $335; Flint enamel, $465.

CRADLES. Since cradles have been known for centuries, it is not surprising that early Pilgrim models with paneled sides and turned spindles abide in museum collections. Although styles varied only slightly over the centuries, there was some attempt on the part of cradle makers to craft them in a manner to blend with contemporary designs. Most cradles have a hood or cover to keep baby draft-free. Wicker cradles have been favorites with the lullaby set since the 1600s. Many Windsor-style cradles appeared during the craze for Windsor chairs in the 18th century. A cradle constructed to be hung on a post, known as a "swinging crib bed," appeared during the Queen Anne period. A sleigh cradle imitative of the sleigh bed held swingers of the 1830s. Painted or stenciled motifs and heart-shaped finger holds were characteristics of Pennsylvania cradles. Cradle value guide: pine, painted with grained pattern, hanging type, circa 1830, $300; pine, painted green with florals, hooded type, circa 1840, $340; sleigh cradle, mahogany, New England, circa 1840, $330; cottonwood, dovetailed, side hand holes, Pennsylvania, circa 1850, $290.

CRAZY QUILTS. The traditional patchwork quilt of the 17th and 18th centuries was revived with vigor in the mid-19th century in the form of a Crazy quilt. The technique was similar to the earlier patched covers, with small irregular-shaped pieces appliquéd to a foundation fabric. On these later quilts, seams were covered with embroidery, such as feather stitching. Very often the patch itself had a design embroidered or painted on it. Makers relied on bits and pieces of brocade, velvet, silk or satin accumulated by the homemaker from various sources. Crazy quilts proved somewhat impractical as bed coverings; therefore many were transformed into coverings for couches, pianos or other furniture. Crazy quilt value guide: fan pattern, necktie silks, black background, circa 1880, $155; multicolored quilt, dated 1885, $140.

CREEPERS. The focal point of a Colonial interior was the fireplace about which family life centered. Some fireplace equipment was custom designed by a local blacksmith or brass worker. A pair of small andirons known as creepers were familiar hearthside accessories. They rested in the grate between a taller pair of andirons. Creepers were typically made with short shafts. Busy cooks transformed them into auxiliary cooking accouterments, as they proved ideal for supporting a pot or pan. As a pair, they held a small spit, sending a tempting assortment of cooking aromas wafting through the air. They creeped into popularity when andirons became too costly for people of average means. Creeper value guide: wrought iron, plain shafts, ball finials, circa 1790, $185.

CRESSETS. Considering the number of modern-day conveniences at our fingertips, it is difficult to imagine some of the primitive lighting devices utilized by early settlers. One such open lamp, called a cresset, was a metal fork or framework of a size to hold a resin-soaked rope or resin-filled pine blank. The cresset was a variation of the firebasket. For indoor use there were small cresset light holders with short handles or bases. To provide a bit of light after dark outdoors, the cresset had a long handle or was attached to a pole. This lighted the path for a pedestrian or furnished a small amount of illumination for a hunter, fisherman or outdoorsman. Cressets could be found perched atop a coach for nighttime travelers. The term "cresset andiron" is applied to an andiron with a basket top on the front post of a size to hold a cresset light. Cresset value guide: wrought iron, 18th century, $160.

CRICKET STOOLS. These small stools or seats were customarily found near the hearth in the 1700s and early 1800s, thus the name cricket stool is most appropriate. The word is supposedly derived from the term "crice," meaning crutch. Children warmed themselves by the hearth on cricket stools or climbed atop them to reach upward toward forbidden territory, more specifically, the cookie container. The cricket stool obviously knew no age barrier as the elderly converted them into kneeling stools for church services. When country woodworkers of the late 1800s crafted three-legged stools, they were affectionately known as cricket tables out of deference to the earlier cricket stools. Finding an early cricket stool is really something to chirp about. Cricket stool value guide: maple, 18th century, $130.

CROCKS. Simple utilitarian crocks of redware, brownware or stoneware proved invaluable for storing liquids, preserves, pickled delicacies and other foodstuffs. Early gracefully shaped redware crocks and jars were made in various sizes. Later straight-sided shapes became fashionable, usually with solid durable handles. Strong stoneware crocks and jars enjoyed widespread use in the 19th century. They came in numerous shapes and sizes, ranging up to thirty gallons in capacity. Some were bellied out in the center, although most were straight-sided. Eagerly acquired are those having the potter's trademark or a date impressed into the clay. Larger pieces lent themselves to surface decoration in the form of stenciling, incising, scratching or handpainted cobalt blue motifs. Country antique dealers are constantly staging a losing battle over maintaining their fine stock of antique crocks. Crock value guide: stoneware, Shenfelder, Reading, Pennsylvania, floral decor, six gallons, $200;

stoneware two-handle type, blue slip decor, three gallons, $120; redware, Smith, Womelsdorf, Pennsylvania, 5″ tall, $100.

CROMWELLIAN FURNITURE. American Cromwellian furniture forms were inspired by English styles dating from Cromwell's regime (1649–1660). As usual it took several decades for the influence to be acknowledged by Colonial craftsmen. Although the spiral rope and twisted turnings met with enormous acceptance in England, they failed to stimulate either cabinetmakers or customers on this side of the Atlantic to any degree. However, there was a limited amount of square-backed pieces having turkey or leatherwork upholstery. Furniture makers replaced oak with more adaptable woods such as pine, maple or walnut. Admittedly, this museum quality furniture is rarely encountered by the casual antiquer outside the walls of a museum. Cromwellian furniture value guide: chair, maple, oak stretchers and seat rails, leather back and square seat, turned legs, circa 1700, fair condition, $1,400.

CURD BREAKERS. Knowledgeable home cheesemakers realized that the dried stomach lining of a young calf, known as rennet, managed to curdle milk or cream rather rapidly. The process involved dissolving rennet in warm water and mixing the fluid with cream or milk. The mixture was patiently turned with a wooden paddle until coagulation resulted. A curd knife was sometimes employed to cut or break the firm curds. However, the wooden curd breaker with inner teeth activated by a crank handle managed to do the job more effectively. These labor-saving devices became obsolete once cheesemaking activities became limited to commercial dairies. Curd breaker value guide: wooden box, inner teeth, crank handle, $135.

D

DATE STONES. The settlers of Pennsylvania perpetuated a charming Rhenish custom of inserting a wood or stone date marker into the wall to commemorate the building of a house. Every peas-

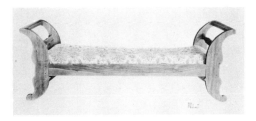

Day bed, Southwestern characteristics

National Gallery of Art, Washington

ant settler worked toward the day when he would own his own home. The date stone presented him with the opportunity to celebrate the occasion with a permanent memento. The stone carver was able to test his talents by cutting these markers with the owner's name or initials and a date. Frequently he exhibited additional skills in the form of folk motifs, symbols or a house blessing. Sometimes a pair of stones commemorated the happy occasion, carrying the names or initials of both husband and wife. These marvelous markers were also visible in the walls of other buildings such as churches, barns, schools and mills. Extremely rare.

DAY BEDS. The American rendition of the day bed first appeared in the mid-1600s in the form of an elongated bench having multiple legs and an angled stationary or adjustable back. This piece for lulling, sitting or sleeping is presently known by the French "chaise lounge." Splat backs became stylish during the William and Mary period, when most day beds had caned, heavy canvas or rush seats and turned legs and stretchers. A vase splat back and cabriole legs denotes an example having Queen Anne characteristics. During the Chippendale period the vase splat back was subjected to piercing, top rails had a cupid's bow, and legs terminated in claw-and-ball feet. Following the Chippendale period, the day bed retired temporarily from prominence, returning as a sophisticated couch as shown in Thomas Sheraton's manuals. Day bed value guide: maple, vase splat back, turned legs, rush seat, circa 1740, $2,300; walnut, vase splat back, cabriole legs, adjustable back, rush seat, circa 1760, $2,650.

DEACON'S BENCHES. The town meeting or deacon's bench is a plainer member of the settee family. It was customarily made with a spindle back beneath a wide rail, and a curved piece above the arm spindles. This style bench made in various sections of the country was either painted or left in a natural finish. Many factories engaged in manufacturing plank-bottom chairs added them to production schedules in the mid-19th century. The mass-produced versions supported by four or eight legs often measured up to eight feet in length. The backs were made in varying styles, matching plank-bottom chair backs. They often submitted to the same type of painted decoration reserved for the "fancy chairs" of the era. Deacon's bench value guide: pine, stenciled fruit and flowers, original decor, 7' 6" long, circa 1840, $225; maple, pine seat, 7' long, $175.

DECORATED TINWARE. The vogue for decorated tinware in America coincided with the rage for painted furniture. This so-called "country tin" was at its peak of popularity in the first half of the 19th century. Attend any auction sale when a piece is offered and you will realize its importance with collectors. Inexpensive tinware with a modest amount of ornamentation was called painted tin. More expensive pieces were known as japanned wares, while elaborately decorated objects were referred to as tole. Some early tinware was handpainted, but later stenciling became widespread. Japanning was a process of imitating Oriental lacquered effects by coating a piece with asphaltum varnish, then heat-drying it to create a lustrous finish. The piece was then ready to be decorated. There were numerous tin centers scattered throughout New England, New York and Pennsylvania, where artists busied themselves using colors derived from earthy substances. Regional characteristics are manifested in American decorated tinware, making attribution possible. Decorated tinware value guide: watering can, floral motif, original, circa 1825, $290; apple tray, stenciled florals, circa 1840, $285; oval tray, stenciled birds, fruits, leaves, medium size, circa 1845, $325; syrup pitcher, handpainted floral forms, brown background, slightly worn decor, $260.

DECOYS. These wood, metal, canvas, rubber or papier-mâché deceivers used in luring fowl within gunshot range date back to the period when America was inhabited by the Indians. As early as the 1790s, legislation was enacted protecting game by inaugurating closed seasons. It was during the 19th century that wooden carved, turned and painted decoys became a minor folk art. These small whittled forms resembling ducks, geese and other waterfowl were so cleverly crafted as to fool fowl and bird watchers alike. Those of 19th-century origin show a high degree of originality, plus signs of wear that distinguish them from their modern counterparts. Decoy value guide: mallard, drake, red-breasted, early, Long Island, original paint, $190; plover, black-bellied, New Jersey, original paint, $160; Canadian goose, handcarved, glass eyes, original finish, circa 1880, $125.

DERRINGERS. Henry Deringer of Philadelphia abandoned work on rifles and dueling pistols about 1825 to concentrate on pocket pistols. The pocket-size percussion pistols he developed ranged in length from 3¾ inches to 9 inches. Since their size made them easy to conceal, they enjoyed tremendous popularity. Soon any short pistol was being called a deringer, or derringer. Unscrupulous competitors attempting to derive financial benefits from Deringer's pistol used his name or close resembling names such as Beringer on some small pocket pistols of the period. Surely even Henry's heart must have been troubled when he read the headlines concerning the assassination of Abraham Lincoln by John Wilkes Booth with one of his pistols. Derringer value guide: pocket pistol, $525; Derringer, model 1843, $575.

DESK BOXES. Prior to the 18th century the word "desk" was used to describe a wooden box designed to hold writing materials or the family Bible. Slope-front, slant-top or flat boxes were made with painstaking care and usually ornamented with carved motifs based on Jacobean themes. Many boxes were made of oak or pine, used either singly or together. This piece was usually placed on a table or chest, thereby lifting it to a more convenient height. Rare dated or initialed specimens have been located but are generally found only in museum collections. Sometimes a desk box or book box will show faint traces of its original paint, pleasing collectors enormously.

Desk box, carved, late 17th century

National Gallery of Art, Washington

Desk boxes enjoyed a revival in the 19th century when they were called lap desks or field desks. The more elaborate examples dating from this period were made of mahogany. However, even the crudely crafted country desks of maple and walnut prompt the appearance of such writing materials as a pen and checkbook. Desk box value guide: mahogany, detailed interior, circa 1770, $265; pine, original red paint, slant cover, two interior drawers, $220.

DESK-ON-FRAMES. A major development toward the modern-day desk was recorded when the desk-on-frame was introduced during the William and Mary period (1685–1720). This was an enlarged desk box, writing box or Bible desk set on a topless frame. Many boxes were supported on frames having four turned legs connected by four stretchers of similar design. Although the country versions were rarely ornamented, the form varied slightly, depending on the skill of the maker and the region. Some prized New England examples were painted red on the exterior and blue on the interior. Maple, pine, walnut, gumwood and tulipwood were among the woods used singly or in combinations. Desk boxes having slanting tops or sloping lids were favored, although some flat-top boxes were also utilized. The sloping lid often served as the writing surface, opening to reveal a compartment for writing materials. Any example with a lip-molded edge suggests a date of production subsequent to 1720. Desk-on-frame value guide: walnut, New England, slant front, detailed interior compartment, cabriole legs, Dutch feet, circa 1760, $2,400.

DESKS. In America this was originally a box for books or writing materials, known as a Bible box or desk box. It functioned as a desk when placed on a stand or table. This gave rise to the desk-on-frame form usually composed of a slanting lid or sloping front set on a matching frame. In the early 18th century the well-known bureau desk evolved as a major form along with the secretary bookcase. These two forms appeared in virtually every known American furniture style of the 18th and 19th centuries. The simplest versions, devoid of extensive cabinetmaking details, emerged from country workshops. Country adaptations never adhered to any particular formula, varying according to the skills of the maker. Local woods were utilized. Kneehole desks were introduced about 1750. The standard type slope front or slant top was joined by other writing surfaces toward the latter part of the 18th century such as the fall front, pull-out writing surface, cylinder front, fold-over writing flap and tambour top. Desk value guide: Chippendale, slant top, cherry, ogee bracket feet, $3,200; Queen Anne style, slant front, walnut and maple, 32½" writing surface, finely crafted interior compartment, $2,800; walnut, Pennsylvania, slant front, brass handles, circa 1820, $2,200.

DOCUMENT BOXES. The document box served as a home version of the safe deposit box in the 1700s and 1800s. A tin or wooden document box held important family papers or other valuables. The wooden versions equipped with lock and key were decorated with elegant papers on the exterior and were lined with newspapers. Any leather-covered example meets with instant acceptance whenever it emerges from its hiding place. Lavishly handpainted or stenciled tin deed or document boxes do indeed rate as choice collectibles. These gaily ornamented tin boxes, which can be correctly described as tin catchalls, were used to store paraphernalia ranging from bibelots to Bibles. The early examples show signs of flecking and a darkening of color giving them an aged appearance appreciated by dedicated antiquers. They should always be left in their original condition. A slightly smaller tin box called a money box was another favored storage receptacle for treasured family possessions. Document box

Desk, Shaker type, mid-19th century

Document box, toleware, mid-19th century

Both photographs, National Gallery of Art, Washington

value guide: wood, pine, painted, brass bail handle, domed, circa 1820, $395; tin, black background, stenciled red and green florals, gold bands, circa 1840, $375.

DOLLS. Among the beloved playthings of the past are the primitive dolls created from natural substances. They represent an alliance formed by mothers with Mother Nature, a combination that produced dolls made from apples, hickory nuts and cornhusks. One enduring favorite in farmhouses was the rag doll, quickly conceived from bits of cloth, having a body stuffing of bran or sawdust and a crudely handpainted face. They were dressed from available materials, which could mean anything from calico to silk. Many carved wooden dolls were made in different sections of the country. Some of the most appealing ones originated in New England and the Southern Highlands. The heads usually showed little concern for details, and when not painted or dressed, the costume was carved in the wood. Unpainted wooden dolls were often left in a natural condition, pleasing lovers of primitive playthings. Doll value guide: hickory nut type, gingham dress, original, $55; rag doll, painted features, red hat and dress, original, 9" tall, $80.

DOLLY PINS. Whether or not the primitive wooden dolly or dolly pin was actually a giant step forward in the development of the washing machine is questionable. However, these heavy wooden clubs having three or four deep grooves in the base and a cross-bar handle did a dandy job of twisting and mangling the clothes in the washtub. Since they were manually operated, these clubs, which resembled butter churn plungers, obviously required some vigorous physical exertion by the user. The washing dolly was usually made of maple, as were the clothes pounders. Dolly value guide: maple, circa 1800, $80.

DOOR LINTELS. Many European customs found their way across the Atlantic, landing squarely in Penn's land from the Rhineland. This was true of the wooden panel carved with lettering in the form of a prayer or blessing, commonly called a door lintel. They were usually incised with Roman lettering and dated. According to the dated examples located thus far, it is safe to assume that the door lintel rage was short-lived, extending primarily between the 1740s and 1760s. Therefore, these carved wooden panels definitely fall into the scarce category, a fact that does not discourage the dedicated collector. Extremely rare.

DOUGH TROUGHS. The dough trough was an essential piece of kitchen furniture specifically designed to the needs of the busy breadmaker. It was a rectangular box with sides and ends that flared outward from the base. A dough tray is merely a smaller version of the dough trough designed to be stored in the base of a flour bin. The top of the dough trough provided the baker with a kneading board, and the dough was set to rise in the trough portion. The finest examples had dovetailed corners, legs attached to the apron by mortise-and-tenon joints and pegged with wooden pegs. The plain or turned legs were angled to furnish maximum support. Most dough trays and troughs remained undecorated, although some were treated to red filler. Occasionally a decorated specimen of Pennsylvania origin comes to light. They were made of such woods as maple, walnut, pine or poplar. Dough trough value guide: maple, dovetailed box, turned legs, sliding top, $325; pine, dovetailed box, grained finish, original, pegged legs, $275.

DOWER CHESTS. The Pennsylvania-type dower chest popular in the late 18th and early 19th centuries was the forerunner of the modern-day hope chest. It was an integral part of a maiden's world from an early age. The dower chest was a simply constructed dovetailed box of walnut, pine or poplar measuring up to four feet in length. They typically had molded edges and were raised to a more convenient height by supports such as ball feet, bracket feet, ogee molded feet or trestles. The earliest chests, often made without

Left: Dower chest, floral decor, Pennsylvania German; Right: Dower chest, birds and flowers, Pennsylvania German

Both photographs, National Gallery of Art, Washington

All photographs, National Gallery of Art, Washington

Top left: Dower chest, heart motif, Pennsylvania German, dated 1788; Top right: Dower chest, rare human form, Pennsylvania German; Bottom left: Dower chest, triple-arch motif, Pennsylvania German; Bottom right: Dower chest, Pennsylvania, circa 1800

drawers, had a sliding tray or till inside the lid. The walnut chests lent themselves to delicate inlay work. Those of pine were painted in a selected background color and enhanced with gaily painted motifs including stars, unicorns, flowers, birds and hearts. The owner's name, initials or a date were usually incorporated into the decorative theme. Preserving the original painted areas maintains the value of a Pennsylvania chest decorated for a dowry. Dower chest value guide: pine, painted, double-arched panels, urns, flowers, original decor, bottom drawers, circa 1820, $4,000; pine, painted, flowers, leaves, stems, overall decor, original, circa 1830, $3,400.

DRAM BOTTLES. Nothing lifts the spirits of a pursuer of early pewter more than a dram bottle, once used to hold a drink of spirits. In the 18th century a drink of spirits was called a dram, thus the term "dram bottle." These shallow round pewter bottles were actually forerunners of the pocket flask. They ranged in size from 4½ to 5½ inches in diameter and had spouts covered by threaded metal corks. Since pewter is a soft metal, the corks often became loose, causing more than a bit of leaking and cussing. If the cork shows signs of teethmarks, it is probably original. Some marked dram bottles have been recorded from such perceptive pewterers as Johanne Christopher Heyne of Lancaster, Pennsylvania, working between 1754 and 1780. His dram bottles were carried and emptied by fearless fighters of the Revolutionary War. However, this is not to be confused with the Spirit of '76! Dram bottle value guide: American, unmarked, 18th century, $260.

DRESSING TABLES. A variety of desirable dressing tables originated in country workshops as craftsmen endeavored to duplicate those made by formal furniture makers. Their efforts were always modified renditions of the more sophisticated models. A typical dressing table of the Sheraton period possessed an oblong top with rounded corners, and frequently a serpentined front. It had a conforming skirt and either a full-width or narrow central drawer. The rear portion of the top usually had a recessed cabinet approximately five inches high containing two or three small drawers for milady's necessities. An oblong mirror often surmounted this section during the American Empire period. When cottage furniture flooded country areas in the late 19th century, painted and grained dressing tables became fashionable. A dressing table of the 1800s featuring spool-turned elements is assured of immediate sale. Dressing table value guide: Sheraton style, satinwood, full-width drawer, turned legs, circa 1820, $530; spool turned, black walnut, full-width drawer, rear gallery piece, circa 1860, $250.

DRIP PANS. Those who spend hours trying to accumulate country things are always pleased to catch an early drip pan. These were the metal pans, generally of tin and iron, employed in catching the drippings from the roast as it slowly turned on the spit in the fireplace. The juices finding their way into the drip pans were utilized by economy-minded cooks in preparing tantalizing ragouts or stews. Some metal drip pans bore a resemblance to dust pans, having a handle and four-sided deep rims. The tin pans had their edges rolled over wire to prevent them from breaking. A wire protruded from the end of the handle to enable the drip pan to join other hearthside swingers. Drip pan value guide: iron, 18th century, $70.

Drop-leaf table, high stretcher
style, 17th century

*National Gallery of
Art, Washington*

DROP-LEAF TABLES. The drop-leaf or falling leaves table made its debut in American homes during the late 1600s. There are many varieties including Pembroke tables, gateleg tables, butterfly tables and others. Long after styles had been supplanted in urban areas, they were still crafted by country furniture makers. Thus the Queen Anne drop-leaf table with its round, oval or rectangular top supported by four gracefully curved cabriole legs terminating in drake or Dutch feet remained popular in outlying areas for generations. The Chippendale drop-leaf table with its oval or rectangular top also had cabriole legs, which terminated in the somewhat showier claw-and-ball feet. Mahogany was often used by city cabinet-makers for these handsome dining tables. However, those originating in country regions were usually made of cherry, walnut or maple. A Hepplewhite-style drop-leaf table usually had square tapering legs. Urn-shaped pedestals, acanthus-leaf and reeded globe columns were popular in the early 1800s. Spool turnings may be noted on some country examples dating from the 19th century. Many Shaker drop-leaf tables had a single drop leaf rather than the usual two leaves. Drop-leaf table value guide: Chippendale, walnut, four legs, ball-and-claw feet, $1,200; curly maple, six legs, fine turnings, $675; cherry, six turned legs, drawer at either end, 46″ long, $525; oak, pedestal base, claw feet, 54″ square, circa 1880, $500.

DRY SINKS. The dry sink came by its name honestly as it was never connected to any supply of water. This forerunner of the modern-day sink was a standard kitchen piece in country areas deprived of indoor plumbing facilities. It was in general use from about the 1820s onward. The form consisted of a cupboard base with an open, often metal-lined trough above. Frequently the maker included a splashboard, or small drawers above the trough portion. A receptacle of water was kept in the zinc-lined well for dishwashing chores. Dry sinks were crafted in many areas of assorted woods including pine, birch, poplar, maple or cherry. A small-size Shaker model dating from the mid-1800s had a drawer below the trough area and a single cupboard door. A Pennsylvania version was decidedly different, having turned legs and a lower shelf instead of the more familiar cupboard base. Some were painted, others remained in a natural wood finish. Dry sink value guide: poplar, high back, two drawers above, 48" high, 24" wide, 46" long, refinished, $390; walnut, one drawer, two doors, rough condition, $275; pine, well top, two doors, one drawer, $300.

DUMB STOVES. Only a highly seasoned and knowledgeable antiquer is likely to recognize an antique dumb stove. The earliest model was patented in 1838, as another improvement in the continuing battle to combat Jack Frost. The dumb stove was aptly named, being an iron device through which heated air passed from a regular stove below it on the same floor or the floor below. From a collecting standpoint the version patented in 1841 is infinitely more interesting. This consisted of a practically life-size hollow metal figure perched on a base, which was actually the stove. Although classical figures were made, the most fiery acceptance is usually afforded the figure of George Washington resplendent in a toga. Dumb stove value guide: classical figure, circa 1840, $1,350.

DUTCH CUPBOARDS. The two-piece Welsh cupboard was converted into a Dutch cupboard with the addition of glass-paneled doors on the upper section. From the 1830s onward they were made of native Pennsylvania woods such as cherry, pine, poplar and walnut. Since it was made in two sections, the tenons on the sides of the top piece fitted into the mortises of the bottom section. The number of glass panes on the upper section varied, but as a general rule the mullions were directly in front of the shelves to provide a clear view of the contents of the cupboard. Some models had spoon racks, cup and saucer rack, or only one glass door rather than two on the upper section. The bottom section also varied in design, with most examples displaying two or more drawers and two doors. Those found in their painted condition are prized, as most cupboards have been repainted repeatedly over the years. Dutch cupboard value guide: pine, top section two doors, six panes each, lower section two drawers, two doors, red paint, original, $2,100; poplar, top section two nine-pane glass doors, lower section two doors, three drawers, bracket feet, $1,950.

DUTCH OVENS. There are those who proclaim that the best bread and biscuits were baked in the primitive Dutch oven. Practically every household had a Dutch oven used for baking and roasting in the period prior to the brick bake oven. The true Dutch oven was a footed kettle or pot with a cover for holding hot coals. When the kettle was placed on the hearth, it was surrounded by embers from above and below, converting it into a form of oven. Although the iron types are best known, some copper examples lined with tin also sent a tempting aroma wafting through the air from their home by the hearth. Dutch oven value guide: cast iron with cover, two legs, $75.

E

EGG BASKETS. The splint egg basket was as common on most farms as chickens. They were used for gathering eggs or in transporting them to market. Most examples had broad bases which enabled them to rest firmly on a surface, thereby minimizing breakage. All examples had stationary or swinging handles extending across the top. Egg baskets were crafted in the cross-woven splint and in the hexagonal weave. The former required less splint but more skill. Basketmakers demonstrated their dexterity by making receptacles for holding exactly one dozen or two dozen eggs. Willow egg baskets were made by many basketmakers, especially in the Southern Appalachian area. Egg basket value guide: splint, cross weave, 11" x 12", circa 1860, $40.

EGGBEATERS. Collectors scramble after the Baby Binge, Cyclone and Dover crank-handled eggbeaters of 19th-century origin. These are just a few of the models guaranteed by their makers to

Early wooden eggbeater

National Gallery of Art, Washington

beat eggs or to whip cream in record-breaking time. Needless to say, they immediately sent the earlier wooden contraptions in this field directly into oblivion. Most of these beaters had tinned blades and sturdy iron handles and cranks. Examine any beater for a maker's name, initials or a patent date, which can furnish a clue to age. However, remember that a patent date should not be misconstrued as a date of production. Manufacturers hatched many eggbeater-cream-whipper combinations, but the A. & J. beater provided a triple threat, as it also functioned as a mayonnaise mixer—and to think it sold for just seventy cents! Eggbeater value guide: Betty Taplin Beater, 5½" long, $14; Lightning Cream Whip and Egg-beater, $13; Holt's eggbeater, 1899, $10.

EMBROIDERED RUGS. The creation of an elegant embroidered rug required the services of a lady blessed with equal amounts of patience and persistence in the early 1800s. Some were several years in the making. Inspiration for these extraordinary floor coverings was derived primarily from 18th-century crewelwork designs. Some embroidered rugs worked in the tent stitch or cross stitch approached carpet size. Against a background of handwoven linen, heavy blanketing or woolen cloth, the selected design was sewn with homespun woolen yarn. The soft colors were achieved from natural dyestuffs, the only type known prior to about 1850. Embroidered rug makers worked in close alliance with Mother Nature and favored flowers, birds, vines, leaves and other naturalistic wonders. These exquisite homemade floor coverings sewn by happy handcrafters were enough to make Persian rugmakers blush with envy. Embroidered rug value guide: small size, flowers and leaves, circa 1840, $290.

EMPIRE VASE-SPLAT CHAIRS. America was awakening to the dawn of industrialization during the Empire period (1815–1840).

Chair factories started springing up in eastern communities, where vase-splat chairs with cane seats originated. Their makers normally employed one or more of the three varieties of maple: bird's-eye, curly or straight-grained. Most chairs of this type had a top rail composed of a wide concave cross member. The large vase-splat and cane seat combined to make this style chair unmistakable. (Should the seat require recaning, the price should be adjusted accordingly.) Furniture factories shipped them into outlying areas, where economy-minded customers responded enthusiastically. That political great, "Boss Tweed," made this style chair in his New York shop prior to abandoning chairmaking for the activity of the political arena. Empire vase-splat chair value guide: maple, cane seat, circa 1840, $155.

F

FAN-BACK WINDSOR CHAIRS. Such notables as James Monroe and John Adams were known to have transacted business with Windsor chairmakers. In the latter part of the 18th century the fan-back Windsor made its American appearance. The back spindles resembled an open fan, and thus the name fan-back is most fitting. The spindles of this high-back chair extended from the seat to the cupid's bow top rail. There was no crosspiece. Sometimes it was used as a side chair along with the comb-back style. There were numerous variations as Windsor chairmakers dotted the landscape in the late 1700s, some later chairs having rockers, arms and combs. Factory-made kitchen chairs based on the fan-back style, including the arrow-back and the rod-back, enjoyed a wave of popularity in the late 19th century. Fan-back Windsor chair value guide: side chair, original finish, seven spindles, New England, bamboo turnings, circa 1830, $425; side chair, H-stretcher, saddle seat, nine spindles, circa 1840, $275.

FANCY SIDE CHAIRS. Cabinetmakers formed an alliance with decorators in the first half of the 19th century to produce lightweight, painted or stenciled chairs influenced by Classical Revival patterns. Practically every village had its own "Fancy and Windsor Chairmaker." Often the term "Hitchcock chair" was employed as a generic reference to these pieces combining the finer qualities of Sheraton and Directoire styles. Most examples in this category had cane or rush seats. Handsome handpainted designs proliferated on the earlier chairs, highlighted by gold leaf or gold stripes. Later, stenciled designs were widely utilized. Chair backs blossomed into small art treasures with stenciled motifs of fruits, flowers, grapevines, tendrils and landscapes. Their shapes changed slightly in accordance with the contemporary furniture style. Fancy prices are paid for "fancy chairs" having their original decoration intact, but repainting or stripping diminishes the value. Fancy side chair value guide: Sheraton, gilt stenciling, yellow stripes, rush seat, circa 1830, $190; maple, painted to imitate graining, gold and bronze fruit and floral stenciling, turned legs, rush seat, $175.

FARM COLLECTIBLES. Every weekend year-round seekers of farming items hit the road hoping to find a barn full of antique agricultural tools and implements. They dream of walking away from a barn sale with a blueberry picker, cranberry scoop, hay fork, grain shovel or corn planter. Local woodworkers and blacksmiths made many of the earliest tools, although more than one was simply conceived by a handyman farmer. Nowadays they excite a segment of the collecting fraternity who find them enormously nostalgic. They also find immediate sale with decorators who realize their importance in creating a country setting. There is no problem keeping them down on the farm once they uncover a building housing such items as a potato digger, rake, calf weaner, ox yoke, corn dryer or scythe. Farm collectibles value guide: corn-husking knife, $20; corn dryer, ten prongs, $14; grain shovel, carved wood, $65; pitchfork, wooden, three tines, $45; potato digger, $35.

FARMER'S CUPS. When a farmer sat down to have a cup of coffee, it was served in a large cup holding up to a pint or more. Those dainty little cups and saucers might be just fine for the lady of the house, but they were hardly appropriate for the gentleman. Coffee drinking was on the upsurge in the latter part of the 19th century and potters responded with giant cups. These so-called "farmer's cups" were made in various kinds of pottery including spongeware, ironstone, Rockingham, blue-printed wares and others. Fancy handpainted china examples were also available with suitable inscriptions, such as "Love the Giver" or "For Papa." Farmer's cups value guide: blue, printed type, landscape scene, circa 1860, $40; inscription "For Papa," Germany, circa 1880, $32.

FARM TABLES. This collector-named table is a direct descendant of the tavern table. These sturdy tables of Pennsylvania origin ranged up to eight feet in length. As a rule they were crafted with one or more drawers under the top, and with plain or turned legs. Apparently the size of the table dictated the type of wood, as smaller ones were normally made of pine and larger ones of walnut and cherry. Smaller sizes were frequently used as kitchen work tables. The large size farm tables, often crafted with removable tops, saw service in the kitchen when guests were invited to dinner. Due to their pleasing size and proportions, they are in demand with present-day antiquers. Farm table value guide: pine, one drawer, 6' long, 3' wide, turned legs, circa 1830, $400; walnut, two drawers, 8' long, 4' wide, turned legs, circa 1840, $525.

FEATHERBED SMOOTHERS. A casual collector is likely to lose forty winks or more trying to identify an early wooden featherbed smoother. These paddles could be found in Colonial bedrooms whenever the featherbed had to be smoothed or flattened. They measured up to eighteen inches in length and were usually made with long tapering handles. This article can be distinguished from close-resembling occupational tools because its edges were never tapered. The featherbed smoother was steeped in sentimentality, as a young suitor frequently crafted one as a love token for his bride-to-be. Featherbed smoother value guide: late 18th century, 16" long, $80.

FENTON, CHRISTOPHER. This gentleman was actively working with his brother-in-law, Julius Norton, in Bennington, Vermont, for several years prior to establishing his own pottery in 1847. He desired to experiment with various types of ceramic productions rather than the standard stoneware associated with the Norton firm. In 1848 a new building and two partners, Lyman and Park, joined forces with Fenton. When Park withdrew a year later, the pottery became known as Lyman, Fenton & Company. This company produced the most diversified pottery and porcelain ever to originate in

America. Among their accomplishments was Fenton's enamel, capable of creating streaks or flecks of color, which when patented in 1849 was an improvement over the brown Rockingham glaze. About 1853 the name United States Pottery was adapted and used by the firm until financial reverses forced its closing in 1858. Fenton value guide: flint enamel pitcher, ribbed, 9″ tall, $360; flint enamel teapot, ribbed, 6½″ tall, $875; flint enamel toby, Benjamin Franklin, 5¾″ tall, $550.

FIDDLEBACK BOSTON ROCKERS. Any chair afforded the popularity of the Boston rocker was assured of spawning offspring; the introduction of the fiddleback Boston with its fiddle shaped or vase-shaped splat was thus inevitable. A lyre-shaped center splat, often associated with Duncan Phyfe, can be found on some of these rockers dating from the mid-1800s. Sometimes the decorating was confined to the headpiece, although on other examples it extended to the center splat. Chairmakers in New England and in the Midwest specialized in crafting this style rocker; many were factory made as the century progressed. Fiddleback Boston rocker value guide: maple, landscape scene, original finish, circa 1850, $240.

FIELD BEDS. The field bed, extensively made in America from the late 1700s onward, has earned the respect and admiration of antiquers. The design won popularity during the Hepplewhite period in Philadelphia, and it was quickly copied by furniture makers in other areas. The country types were customarily made of curly

Fiddleback Boston rocker, stenciled decoration

National Gallery of Art, Washington

85

maple, maple, birch, cherry or mahogany. A field bed can be recognized by its arched tester frame (the usual tester bed had a rectangular frame). Several different designs were featured in George Hepplewhite's design book. According to Thomas Sheraton, the style was similar to a type used in Army camps. However, those designed for camping or traveling differed from those designated for domestic use as they could be easily assembled and taken apart. They are also known as tent beds. Field Bed value guide: maple, simply turned posts, peg feet, 6' long, 4' wide, tester arch, circa 1830, $650; pine, stained, single bed size, 36" wide, circa 1840, original finish, $475.

FILLEY TINSMITHS. The Filley family tin shop was founded in Bloomfield (now Simsbury), Connecticut, about 1800. Oliver Filley was a former Vermont tin peddler who brought prior knowledge of the tinsmithing business to his new venture. He married Annis Humphrey in 1805 and together they set about building a budding business and family. Oliver traveled to Elizabeth, New Jersey, briefly in 1810, setting up a tin shop that prospered momentarily but soon faltered. Returning to the well-established Bloomfield location, he attracted some of the finest decorators, tinsmiths and peddlers to his employ. Filley might be accused of being somewhat clannish as he trained brothers, sons and cousins to enter the tin trade. The Filleys outdistanced competitors mile wise by organizing tin shops in such faraway places as Philadelphia, St. Louis and Troy, New York. Oliver was kept busy with his own shop while continuing to supply his relatives and offspring with supplies and advice in the early 1800s. Filley tinsmiths value guide: Filley-type bread tray, fruit, flowers, leaves, vermilion repeat border, original finish, $475.

FIREBACKS. A fireback is a cast-iron plate, also known as a chimney back, attached to the rear wall of a fireplace to protect the wall and to reflect heat. In the 1700s, when the fireplace was the focal point of country living, firebacks were cast by many foundries. They were typically made with a curvature or wide crest at the top. The decorative designs in low relief frequently included the name of the furnace and a date. English and Welsh foundries accommodated their German immigrant clientele with firebacks warmly enriched with tulips, lilies, stars, sheaves of wheat and sunbursts. In other areas patriotic, religious, and leaf and scroll motifs adorned these delicately decorated fireplace fixtures. The reproductions have not cooled collectors' ardor for antique firebacks. According to legend, Benjamin Franklin frowned upon the fireback as being an ineffective piece of fireplace garniture, prompting him to develop the Franklin stove. Fireback value guide: floral decor, 18th century, $820.

FIREDOGS. As interest mounts in collecting antique metalwork, many people are seeking firedogs. This is a modern term for andirons of simple design. The earliest ones had straight flattened shafts, enlarged heads and curved feet. Later blacksmiths strived for versatility, crafting them with various shaped shafts and top design. Those destined for kitchen use were always quite plain. Some were made with a hook to hold a spit. Cast-iron foundries produced them in shapes influenced by contemporary furniture styles in the late 18th and early 19th centuries. Firedog value guide: wrought iron, simple design, late 18th century, pair, $150.

FIREFIGHTING COLLECTIBLES. Volunteer firefighters working under primitive conditions were ready for duty round-the-clock well into the late 19th century. They have willed collectors an array of objects associated with their various firefighting activities. Few antiquers are able to boast a handsomely carved or painted "enjine." But there are triumphantly designed silver trumpets, some engraved or embossed as presentation pieces. Firemen's helmets are other revered relics, many of which could be reversed to form a face shield. Handpainted stovepipe hats popped proudly onto heads for dress parades. Fire buckets of oiled leather crafted by local shoe-

Right: Fireman's hand-painted stovepipe hat

Far right: Fireman's leather water bucket

Both photographs, National Gallery of Art, Washington

makers bore identifying information relating to the fire company. Collectors also fight for such firefighting finds as belts, badges, uniforms, hose holders, hose and reel carts, wooden fire hydrants, company signboards, firemarks and engravings and lithographs depicting fire laddies in action. Firefighting collectibles: coal bucket, tin, painted flowers and leaves, circa 1860, $225; fireman's belt, metal letters, circa 1850, $95; fire bucket, leather, circa 1830, $150; sterling silver horn, presentation, flowers and scrollwork, dated 1878, $450.

FIREHOUSE CHAIRS. This 19th-century version of the low-back Windsor chair proved so popular in public buildings and firehouses that it was dubbed a "firehouse chair." Mass produced by furniture factories of the period, these sturdily constructed chairs continue to rate as hot sellers. On most examples the horseshoe-shaped arm was supported by seven to nine spindles and had a finger-hole center. The deep U-shaped seats were either all wood or caned. Many were painted or grained, including the small child's version and highchair. The moderately splayed legs were braced by a stretcher on these chairs made of assorted softwoods and hardwoods. In the closing decades of the century, many firehouse chairs were marketed in a natural-finished oak. Firehouse Windsor value guide: pine seat and arms, maple legs, stretchers and seven spindles, wooden seat, original finish, circa 1870, $135.

FIREMARKS. Fire insurance company plaques were issued to customers, who attached them to their homes or buildings, to indicate that the property was insured. Amateur firefighters realized

Far left: Fireman's hand-powered pump
Left: Fireman's silver presentation trumpet
Both photographs, National Gallery of Art, Washington

Right: Eagle firemark, Insurance Company of North America

National Gallery of Art, Washington

that a reward would be paid for battling the blaze. Firemarks were made of iron, lead, tin and terra-cotta. The well-known clasped hands plaque was issued by the Philadelphia Contributorship for the Insurance of Houses from Loss by Fire founded in 1752. This firm objected to insuring homes surrounded by trees. But the Mutual Insurance Company of Philadelphia, established in 1784, would insure such properties, their "flowering trees" mark clearly indicating their position. Through the late 19th century firemarks were made in numerous motifs, particularly stars, hydrants, eagles, speaking trumpets, fire engines, firefighters and other closely related designs. Firemark value guide: brass, embossed tree, $100; cast iron, Germantown National Fire, circa 1845, $125; cast iron, fire hydrant with hose, circa 1820, $110.

FIRE PANS. Before friction matches lighted the way in the 1830s, striking a spark to start or rekindle a fire was a mighty troublesome chore. On more than one occasion it was easier to fill a fire pan with burning coals from an existing fire. Fire pans were used to carry a fire from a hearth in the same house or to fetch one from a neighboring fireplace. In securing hot coals from a neighbor, a distance of a mile or more was traveled in remote areas. Local craftsmen fashioned fire pans of iron, tin, copper or brass, with short handles generally attached to scoop-shaped pans. The form varied slightly depending on the individual artisan. Later factory-made models generally possess a maker's trademark. In the pre-match era a fire carrier was deemed a suitable gift for a pair of perfectly matched newlyweds. Fire pan value guide: iron, hand forged, wooden handle, circa 1820, $75.

FIRE TOOLS. When the fireplace was the center of activity in homes and taverns, sets of fire tools were necessary to accomplish various hearthside housekeeping functions. A complete set generally consisted of a toolbox, tongs, brush, shovel, poker and irons. Fire shovels were employed to transfer coals or ashes. There were also ember carriers with either open or closed lids. Brass or polished steel equipment was considered proper for chamber and parlor fireplaces, while iron tools were used in the kitchen. Most tools could be purchased separately. The brass tankard with an oil-soaked stone on a handle for igniting fires was known as a Cape Cod lighter. Simple metal coal scuttles were important items in rural America, while fancier versions were favored by proper city folk. As more collectors warm up to antique fire tools, prices edge ever higher. Fire tools value guide: bronze fire bin, ornate florals, $130; coal scuttle, cast iron, urn-shaped body, lion's head, ring drop handles, 32" long, $190; ember tongs, brass, 14" long, $70; fire tools, set of three, with stand, $200.

FISH BASKETS. Have you noticed how many fish baskets catch collectors? At first glance they bear a resemblance to fruit-drying baskets, but closer examination reveals minor differences. They are at least a foot deep, whereas fruit-drying baskets are quite shallow. Fish baskets were more sturdily constructed, with heavy hickory handles rather than splint handles. They typically had loosely woven bottoms to permit the proper amount of drainage. These rectangular splint baskets were being shipped to coastal areas by basketmakers throughout the 19th century. Fish basket value guide: splint, hickory handle, circa 1860, $50.

FIVE-PLATE STOVES. These early warming or cooking stoves are also known as "Jamb stoves," "carved stoves" or "German stoves." The German settlers introduced these cast-iron box stoves bearing a striking similarity to European models in the late 1720s. They were simple rectangular boxes with five sides and one open end. The open end fitted into an opening in the wall, where it was pushed into an adjoining room against the fireplace. The stove protruded from the wall in the room it was meant to heat and was supported by a platform or legs. Not only did the five-plate stove heat an additional area of the house, but it also functioned as a cooking stove when filled with hot embers from the fireplace. There was one slight problem—no ventilation. Therefore they had to be constantly replenished with hot embers. The outside plates were handsomely decorated in the German tradition with Biblical subjects and folk motifs. A collector will positively glow if the name of the casting furnace appears on one of these mid-18th-century stoves. Extremely rare.

FLAGONS. Throughout the Golden Age of American Pewter (1700–1850), these large vessels for dispensing liquids were gracefully executed. A flagon resembled an enlarged tankard and was made with a handle and cover. It was crafted with or without a spout. Some of the finest flagons had handles composed of parts from two tankard handles. American pewterers resisted ornamenting their flagons except for an occasional decorative band around the center body portion. The touch marks found on flagons read like a Who's Who in American Pewter, as they reveal such revered workers as Johanne Christopher Heyne (1745–1780), Samuel Hamlin (1767–1801) and Samuel Danforth (1795–1816). Flagon value guide: American, unmarked, 11" tall, $280; Samuel Danforth, 10" tall, $725.

FLASKS. Originally the terms "flask" and "pocket bottle" were used interchangeably in describing these bottle-shaped containers for holding liquor. Between the War of 1812 and the Civil War, American glass houses issued them in various colors and in over five hundred designs. Therefore, opportunity for specialization exists.

Flasks, eagle and agricultural motifs

National Gallery of Art, Washington

People with a preference for patriotic motifs will find a mélange of motifs including the American flag, stars, eagles, portraits of political figures, famous heroes and historical events. George Washington was immortalized on over sixty different designs. Other decorations, such as agricultural motifs, Masonic emblems, transportation themes and geometric and naturalistic patterns, were freely used on American-made flasks. The violin flask and .the Jenny Lind flask are among the finds in which collectors bask. Flask value guide: Washington and Jackson, olive amber, $275; double eagle, golden amber, pint, $230; Pitkin, green, $260; Jenny Lind, calabash, aqua, $135.

FLOOR CLOTHS. The painted floor cloth caught on as a substitute for expensive woven carpets when it was first found underfoot in England in the 17th century. Shortly thereafter they were loaded into ships bound for America, where they met with immediate acceptance from bare-floored colonists. The floor cloth made of sturdy canvas or linen treated to several coats of sizing suddenly turned floors into focal points. They flourished throughout the 18th century, when imported and domestically made designs were offered in stenciled, painted or stamped patterns. There were ready-made floor cloths and others made to order. Designs imitating marble-tiled floors proved enduringly popular. Some householders painted their own carpets, but for the less talented there were "carpet painters" or "oil cloth painters." For the poor folk who could not afford this early form of inlaid linoleum, there was no recourse but to paint their own floorboards in imitation of a painted carpet. The floor cloth was afforded a hint of historical significance when George Washington purchased one for $14.82 in 1769. Extremely rare.

FLOUR BINS. Once packaged flour reached country store shelves, the flour bin slowly disappeared from country kitchens. In the prepackage period, this one-piece bin provided a valuable storage area for flour. Typically made of pine, it was divided into two compartments beneath the lift-top lid. Fine flour was stored in the smaller section, common flour in the larger. The two doors comprising the lower section swung open to reveal a storage area for a dough tray. Some models had a small drawer located on one side of the bin between the upper compartment and the lower storage area. Many individuals designed and made their own flour bins, accounting for the numerous variations. Their present popularity is based on adaptability to modern-day use. Flour bin value guide: pine, Pennsylvania, lift-top lid, original finish, circa 1870, $390.

FLUTING IRONS. Specially designed crimping or fluting irons were made by iron manufacturers to facilitate the crimping or pleating of materials. They were composed of two corrugated sections, a stationary base and a movable top hand piece that could be locked together for pressing chores. The presser first heated the base part and placed it on an ironing board or tabletop. Then the material to be pressed was placed on the lower section and the top section was rolled back and forth over it to complete the crimping. The Geneva Hand Fluter, patented in 1866, appeared in white metal and brass. Metal models sold for about a dollar each, while the brass types were priced at a dollar and a quarter. Fluting iron value guide: Geneva Hand Fluter, brass, two parts, $35; "The Best," two parts, $25.

FOLDING BEDS. The folding trestle bed of the early 1700s was usually found in the main living room awaiting the arrival of guests. When not in use it could be folded back and concealed behind curtains. Since this style bed was clothed with curtains, it was often called a slaw bed, from the word "slough" meaning "clothed." A small tester frame supported the valance and curtains. The valance, curtains and coverlet were always made in a matching crewelwork design. The Jacobean influence may be noted in the turned footposts and headposts found on some models. Their New England makers favored a variety of local hardwoods. Folding bed value guide: maple, six legs, 6'3" long, 4'4" wide, original finish, circa 1760, $475.

FOLK PAINTINGS. The word "folk," as used in "folk painting," relates to the common folk. The type of paintings which were hung on country walls definitely fit this description. Very few people residing in rural areas could afford to own a painting by a professional artist. However, they could purchase one from an itinerant painter, who often charged from three to twenty dollars for a portrait, a dollar or less for a child's portrait. They usually painted in oils on canvas or wood, with portrait subjects dominating their output. Landscapes and scenes of everyday life are somewhat less available. Perspective was of small importance to the folk artist, as can be evidenced in their output. A decline in folk painting occurred in the mid-19th century, hastened considerably by the invention of the daguerreotype in 1839. Folk painting value guide: child's portrait, oil on canvas, large size, New England, circa 1840, $1,100; farmyard scene, oil on canvas, 12" x 12", Pennsylvania, circa 1870, $525.

FOOD CHOPPERS. Without mincing words, it is safe to state that food choppers can be classified as neglected antiques. This is unfortunate as the variety is endless, and many one-of-a-kind chopper begs to be adopted. When homemade sausage and mince pies were considered gourmet delights, these choppers, mincers or mincing knives were pantry staples. The earliest types were homemade or fashioned by the local blacksmith. People who prefer primitives pay premium prices for all-iron choppers. Others were made entirely of tin, although many were fitted with more convenient wooden handles. The shape of the handles and the blades varied considerably on the handcrafted models. Those made with a double blade or rotating blade show additional versatility. By the 19th century factory-made choppers, including crank-handled versions, were being produced for domestic and commercial use. Some bear a patent date or maker's name, such as the cast-steel model originating at the C. W. Dunlap firm of New York City. Food chopper value guide: C. W. Dunlap, cast steel, circa 1890, $22; Enterprise Meat & Food Chopper, $18; handcrafted iron chopper, $34.

FOOD MOLDS. The food mold of metal or ceramic with an intaglio design on the base was used in preparing jellies, puddings and other desserts. They were made of many materials, such as silver, tin, copper, wood, glass, iron, stoneware, brownware, redware, creamware and ironstone. The shape and decorative design of the mold was automatically transferred to the food. Most molds were either round or oval. A ceramic mold of 19th-century origin often had a maker's name or trademark providing a source of identification. Toward the latter part of the century granite molds in octagonal, turban and turk's head shapes appeared in various mottled colors. Food mold value guide: ice cream mold, eagle, pewter, $65; chocolate mold, rooster, tin, $30; jelly mold, lamb, pottery, $35; pudding mold, melon-ribbed, tin, $18.

FOOTSTOOLS. The major difference between a footstool and a seating stool is primarily one of height. Footstools usually ranged up to about eight inches high. More than one doubled as a seating stool for a minor family member. Elegant upholstered types can be attributed to urban cabinetmakers, while all-wooden examples proliferated in country areas. One early style was made without nails or bracing and had scalloped legs tenoned into the top and wedged from above. Construction varied according to the skill of the maker, with the finest examples having an apron on four sides, a drawer, center brace, or sides extended to form brackets. However, some of the crudest stools are also the most charming. Beautifully decorated footstools protected users from chilly drafts in Pennsylvania areas, but alas, frequent use has usually removed a substantial amount of original ornamentation. Locating a mid-19th-century spool-turned footstool is quite a feat! Footstool value guide: Pennsylvania, red-and-black grained background, stenciled, eagle top striping, circa 1850, $285; curly maple, oblong, circa 1800, $220; spool turned, circular top, 12" diameter, $90.

FOOT WARMERS. Following several serious fires in New England churches, some communities outlawed all-wood foot stoves, much to the chagrin of shivering congregations in the early 1700s. These early foot stoves, made with sliding doors to accommodate the tin pan of coals, often had carved motifs. The primitive all-tin models also posed a problem as they managed to scratch the floor while warming the feet. Foot warmers appeared over the lengthy winter season in as many different assorted sizes and shapes as the feet they warmed. When a wire handle and wooden frame were added to the pierced tin warmer, a standard form evolved, proving popular well into the 1800s. The earliest versions can be recognized

Foot warmer, pierced tin panels, 19th century

National Gallery of Art, Washington

95

by the detailed turnings on the posts. Other shiver stoppers of the period included a combination lantern foot warmer, an oil-burning portable stove, U-shaped tin warmers of copper and brass, and oval and round hot-water bottles. People with a penchant for portable warmers comb the countryside searching for redware, stoneware, Rockingham and soapstone warmers. Foot warmer value guide: tin, pierced heart design, wood frame, $85; soapstone, slab with handle, $70; brass foot warmer, oval, loop handle, $65; carpet covered, tin, with handle, $60.

FOUR-O'CLOCK STOVES. This name is applied to a type of small box stove of the 1800s. Many eastern cast-iron foundries shipped these stoves into agricultural communities, where they performed beautifully on cold winter nights. The unusual name is derived from the fact that the stoves were lighted about four o'clock in the afternoon to warm the bedroom before retiring ("Early to bed, early to rise" was the motto of the moment). Many of these small heating devices were cast in decorative folk motifs. Four-o'clock stoves still manage to sell at an alarming rate to antiquers bent on reviving an authentic country bedroom decor. Four-o'clock stove value guide: flowers and leaves motif, $750.

FRAKTURS. This term is applied to the hand-lettered, illuminated manuscripts and ornamental drawings attributed to the Pennsylvania Germans of the 18th and 19th centuries. Although the true masters of Fraktur illuminations were the educated schoolmasters, clergymen and others, many a child or adult also attempted some multicolored penmanship or brushwork. Birth and baptism records, marriage certificates, house blessings, broadsides and book plates were among the Fraktur subjects. They were decorated with typical flourish in a multitude of folk designs such as flowers, birds, hearts and angels. A nod of gratitude should also be paid the Pennsylvania papermakers who provided superior handmade papers for these records. These calligraphic creations are dearly coveted by dedicated antiquers. Preprinted Frakturs came into widespread use in the mid-19th century, and few calligraphers could successfully compete against the printing press. Fraktur value guide: house blessing, Jacob Schultz, hearts, prayer, original red frame, dated 1814, $1,200; bookmark, tulip and heart, framed, circa 1846, $350;

Top left: Fraktur,
Pennsylvania German

Above: Fraktur, plant and
floral forms, Pennsylvania
German

Left: Fraktur, elaborately
embellished, Pennsylvania
German

*All photographs, National
Gallery of Art, Washington*

birth certificate, Anna Miller, 1854, birds and hearts, circa 1835,
$750.

FRANKLIN STOVES. Benjamin Franklin is warmly remembered
as the inventor of the Franklin stove. He referred to his 1742 creation as the "New Invented Pennsylvania Fireplace." Who could
better describe this portable cast-iron fireplace, which distributed
more heat at less cost, than its inventor? While originally designed to
be partially set into an existing fireplace, it actually operated more
efficiently outside the fireplace, connected by a chimney. It was
made with straight or flaring sides in many variations. Most were
constructed so that the flame could be viewed, although some versions had movable front doors. Franklin failed to patent his invention, possibly due to his preoccupation with weather forecasting.
The decoration on a Franklin stove can help determine its age. A

sun face with sixteen rays favored in the 1740s and 1750s was superseded by classical designs reflecting prevailing furniture forms in the 1760s. Patriotic motifs dominated designs in the post-Revolutionary War period. The "Be Liberty Thine" design vied for customer approval with profiles of Washington and Franklin. Throughout the 19th century various interpretations of the Franklin stove blazed brightly in country interiors. Franklin stove value guide: cast iron and brass, H. W. Cobert Co., N.Y., circa 1835, $600; sliding door, elaborate decor, circa 1850, $525.

FROST, EDWARD SANDS. How can a Yankee soldier returning to his home state of Maine in ill health strike it rich following the Civil War? Simply by turning his attention to stenciling designs for hooked rugs. Mr. Frost became a tin peddler, and while roaming about the hinterlands received numerous requests from customers for hooked rug patterns. He obliged by developing metal stencils to be used in tracing designs in color on burlap. The patterns he created pleased rugmakers, and soon fame and fortune came his way. Eventually he opened a factory and salesroom, furnishing many peddlers and dealers with rug patterns. Mr. Frost was undisturbed by those who argued that his designs were responsible for hooked rugs losing their originality; he was too floored with orders to pay any attention to nasty rumors! Frost value guide: floral pattern, red and green roses on black background, small size, $155; house pattern, medium size, $140.

FRUIT BASKETS. Fruit growers and packers relied on basketmakers to furnish them with suitable containers for their products during the 19th century. Basketmakers responded with a barrage of splint and willow baskets generally made in half pint, pint and quart sizes. Rarely was one crafted in excess of two-quart capacity, lest the weight crush the bottom berries. As new patents were granted, the shape of the berry basket underwent minor alterations. The reliable circular splint type known in the early 1800s was supplanted in popularity by a similarly shaped factory-produced veneer version known as "The Star," patented in the 1860s. However, The Star fell from favor faster than a meteorite when square-shaped "Delaware" baskets reached marketplaces in the 1870s. Some basketmakers stamped their containers with name or initials. Shaker berry baskets are unmistakable, resembling lopped-off triangles with air-hole sides. The berry basket was tinged with patriotism in 1876, when the Hudson River Basket Depot distributed them under the topical trade names Eureka and Centennial. Fruit basket value guide: Shaker berry basket, circa 1850, $35; splint berry basket, one pint, $30.

FRUIT JARS. Simply by examining the information found on a fruit jar it is possible to obtain some information regarding age or origin. Many bear a trademark or factory monogram or patent date (of course, a patent date should never be misconstrued as a date of production). Commercial canning started in America in the first quarter of the 19th century. By the 1830s various glass houses were advertising fruit jars. From the 1850s onward the United States Patent Office was besieged with requests for improvements. The patents reveal the numerous types of sealing methods employed on jars. Earlier jars were simply lettered, while those made from the 1870s on possessed ornate monograms or initials. After a trademark has been accurately identified, it is necessary to learn the date it was initially used. Although machine-made jars were first made in 1904, it took many years for manufacturers to make the transition to modern methods. Fruit jar value guide: Fruit Keeper, ½ gallon, $45; Mason's Patent 1858, snowflake back, blue, quart, $35; Mansfield Improved Mason, aqua, quart, $18; Atlas E. Z. Seal, aqua, ½ pint, $12.

FUNNELS. With the exception of the earliest woven splint and lathe-turned funnels of birch and maple, there are many affordable finds in this category. Throughout the 19th century they were produced in a variety of materials, including pottery, tin, wood, ironstone, copper, pewter, pressed glass, blown glass and enamelware. Upon close examination a factory-produced example may show a maker's name or patent date. The ceramic funnels were often marked with the potter's trademark. There is opportunity for specialization should the funnel fancier decide to concentrate on examples made specifically for home canning jars. The tin funnels marked "C. D. Kenny's Co.'s, Teas—Coffees—Sugars" were distributed by this Baltimore-based firm around the turn of the century. Funnel value guide: brass, round, copper ribs, 10″ long, $50; sap, turned maple, $40; tin, gallon, $25.

G

GALLERY TRAYS. The Revolutionary War brought the supply of tin plate from England to a swift halt. However, when hostilities ceased it was again available to American tinsmiths. Gifted craftsmen supplied their country buyers with strikingly beautiful gallery trays having narrow solid rails, pierced rails or rails with handles. The tinsmith was afforded an opportunity of showing his skills by piercing the rails in eye-catching patterns. In addition to pierced motifs, these trays were also ornamented in a spontaneous style which automatically insured their survival to the present day. Weight is a determining factor in judging quality, as the heavier trays are considered finest. Gallery tray value guide: oval, pierced rail, floral motif center, 16″ x 10″, original finish, $140.

GATE-LEG TABLES. The American version of the gate-leg table appeared in the mid-17th century and immediately supplanted the earlier stretcher table for dining. This style table had been popular in England at an earlier date. It achieved its descriptive name due to the gatelike construction of legs and stretchers. A series of turned legs were opened to support an extension or leaf. Most gate-leg tables ranged from 3′ to 6′ in diameter, with collector interest centering on the smallest and largest examples. Although the general form remained fashionable throughout the 18th and 19th centuries, later versions were less elaborate. The style of the turnings changed slightly in various periods. The plainer the turnings, the later the table. The finest tables have the greatest number of legs. New England craftsmen favored walnut, maple or cherry, while workers in Pennsylvania and southern regions showed a distinct preference for walnut. Gate-leg table value guide: maple, William and Mary style, oval top, turned legs, circa 1720, $1,700; walnut, Pennsylvania, two drawers, 44″ long, 30″ high, circa 1820, $985.

GAUDY DUTCH. This type of pottery produced in the Staffordshire district of England between 1810 and 1830 was supposedly earmarked for export to the Pennsylvania area. There are those who debunk this theory, claiming it was shipped to America only because it failed to excite English consumers. It certainly appealed to country customers, who did not object to the fact that the ware imitated Imari-type English porcelains, which in turn copied true Imari from Japan. Gaudy Dutch pieces were devoid of lustre decoration. The patterns were painted in exciting color combinations, including red, green, orange, pink and yellow over the glaze and blue under the glaze. Among the collector-named designs are Urn, Grape, War Bonnet, Single Rose, Zinnia, Dahlia, King's Rose, Oyster and Strawflower. Originally, Gaudy Dutch was known as "Rileyware" due to marked examples that originated at the J. & R. Riley firm in Burslem, England, active between 1802 and 1828. Gaudy Dutch value guide: teapot, King's Rose pattern, $950; plate, Urn pattern, 7½" diameter, $600; cup and saucer, Oyster pattern, $575; bowl, Butterfly pattern, 6½" diameter, $475.

GAUDY WELSH. A check of an abandoned country cupboard may yield one or more pieces of Gaudy Welsh, dating from the 1830s and 1840s. The potters operating in the Swansea district of England captured country customers with this translucent porcelain teaware. They found the lovely range of floral patterns highlighted by gilding or copper lustre absolutely irresistible. This colorful teaware met with enormous success in areas populated by German settlers. Gaudy Welsh was decidedly reminiscent of the bold and beautiful Japanese Imari porcelains. The ware is related to Gaudy Dutch and Gaudy Ironstone in name only. Gaudy Welsh value guide: teapot, Strawberry pattern, $135; cup and saucer, Grape pattern, handleless, $80; creamer, Daisy and Chain pattern, $75; plate, Tulip pattern, 6" diameter, $65.

GERMAN BLUE STONEWARE. This flea market staple dates from the late 1800s and early 1900s. Although it was also produced with a brown or shaded green glaze, it is the blue and white that fascinates collectors. Decoration varies considerably, as some pieces have a shaded smooth surface while others have appealing embossed patterns. The embossed designs cover a wide range, including birds, butterflies, animals, apricots, swans and buildings.

Marked pieces are extremely difficult to locate. Collectors simply cannot agree on the proper term for this ware, calling it by such names as blue-and-white stoneware, salt-glaze pottery, blue crockery, blue Flemish and German blue stoneware. Regardless of what you choose to call it, be certain not to miss a buy in this utilitarian stoneware as prices are climbing faster than a kite on a March afternoon. German blue stoneware value guide: bowl and pitcher set, embossed, tree pattern, $100; cookie jar, embossed butterflies, $60; saltbox, hanging, embossed bird, $35; milk pitcher, smooth surface, $30.

GLOBE STOVES. Prior to engaging in a heated argument about the age of a globe stove, remember that this bit of cast-iron whimsy was patented on February 8, 1834. Resembling the shape of a mounted globe, it helped lower the chill factor on cold country nights for several generations thereafter. The pedestal portion of the stove concealed the grate, which could be raised or lowered. Benjamin Franklin made a vase stove based on the same principle in the 1770s. The globe stove is absolutely unmistakable due to its highly descriptive shape. The word "globe" was also employed to describe large heaters found in public buildings, factories and rest rooms in the 1800s, although these heaters were not globe-shaped. Globe stove value guide: circa 1840, $730.

GRANDFATHER CLOCKS. The majority of American-made clocks dating from the 18th century were of the long-case, or tall-case style, known presently as a grandfather clock. Each one was completely handmade and the case (which conformed to contemporary furnishings) was made in the same shop or was supplied by a local cabinetmaker. Most early clocks had brass eight-day movements, although some thirty-hour movements are known to exist. Brass dials with engraved or etched designs and Roman numerals were favored along with cast-brass spandrels. They were almost always custom made, thereby making the tall-case clock too costly for country customers. In the early 1800s this style was made in increasing numbers by New England clockmakers at more affordable prices. Often the papers inside a clock provide information regarding the clockmaker or cabinetmaker. Grandfather clock value guide: Seth Thomas, pine and maple case, arched and white-painted dial,

7′3″ tall, circa 1830, $2,100; Silas Hoadley, pine case, painted eagle motif, 8′ tall, $2,300; Shaker style, $900.

GRATERS. A grater is a great collectible for anyone working within the framework of a limited budget. The earliest finds in this category are the handmade, hand-pierced graters dating from the 1700s. Old square-cut nails were utilized to pierce the tin, ornamenting it with stars, dots and dashes. Once the piercing was accomplished the tin portion was crudely attached to a wooden base with the rough side facing forward to function as the grater. The persistent pursuer may be rewarded by finding a grater-strainer combination. Most country kitchens boasted an assortment of graters in various sizes. Some nutmeg graters were small enough to carry about in a vest pocket for flavoring a drink to the individual's taste. The factory-made graters of the 1800s offer exciting possibilities: many bear a patent date or maker's name, providing the browser with a clue to age or origin. Grater value guide: pine, wooden, paddle-shaped back, pierced stars, handcrafted, $45; pine board, half round, pierced tin, circa 1800, $42; nutmeg, tin, swing action, $25; Edgar nutmeg grater, patented 1891, $18.

GREASE BUCKETS. Searching for a primitive bucket with storytelling possibilities? Then try acquiring an early grease bucket. Would you believe these receptacles were actually made from hollowed-out logs? They had set-in wooden covers equipped with ears through which was strung a leather carrying strap. That hole in the middle of the lid accommodated a stick for gathering enough tar or grease to keep the wagon's axles and hubs greased. The grease bucket was a familiar sight hanging from the rear axle of a covered wagon wending its way over hill and dale. Depending on its origin, this wooden container paraded under such awesome names as slush bucket or tar bucket. Grease bucket value guide: Conestoga wagon, one-piece type, 10″ high, $70.

GRIDIRONS. The gridiron should not be confused with the griddle, as this utensil served as a portable grate for broiling meat on the open hearth. They were also favored as campfire cooking companions. The handled gridiron, usually set on three short legs, had a flat openwork top surface which was either round, square or oblong.

Guilford painted chest

National Gallery of Art, Washington

The earliest wooden types are extremely scarce. Those of iron are more likely to be encountered by the casual collector than the tin or soapstone versions. Some unusual gridirons slanted slightly toward the front, permitting the juices to run from the grooved slats into a small cup. Collectors can be counted upon to make a fifty-yard dash in record-breaking time at the sight of an early gridiron. Gridiron value guide: wrought iron, slanted top, $85.

GUILFORD CHESTS. The clever cabinetmakers of Guilford, Connecticut, actively practicing their chosen profession in the late 1600s and early 1700s, crafted a type of chest which broke with tradition. Rather than following the standard custom of the period by decorating their chests with carved motifs, they treated them to all-over painted designs. Flowers, foliage and bands of scrolls and leaves were among the dominating themes utilized by this group of craftsmen. Guilford chests were customarily made with a wide front panel and a single drawer. Chest decorators from this region were apparently inspired by contemporary European patterns. Extremely rare.

H

HADLEY CHESTS. The highly regarded Hadley chest was chiefly made by Colonial workers residing in and around the town of Hadley, Massachusetts, between 1675 and 1740. These chests, with a hinged top, were characteristically made with three rectangular upper panels and one or two drawers. Made of oak with pine parts, they were painted red, green, brown or black. Some makers incorporated the initials of the owner, customarily found on the front center panel. The chests were decorated in a distinct manner, with overall shallow carving in floral and leaf designs. John Allis and Samuel Belding made them, as did their sons, Ichabod Allis and Samuel Belding Jr. Hadley chests were also made by other capable craftsmen scattered about the Connecticut River area. Extremely rare.

HARDWARE. There are several categories open for investigation in the field of wrought-iron hardware. Apparently the village blacksmith kept the midnight oil burning to meet the demand for his products. Builders' hardware constitutes one group, covering such collectibles as nails, hasps, door latches, locks, shutter fasteners, hinges and footscrapers. Of course, many of these items are still securely attached to the homes for which they were made, but any such homes destined for demolition should have their hardware salvaged. Frequently the blacksmith designed some truly magnificent pieces of cabinet hardware to adorn early furniture. Locks and latches were made in abundance, some factory produced. The decorative hardware found on coaches, carriages and other vehicles also brings hardware buffs to a fast halt. Hardware value guide: wrought-iron escutheon, stylized horse head, $225; wrought-iron thumb latch, daisy top and bottom, $100; handwrought iron bean latch, pair, $65.

HARVEST TABLES. Normally reserved for seating large groups of people during harvesting periods, this special type of drop-leaf table was particularly favored by provincial carpenters in the 19th century. It was made with a wide drop leaf and a narrow top. Therefore, this style table was rather long and narrow. They were simply crafted by local woodworkers, who crafted them from readily available woods. The harvest table can be correctly identified as a country variation of the ever-popular Pembroke table. Harvest table value guide: pine, two drop leaves, 8' long, 24" wide, $425.

HASTY PUDDING SPOONS. The name "hasty pudding" seems inappropriate, for this gruel necessitated long hours of preparation by the hearth. Actually, the early settlers who indulged in eating this nourishing concoction two or three times daily referred to it as mush, Indian pudding or corn meal pudding. The mixture was boiled in a large kettle by the hearth and slowly stirred with a long-handled spoon or stirrer. Some spoons were ingeniously crooked so that they could be held easily, even by minor family members who spent stirring hours by the fireplace. The spoon bowls should show signs of wear from being scraped against the bottom of the kettle. The hasty pudding stirrers typically had long handles and rather short heads. Hasty pudding spoon value guide: 17" long, crooked handle, $45.

HEPPLEWHITE CHEST OF DRAWERS. The Hepplewhite chest of drawers with its straight front was widely constructed in rural regions from the late 1700s onward. These chests had overhanging tops, square corners and usually four full-width drawers. Oval plate brasses with bail handles and matching keyhole escutcheons adorned drawer fronts. Most models were supported by outcurved French feet. Frequently, in the hands of a skilled craftsman, the feet were connected by a deeply valanced skirt. Forsaking elaborate carved motifs, inlay and veneer work, the country adaptations were simply made from native hardwoods, often stained in imitation of mahogany. Hepplewhite chest of drawers value guide: walnut, four drawers, scalloped apron, original brasses, French feet, $1,450; cherry, four drawers, inlay, French feet, $1,175.

HEPPLEWHITE DESKS. Several innovative style changes occurred on desks of the Hepplewhite period (1785–1800). Slant-top and fall-front bureau desks displayed oval or round hardware and curving high bracket feet. The veneered surfaces lent themselves to inlaid decoration, eagle motifs being enormously popular. This elaborate form of embellishment was never attempted by unskilled cabinetmakers in outlying districts. Many models crafted from assorted hardwoods had six or eight pigeonholes, and an equal number of small drawers in the interior compartment. Special mention should be made of the roll-top tambour desk, although its fame eluded country folk. A variation had the tambour shutters in a vertical position, opening horizontally in two sections to reveal pigeonholes and small drawers. Hepplewhite desk value guide: mahogany, inlaid, fall-front, four drawers, valanced skirt, French feet, $1,400;

cherry, slant-front, inlaid, four drawers, French feet, 44″ high, 39″ wide, $1,200.

HERB BOXES. The Shakers were American pacesetters in marketing herbs on a commercial basis in the United States. Consequently, their oval herb boxes are always in demand. Often the largest box in a set of nested boxes was designated for herbs. They made shallow and deep boxes for storing herbs, which can be recognized by side and cover laps uniformly pointing in the same direction. A paper label often bore the name of the contents. Shaker-made herb trays and boxes are considered best by box buffs. Of course, other boxmakers made them in round and oval shapes with close-fitting overlapping tops thus keeping the contents fresh and hopefully rodent protected. Herb box value guide: Shaker, copper tacks, oval, 12″ x 6″ x 2¾″, $55.

HIGH-POST BEDS. The high-post bed reached the height of its popularity in America between the 1720s and 1830s. Country cabinetmakers endeavored to copy the contemporary furniture designs, but with modest success. Queen Anne style beds having cabriole legs terminating in club feet were supplanted in the Chippendale period by cabriole legs with claw-and-ball or square-block feet. Those based on the furniture designs of George Hepplewhite fea-

High-post bed, Southwestern characteristics

National Gallery of Art, Washington

tured tapering, finely reeded posts which were wider at the base. A square leg and spade foot was clearly visible below the bed rail on most examples from this period. Hepplewhite beds made by American craftsmen often had a movable metal decoration concealing the bolt. It held the posts and sides together. The Sheraton styles of the early 1800s were characterized by round tapering posts, carved motifs and casters. Bedposts became heavier and thicker, and carved motifs became more elaborate during the American Empire period (1815–1840). The high-post bed with its tester and valance fell from favor during the late 1800s. High-post bed value guide: Hepplewhite style, curly maple, turned and reeded posts, spade feet, circa 1810, $725; butternut wood, four-poster, carved posts, scrolled headboard, New York, $675.

HIGH-POST SPOOL BEDS. There were infinitely more low-post spool beds made during the 19th century than high-post spool beds; thus the latter command premium prices. Their limited production was primarily restricted to furniture factories operating in the midwestern section of the United States. They had four spool-turned posts ranging up to seven feet in height. Some had ball-turned finials while others were made with arched tester-type frames. Spool-turned spindles in varying numbers, combined with matching top rails, created a beautiful bed. A pleasant variation was the triangular arched top rail found on some models. Side pieces on these turned treasures were secured with iron bed latches, or bed screws. Highly regarded high-post spool beds were generally made of black walnut or of maple stained a rich brown. High-post spool bed value guide: black walnut, 6' tall, 6½' long, 5' wide, iron bed latches, circa 1865, $565.

HIGH-STRETCHER TABLES. From about 1650 to 1720 many New England furniture makers crafted tables with high stretchers, known as high-stretcher tables. This style table with its oblong top usually had a full-width drawer. The turned legs generally terminated in small knob or pear-shaped feet. Since the stretchers were unusually high, the tables were somewhat uncomfortable. When five stretchers appear on this style table, it is often referred to as a five-stretcher table. A number of these tables display characteristics of the William and Mary style. They were often made of walnut or oak, used singly or combined with a top of pine. High-stretcher table value guide: William and Mary style, oak and pine, turned legs, matching stretchers, one drawer, circa 1720, $2,160.

HIRED MAN'S BEDS. This is a collector's term for a low single-width bedstead, also known as an under-the-eaves or attic bed. Although they may have been used in servants' quarters, they were also utilized as beds for the sick or elderly. Most early types were made of poplar and were painted green. In the 19th century factory-made spool-turned beds of this type became fashionable. Their production was confined to small furniture factories engaged in distributing cottage furniture. The mattress rested directly on the slats without the aid of springs. Maple, birch, black walnut and other hardwoods were favored for the factory-made specimens. Hired man's bed value guide: maple, circa 1870, $185.

HITCHCOCK, LAMBERT. Will the real Lambert Hitchcock please stand up and take a bow? His name is associated with fancy chairs bearing stenciled-decorated surfaces produced from about 1818 to 1852. The true Hitchcock chairs originated in Connecticut, where Lambert began making chair parts in 1818. A few years later he was making chairs of every description, which were shipped to various sections of the country. About 1825 he opened a large factory and adopted the signature "L. Hitchcock, Hitchcocksville, Conn. Warranted." The chairs he produced followed Sheraton and American Empire designs and were enlivened with stencil-decorated surfaces. The firm manufactured a variety of chairs, rocking chairs, settees and children's chairs. Following financial difficulties the company was reorganized in 1832. Lambert's brother-in-law Arba Alford became a partner and the signature was changed to "Hitchcock Alford & Co. Hitchcocksville, Conn. Warranted." The signature remained in use until 1843, when Lambert withdrew from the firm to establish his own cabinetmaking shop in Unionville, Connecticut. He adopted the signature "Lambert Hitchcock, Unionville, Connecticut." Arba Alford continued operating the factory in Hitchcocksville, labeling his products "Alford and Company." Any piece of furniture having an authentic Hitchcock signature should never be altered in any manner. The chairs currently being manufactured in Hitchcocksville, (now Riverton, Connecticut) are marked with the initials "H.C. & Co." under the front of the seat. Hitchcock chair value guide: black slat-back pillow top, plank seat, signed, original stencil, circa 1835, $285; black button back, crown top, cane seat, signed, stenciled florals, original finish, $285; Salem rocker, plank seat, signed, stenciled florals, circa 1830, $350; black, slat back, pillow top, plank seat, signed, original stencil, circa 1835, $250; natural finish, slat back, crown top, cane seat, signed, undecorated, $155.

HITCHCOCK CLOCKS. This collector-named shelf clock having painted and stenciled splats and columns was fashionable in America during the fad for "fancy furniture." The decorations were so similar to those found on Hitchcock chairs between the 1820s and 1850s that a borrowing of themes seems apparent. Frequently they are called "stenciled clocks." Most clocks in this category were made with wooden works and painted tablets. The decorative treatment often suggested Federal period forms. Eli Terry and talented Eli Terry Jr. of Plymouth, Connecticut, were among the clockmakers inspired by Hitchcock motifs. A clock with a minimum amount of original decoration is far more salable than a recently retouched model. Hitchcock clock value guide: Eli Terry, crotched veneered, hand stenciled, circa 1830, $450.

HITCHING POSTS. When the horse and buggy was replaced by more modern means of transportation, the hitching post found itself relegated to collectible status. There was a time when every main street was lined with variously designed hitching posts. Early

Jockey hitching post
National Gallery of Art, Washington

wooden versions proved perishable when subjected to prolonged exposure to the elements; therefore they are scarce items. Somewhat more available are the durable wrought-iron or cast-iron models. Blacksmiths usually made the hitching post a simple affair, varying the base but generally topping it with a horse's head, complete with a ring for the handle. Fancy designs originated at cast-iron foundries particularly in the mid-19th century. Figural forms proved customer-catching, as foundry catalogues offered such selections as jockeys, footmen and Black Sambos. Hitching post value guide: cast-iron stable boy, circa 1870, $420; horse head and rings, $185; cast-iron horse head, ring for reins, circa 1860, $210.

HOG SCRAPER CANDLESTICKS. Is it possible that a candlestick could also function as a hog scraper? People engaged in the hog-scraping business, particularly between the 1780s and 1850s, found it feasible. These tin or iron lighting accessories had circular convex bases with very sharp edges, which were frequently used to scrape bristles from the backs of slaughtered hogs. Needless to say, these candlesticks were quite sturdily constructed. When not being used for scraping chores, they served as simple candlesticks. They were made with or without a projected lip at the top edge. Any example having a lip could be hung from a slat, settle or chair rail to shed a bit of light between scraping sessions. Hog scraper candlestick value guide: wrought iron, circa 1850, $65.

HOLLOWWARE. A pewter collector who specializes in hollowware articles is showing a preference for all the hollow forms. This term can be applied to any vessel designed to hold liquids. The same terminology is used in silversmithing. It encompasses many pewter forms, including tankards, porringers, loving cups, measures, beakers, flagons, creamers, pitchers and bleeding bowls. The casting of these items required the services of a skilled pewterer—one who could competently create articles consisting of more than one piece of metal and expertly fit them together to form an attractive assemblage. Less expertise was required for crafting articles conceived from one piece of metal, such as spoons, basins and plates. Local pewterers were kept busy supplying their clientele with hollowware items well into the 19th century, when less expensive glass and pottery vessels caused the demand for pewter to diminish. Hollowware value guide: tankard, Manning Bowman & Co., 8½″ tall, circa

Hooked rug,
floral design,
19th century
*National Gallery of Art,
Washington*

1865, $390; porringer, American, heart handle, unmarked, 3¾″ diameter, circa 1820, $225; measure, baluste⁻ shaped, American, unmarked, S-scroll handle, circa 1830, $140.

HOOKED RUGS. The hooked rug became an underfoot favorite in America during the early 19th century. For a foundation many homemakers relied on burlap sacking, often using sugar or meal bags, factory-woven cotton or homespun linen. Discarded family clothing was carefully acquired and cut into narrow strips suitable for hooking. Then the selected strips were dyed with vegetable dyes. Next came the creative part of the project when the rugmaker turned designer and sketched the design on the background prior to stretching it on a frame. Then the hooking started with something resembling a crochet hook. Naturally, the finished product was a tribute to the hooker's ability. Many hookers played it safe with geometric and floral motifs, while more adventuresome ones attempted barnyard scenes, buildings and patriotic designs. Rugs were made in many sizes and shapes, and the earliest types show the softest colors. Hooked rug value guide: geometric design, small multicolored squares, 28″ x 38″, $185; flowers with floral border, reds, yellows, blues, 28″ x 40″, $155; four-corner leaves, green on a beige background, 24″ x 42″, $135.

HOOP-BACK WINDSOR CHAIRS. Philadelphia chairmakers borrowed the Windsor chair design from their English cousins in the 1720s when they were first introduced to the American public. The hoop-back style originated in Philadelphia about 1750, and within the next century was produced throughout the United States. This low-back style had a curved top, the spindles extending through the lower semicircular rail in the center area upward to the curved top piece. Many people call this style a bow-back. The hoop-back was often made from hickory combined with other woods. Some later chairs in this category had a comb or an exceptionally high back. When a chairmaker labeled his product he often did so under the seat. Hoop-back Windsor value guide: child's highchair, oak and hickory, stained dark brown, circa 1790, $340; hickory, pine and maple, seven-spindle back, New England, circa 1780, $335.

HOUND-HANDLED PITCHERS. The hunt continues for hound-handled pitchers produced in Rockingham, Parian, stoneware and brown salt glaze in the 19th century. The pitchers are quite distinctive, with a dog's body forming the handle and with hunting or game scenes in relief on the sides. English modeler Daniel Greatbach introduced the design to American audiences while in the employ of the American Pottery Co. of Jersey City about 1840. Thereafter, Rockingham hound-handled pitchers galloped out of potteries for the duration of the century. On the authentic Bennington version, the hound has an arched neck, and a sharp mold mark appears on the belly. The duck-billed hound has a chain link collar with sufficient room between the paws to insert a finger. On Bennington examples the ribs are always clearly defined. A mask or eagle beneath the spout denotes a remarkable pitcher. Hound-handled pitcher value guide: Bennington, hunt scenes in relief, 7″ tall, $485; Rockingham, East Liverpool, Ohio, $180.

HOUSE BOXES. Every box collector yearns to have a Pennsylvania type "house box" around the house. These boxes date from the mid-1800s, when they served as convenient catchalls for tons of treasures and trinkets. This style wooden box with its curved lid and thin metal hasps bears a striking resemblance to an old-fashioned trunk or deed box. The background colors employed on house boxes are as varied as the rainbow's hue. Garlands of flowers adorn the lids of some models. Expect the unexpected in painted motifs and you will be disappointed—decorators ornamented them with designs indicative of the region. Since the original boxes were hand-pegged and painted with water-base paints which tend to show signs of age, reproductions should not prove troublesome. House box value guide: curved lid, painted flowers, original, slightly worn decor, Pennsylvania, circa 1850, $375.

HUNT BOARDS. Before and after the hunt, refreshments were served on these pieces in southern areas. Formal furniture makers made elegant long and high tables in graceful Hepplewhite or Sheraton styles, known as hunting boards or hunting tables. While the formal examples are quite impressive, the smaller models resembling sideboards, crafted in rural areas, are worth the hunt. From Virginia south and westward, the hunt board was a plantation staple from the late 1700s onward. These tables, which ranged from four to six feet in length, had cupboards or drawers. They were devoid of ornamentation except for brass or turned wooden knobs, brass keyholes or brass pendant ring handles. Some doors had slightly sunken panels. Four or six slender tapering legs supported the carcase of these walnut or southern pine pieces. Hunt board value guide: walnut, 5′ long, 18″ wide, 40″ tall, turned legs, Virginia, circa 1830, $1,750.

HUTCHES. Provincial furniture makers developed the hutch cupboard in the early 1700s. This two-part form consisted of an upper section of two or more railed shelves and a lower one with an arrangement of either doors, drawers or both. As a dating guide, it is best to examine the drawers, hardware and type of wood used on the back. The 18th-century cupboards had detailed handiwork in the form of scalloping, notching and other decorative trim. By the 19th century their makers offered simplified renditions. Those originating in Pennsylvania tended to be more elaborate than their New England counterparts. Spoon notches were rarely found on New England models. There was no attempt on the part of country cabinetmakers to adhere to any set formula. They constructed them from available pine, birch, cherry, maple and other local woods. Many were painted, while others received a natural waxed or polished finish. Hutch value guide: pine, four shelves in upper section, two drawers and two doors in lower section, original red paint, 6′ x 8′ tall, circa 1865, $750; cherry, three shelves in upper section, one drawer and two doors in lower section, 6′ tall, $625.

HUTCH TABLES. The space-saving hutch table can be classified as a twin to the chair-table. When the top tips back to reveal a chest under the tabletop, it is a hutch table. This dual-purpose furniture form was crafted from the early 1700s onward. Sometimes there is a simple boxlike storage area, while other models have a small chest of drawers. The top could be placed in a vertical or horizontal position to function as either a table or a chair. The added storage area beneath the top made this piece a triple threat. Finely crafted examples can usually be traced to a skilled cabinet-maker. A more primitive model may be the work of a householder, or even a journeyman carpenter. Coveted finds in this category are the painted pine chests originating in the southwestern part of the United States dating from the mid-1800s, with handsomely painted designs reflecting the Spanish influence. Hutch table value guide: pine and oak, rail feet, shaped sides, circa 1790, $1,875; pine, original red paint, primitive type, 46″ round in diameter, $1,400.

I

ICE CREAM FREEZERS. Dolley Madison melted the hearts of her countrymen when she served ice cream at a party honoring the second inauguration of President Madison in 1813. Ice cream machines were first advertised in America during the 1700s. However, the first patent was not issued until the mid-19th century. As each new ice cream freezer for home or commercial use appeared, its maker proclaimed it made "the most perfect ice cream ever." Depending on size, a freezer made from one quart to twenty quarts of delicious ice cream. There were many innovative models which operated by means of a crank, flywheel or pulley. Among the numerous named styles were the "Arctic," "The Gem," "White Mountain," "Freezer King" and "Blizzard." The North Manufacturing Company of Philadelphia was rightfully proud of its "American Twin Freezer," which froze two flavors of ice cream at the same time. Ice cream freezer value guide: American Twin Freezer, circa 1900, $40; The Gem Freezer, revolving can and dasher, tinned inner parts, $35; White Mountain Ice Freezer, $30; Arctic Ice Cream Freezer, $30.

INDIAN COLLECTIBLES. Aware antiquers, ever with an ear to the ground for potential profits, should consider investing in Indian arts and crafts. Due to the tremendous interest in authentic examples, numerous reproductions have surfaced. Working with materials supplied by Mother Earth, American Indians produced some of the most sought-after baskets ever crafted. The dyes used by them in basketmaking were derived from natural substances. Homespun and home-dyed yarns were also utilized in Navajo rugs; these are actually blankets, with the earliest types made to be worn over the shoulder. Light and dark stripes formed the pattern on early specimens, but eventually it was broken by a zigzag line in what is known as the terrace pattern. Later, diamond designs dominated their output. American Indian clothing, jewelry, pottery work, beadwork and other crafts are in strong demand and short supply. This situation causes increased values to be posted in practically every category of Indian collectibles. Indian collectibles value guide: clay pipe, $22; Apache bag, turquoise and white beads, circa 1890, $225; Hopi basket, coiled deep bowl, polychrome geometric pattern, 12" diameter, $175; Hopi doll, Katahina, ceremonial figure, 12" tall, $190; Navajo rug, red, white, black and gray, zigzag lines, 3' x 2'6", $275; spearhead, flint, $9.

IPSWICH CHESTS. These oak chests of stile and rail construction are attributed to cabinetmakers active in and around Ipswich, Massachusetts, between 1660 and 1680. They had slightly sunken panels, three on the front and two on either end. The famed craftsman Thomas Dennis fashioned such chests, which had elaborately carved intaglio designs. They typically had a plain pine board top, which often served as a seat. Ornamentation in the form of arcaded panels, lunettes, stylized tulips, leafage, lozenge-shaped medallions and rose-motif bands gave these chests their individuality. End stiles were extended to form straight legs. Extremely rare.

IRONING BOARDS. Prior to the development of the folding ironing board in the 19th century, plain old wooden boards were used in makeshift fashion for ironing chores. These ironing boards, made in various lengths up to six feet, were advertised as being warp and crackproof. A shirt board or bosom board is a shorter version of the ironing board designed for pressing smaller items. When manufacturers marketed folding ironing boards in the 1800s, they resembled hutch tables. They had movable tops above a storage compartment where ironing incidentals could be stored. All wooden folding ironing boards were offered under various trade names around the turn of the century, including Ezy Fold, E. Z. Hour and Universal. One widely advertised model capable of being adjusted to three different heights sold for the affordable price of $1. Ironing board value guide: basswood top, maple legs, adjustable, circa 1900, $45; Acme Sleeve Board, circa 1899, $22.

ISLE D'ORLEANS CHAIRS. This style chair is thought to have been crafted exclusively by chairmakers residing in the lower St. Lawrence region. Patterned after an earlier French style, it found its way into country homes during the 1700s and 1800s. The back of the chair is different enough to make it easy to identify. It is rectangular. There are no slats or spindles. The chair seat is similarly shaped. They were made with square, chamfered or turned legs. Pine was the favorite wood, painted in solid colors. Repainting one of these regional chairs lessens its value. They are also known as Côte de Beaupré chairs. Isle d'Orleans chair value guide: pine, original paint, $275.

J

JACQUARD COVERLETS. Beautiful flowered coverlets known as Jacquard coverlets appeared in America about 1820. They represent some of the most outstanding designs ever to appear in American weaving. The earliest ones were supposedly the work of professional weavers who wove them on the draw loom. Sometimes their makers referred to them as "carpet coverlets." Later, with the aid of a Jacquard attachment, they were made on home looms. The makers employed a stunning variety of fanciful floral motifs, giving special attention to the borders, which frequently contained patriotic motifs, flowers, birds, trees, buildings, portraits or mottoes. A certain amount of restraint may be noted in the design treatment on earlier specimens. Within the border a maker often placed his name and/or the name of the owner, and a date. Jacquard coverlet value guide: floral center, bird border, made by Samuel Dornbach, dated 1846, $425; eagle pattern, eagle border, stars, circa 1850, $350.

JELLY CUPBOARDS. The jelly cupboard or jam cupboard frequently suffers an identity problem with present-day collectors. It is commonly referred to as a small cupboard rather than being distinguished by its original use. These small cupboards, crafted by various rural woodworkers, were always well stocked with jellies or other preserves in the autumn season. The form varied slightly with some of the earliest cupboards, having a door with several stationary shelves in the interior. They were usually fitted with a wooden catch. Many jelly cupboards dating from the late 1800s were made with two drawers above the two cupboard doors. The doors usually opened outward from the center to reveal stationary shelves for storing precious preserves. Jelly cupboard value guide: pine, two dovetailed drawers above two doors, original red paint, slightly worn, circa 1850, $290; pine, two dovetailed drawers, two doors, paneled ends, refinished, circa 1860, $220.

JEROME, NOBLE. Thanks to urging from his brother Chauncey, Noble Jerome developed an ingenious thirty-hour movement of rolled brass about 1838. Prior to this development only more expensive eight-day clocks had this style movement. This was an important moment in the annals of American clockmaking, as it immediately made wooden movements obsolete. Brass was not only durable but possessed weather-resistant qualities. Thereafter, this newly devised movement brought about the mass production of inexpensive eight-day clocks and some thirty-hour versions. The ogee case originally made with wooden moyements was so widely manufactured with rolled brass movements that it was exported extensively in the mid-19th century. Jerome value guide: ogee case, hand-painted landscape scene tablet, original, time and strike, $150; cottage shelf clock, 12″ tall, $120.

JOINT STOOLS. The joint stool, sometimes referred to as a joint table, is one of the earliest American-made stools of importance to collectors. Since it was composed of parts united by a skilled woodworker known as a joiner, it obtained its usual name. The parts were joined together by mortise-and-tenon joints. They usually had raked or splayed legs slanting slightly outward, and were made with or without a small drawer. The legs were turned and braced with stretchers. Discovering an early Jacobean oak joint stool with baluster-turned legs outside the confines of a museum is cause for celebration. When baluster turnings appeared on later versions, they were simplified. Most joint stools of a later date showed vase and ring turnings. They were made primarily of oak, maple, pine and cherry, used either singly or in combinations. Joint stool value guide: oak, maple splayed legs, $235.

JUGS. From the early 1600s onward American potters produced redware jugs and other simple utilitarian articles. Made from local clays, these deep vessels for holding liquids appeared in many sizes. Since the needs of the homemaker dictated the products of the potter, jugs were made in many localities from available clays. Various colored glazes were used, such as brown, yellow, green, orange-red, dark red and black. By the early 1700s village potters in certain areas introduced stoneware jugs. Their production escalated in the 19th century, when saltglazed jugs became a standard item with leading potters. These functional pieces were made in varying sizes and shapes with simple designs. Collector interest intensifies when a jug bears a maker's mark, has an unusual shape or is elaborately decorated with cobalt blue designs. Jug value guide: stoneware, cobalt blue band, "Rum" impressed in blue, large, 18th century, $230; stoneware, cobalt blue decor, two-gallon size, Pennsylvania, $190; pottery jug, onion shaped, black manganese glaze, 7¼" high, $130; redware, speckled glaze, strap handle, 8" high, $100.

JUGTOWN POTTERY. Peter Craven, a potter from the Staffordshire district of England, started a pottery in Steeds, a section

Jug, stoneware, cobalt blue decor, 19th century
National Gallery of Art, Washington

of Moore County, North Carolina, about 1750. Following the Civil War, members of the original Craven family were still engaged in producing pottery. The potters active in the community concentrated their efforts on little brown jugs made for the whiskey trade. This gave rise to the name Jugtown, although a town by this name did not exist. The potters were faced with loss of business with the advent of Prohibition. Collector interest centers about the 20th-century pieces originating at the Jugtown Pottery established by Jacques and Juliana Busbee. Their pottery was the first to bear the name Jugtown. Jugtown pottery value guide: bowl, blue and gray, 3¼" x 4¼", $40.

K

KAS. This large clothes cupboard was made primarily by Dutch-American colonists of the Hudson River Valley, New Jersey and Long Island. The earliest examples followed 17th-century furniture styles, having large ball feet, heavy cornice and wide molding. Later, during the Chippendale period, some wardrobes were made with bracket feet. Most examples had a paneled front with two doors above two drawers. The inside was fitted with shelves. Some had a natural finish while others were painted with fruits or flowers

Kas, elaborately hand-painted, late 17th century

National Gallery of Art, Washington

in grisaille. Walnut was the favored wood for these massive wardrobes. The Edgerton family of cabinetmakers, active in northern New Jersey in the 18th century, labeled some of their pieces. Despite its awesome proportions, a kas was constructed with pins or wedges easily removed, making it quite portable. Kas value guide: walnut, two doors, rat-tail hinges, two drawers, bracket feet, original hardware, raised panel doors, panel sides, $1,400; pine, two raised panel doors, two drawers, original red paint, Pennsylvania, circa 1790, $950.

KEELERS. This woodenware keepsake obtained its name from the German word "kiel" meaning to rise. Apparently it was appropriately named, as these shallow-hooped round or oval containers were used in cooling milk, thus allowing the cream to rise. This piece was of European origin, with the first American examples dating from the mid-1600s. Keelers had two protruding staved handles, oversized in relation to the depth of the vessel. Earlier handmade versions had wooden hoops, while factory specimens invariably exhibit iron hoops. This milk container was still kicking around in the late 19th century when keelers were being sold at country stores. Keeler value guide: pine, staved and pegged, wooden hoop, 16" diameter, $165.

KEGS. The white cooper possessed the know-how for crafting water kegs, rum kegs, molasses kegs and oyster kegs among others. Because these receptacles for holding various liquids deteriorated rapidly, antique specimens are surprisingly scarce. Their makers favored durable oak wood for these staved and hooped containers, which resembled barrels or buckets sealed at one end. Most examples were crafted with a bung hole in the top and body portion. Pewter bung holes appeared on some models. The term "rundelet" is applied to any triangular shaped keg. When rum kegs were made of pine, these spirit lifters were quite portable due to their light weight. Oyster kegs are at the bottom of the barrel craft-wise, as these hastily constructed kegs rarely show careful handiwork. They have an opening in the top of a size to accommodate even an oversized oyster. During the oyster season these kegs traveled miles to satisfy the demand for deep sea dwellers. Keg value guide: handmade, oak, wooden bands, 20" high, $60; oyster keg, staved and hooped, metal hoops, $25.

KENTUCKY RIFLES. The Kentucky or Pennsylvania rifle was brought to perfection by German and Swiss colonists in the early 1700s. They strived to make a rifle capable of meeting the demands of the settlers, and accomplished their task by lengthening the barrel and decreasing the caliber. The earliest examples had thick butts and straight lines, but in the post-Revolutionary War period elegant inlays and engraved motifs were introduced. Another added feature was the sharply dropping butt. Because these rifles were made in Pennsylvania, the term Kentucky rifle may need some clarifying. It was so named based on its widespread use by pioneers settling sections of the Kentucky and Ohio frontiers, just like they did in the movies. Kentucky rifle value guide: McCann, full stock, brass trim, $600.

KEROSENE LAMPS. Kerosene-burning lighting devices became after-dark favorites in America about 1860. The kerosene flame was brighter, better smelling and cleaner than that previously provided by whale oil. Lamp designers worked long and lovingly over innovative lighting accessories of metal and glass. The famous "Gone with the Wind" lamps, with their beautifully decorated shades and cast-brass trim, suddenly appeared on marble-top tables everywhere. Other lamps were purely utilitarian. During the 1880s and 1890s two kerosene-burning lamps having metal bases became household favorites: the currently collectible Rayo and student lamps. Tin and pressed-glass kerosene-burning lamps are somewhat neglected by collectors; thus they merit consideration from farsighted antiquers. Kerosene lamp value guide: brass, student lamp, milk glass shade, circa 1880, $190; brass, turned standard, urn-shaped font, cranberry shade, 22" tall, $290; Rayo, nickel, frosted shade, $80.

KITCHEN CLOCKS. A craze for fretwork or gingerbread work seized the American populace following the Philadelphia Centennial Exposition of 1876. Scrolled and carved clocks, often of oak or walnut, became the fashionable timepieces of the moment, especially in kitchens. They were made in elaborate shapes and in many sizes by such clockmakers as E. N. Welch, E. I. Ingraham and the New Haven Clock Company, among others. A stamped design on the glass usually afforded a view of the decorated pendulum. There were even do-it-yourself kits with Seth Thomas movements, for those wanting to indulge in some downhome clockmaking. Identification is possible, for most clocks bore a company monogram. The fancier the clock, the higher the price tag. Kitchen clock value guide: E. Ingraham and Co., time and strike, walnut case, fancy, $160; New Haven Clock Co., fretwork case, walnut, $150; Waterbury Clock Co., time and strike, oak case, elaborate, $145.

KITCHEN CUPBOARDS. The skilled cabinetmakers of Pennsylvania furnished their clientele with variously styled kitchen cupboards in the late 19th century. They were normally constructed from available local woods such as pine or poplar. Most types were treated to a coat of blue, gray, brown or green paint. Others were permitted to remain in a natural finish, although they are rarely found in that state nowadays. They are easy to recognize despite the fact that there was no strict adherence to any set pattern. A simplified rendition of the Dutch cupboard with two wooden paneled doors in the upper section and two drawers above the two doors in the lower section was offered by many woodworkers. Another style having a high counter kitchen top with two drawers and two doors beneath was also of Pennsylvania German provenance. Kitchen cupboard value guide: pine, red finish, two solid raised panel doors upper section, three drawers above, single door lower section, 6' tall, circa 1860, $550; pine, painted blue, two solid doors upper section, two drawers above, two doors lower section, original finish, circa 1870, $450.

Kitchen cupboard, Pennsylvania, 18th century

National Gallery of Art, Washington

KNIFE BOXES. Stately city dwellings had elegant knife boxes or urns with slanting tops ornamenting sideboards in the 19th century. However, in rural areas simply constructed knife boxes or trays held family utensils. Generally, they were made of pine, poplar, maple or walnut. The simplest and best-known version was a shallow rectangular box divided into two compartments. The divider was fitted with a handle grip. Any antique example is certain to show signs of heavy usage. Fancier versions often had sloping or hinged lids. There were straight-sided models and others with flaring sides. A sharp-eyed scavenger may discover one composed of light and dark contrasting woods. Pennsylvania craftsmen made them in numerous variations, usually with painted or carved motifs. While New England knife boxes were typically painted a solid color, those originating in Pennsylvania displayed more color variation. Knife box value guide: pine, slanted sides, floral decor on sides, original, circa 1840, $175; walnut, dovetailed, chip carved, two compartments, center handle, $150; pine, dovetailed, cutout handle, original red paint, $90.

L

LACE EDGE TRAYS. Paul Revere was known to have been crafting lace edge trays in the pre-Revolutionary War period. Is it any wonder that some collectors call them Paul Revere trays? During the late 1700s and early 1800s they were made by many American tinsmiths in round, oval, oblong and rectangular shapes. They frequently were crafted in graduated sizes. The delicately pierced narrow borders are a lasting tribute to the tinsmiths' creativity. Naturally, the type and amount of piercing varied in accordance with the capabilities of the craftsman. Most trays were treated to a background of black paint and enhanced in the center area with small flower or fruit designs. Since their makers rarely marked them, it is next to impossible for collectors to distinguish them from similarly designed imported trays. Lace edge tray value guide: rectangular, elaborate pierced border, roses and leaves in center, 26" long, 14" wide, original finish, circa 1840, $185.

LADDER-BACK CHAIRS. Distinguished by its horizontal back slats resembling the rungs of a stepladder, this chair of English origin is known as a ladder-back chair, or a slat-back chair. The earliest American versions dating from the late 1600s had square or turned posts and two or three horizontal slats. A change occurred in the early 1700s, when the backs became higher and the slats increased in number and in width. Another innovation was the development of bolder turnings and decorative finials. By the late 1700s most makers were favoring plain posts and two or three back slats. Regional differences abounded. Chairs of Pennsylvania origin had plain posts and curved slats, while New England versions sported turned posts and straight slats. As the form persisted into the 1800s, ladder-back chairs were fabricated from local woods with lower backs and two slats. Most makers favored rush seats, although the Shakers showed a preference for tape seats. The greater the number of slats, the earlier the chair. Ladder-back chair value guide: armchair, ash and maple, turned posts and legs, sausage-turned stretchers, four shaped splats, circa 1780, $420; armchair, maple, plain posts, four curved splats, ball feet, $400; rocking chair, maple, four slats, intricate turnings, rush seat, painted black, $290; side chair, hickory, rush seat, three splats, plain posts, plain stretchers, $165.

LADLES. A notable ladle transaction was recorded in 1806 by Georgetown tinsmith William Thomas, who listed as a customer Francis Scott Key, a lawyer turned songsmith. A check of Colonial household inventories reveals that nary a kitchen lacked a ladle. Local coppersmiths, blacksmiths and braziers endeavored to keep ladies supplied with ladles of copper, iron and brass. Those smitten by the lure for old ladles should never abandon the search before acquiring an early hornware ladle, frequently crafted of exotic musk ox. Fine pewter ladles with gracefully curved handles and beaded bowls fetch premium prices, particularly signed specimens. The wooden ladles are winning acquisitions, with those whittled in Pennsylvania possessing typical folk motifs sometimes incorporating a date or initials; there is no problem distinguishing them from plain and simple Shaker ladles. Ladle value guide: iron ladle-strainer combination, decorated handle, 17" long, $45; wooden, curly maple, $35; iron tasting ladle, circa 1870, $40; brass, large, long handle, $35.

LAMP STANDS. Shortly after whale-oil lamps were introduced in the late 18th century, lamp stands started emerging from country workshops. A four-legged lamp stand was thought to be safer for supporting this source of light than a three-legged candlestand. Country versions of assorted woods, including maple, cherry, walnut and pine, held lamps of every description well into the 19th century. Sometimes an inexpensive wood was stained to resemble the more expensive mahogany. Rural craftsmen usually made them with plain undecorated square tops. Most models had a shallow front drawer, either full-width or narrower. Often the original brass knobs have been replaced. Lamp stands with slightly oblong tops and drop leaves became fashionable during the American Empire period (1815–1840). These stands made with anywhere from one to three drawers were usually fitted with wooden, pressed glass or brass rosette knobs. In the closing decades of the 19th century, cottage-type pedestal lamp stands were favored by furniture factories. Lamp stand value guide: pine, square top, one drawer, circa 1800, $275; pine, square top, painted, pedestal type, baluster-turned shaft, cottage furniture type, circa 1885, $125.

LANTERNS. As a source of light after dark, the lantern was always close at hand in Colonial America. It has been rightfully described as a transparent case for a candle. Originally the translucent sides were composed of sheets of horn; later, glass and mica were utilized. The variously shaped open framework was made of copper, silver, brass, iron, tin, lead or wood. Smaller sizes were destined for outdoor use, while larger sizes often hung in entrance halls. Many lanterns were made for specific uses, such as the miner's lantern or pocket lantern. Every farmer had one or more lanterns hanging by the rear entry and by the barn door for nighttime walks or emergencies. Tin types met with popularity in country regions, where the quality of the workmanship varied according to the dexterity of the tinsmith. A note of caution pertaining to pierced tin lanterns: they are being widely reproduced. Lantern value guide: wood, candle lantern, four glass panes, $120; Tin, pierced, early, cylindrical, 14″, $85; iron, lacy, four glass panes, 14″ high, circa 1880, $45; farm lantern, red globe, $25.

LARD-OIL LAMPS. Noah Webster relied on illumination from a pair of lard-oil lamps while compiling the dictionary bearing his

Lard-oil lamp, 19th century

Pierced tin lantern, early 19th century

Both photographs, National Gallery of Art, Washington

name. When the westward movement materialized, lard-oil lamps were in demand because fish and chemical fuels simply were not available in far-flung outposts. Inventors kept developing new improved models all conceived with the same purpose: to keep the lard in contact with the wick. Country tinsmiths and pewterers worked on the trial-and-error basis, as scientific principles eluded them. Several patents were issued for lamps relying on gravity as well as heat conductivity. Others relied on mechanical pressure of one sort or another to furnish ample illumination. Lard-oil lamp value guide: tin, Kinnear patent, $110; pewter, 7″ tall, early, $120.

LARD SQUEEZERS. Hogs were as commonplace on most farms as chickens. Cooking lard was derived from hog fat in the following manner: after being cooked, the fat was tied in a cloth or bag and vigorously squeezed by wooden pincers. The liquid was caught in a suitable container, where it cooled into lard. The wooden lard squeezer was simply constructed of two whittled strips of wood secured together by a wooden peg, leather strap or metal hinge. Factory-made examples show the leather strap secured by machine-made screws. A similar type of wooden squeezer was utilized in cracking lobster shells. Lard squeezer value guide: early hand-crafted type, leather strap, $85.

LAZY SUSANS. The lazy Susan table is a tribute to the ingenuity of American woodworkers. The raised revolving tray in the center of the tabletop provided this table with its individuality. The lazy Susan generally measured from two to three feet in diameter. Happy homemakers found it saved them having to jump up and down repeatedly during dinnertime. The actual tabletop upon which the tray rotated measured between four and six feet in diameter, its width in proportion to the size of the tray. Pennsylvania craftsmen excelled in producing them, as did workers in southern communities. As a general rule they were made from native hardwoods, except for the tops which were usually of pine. Those originating in Pennsylvania were often treated to Amish blue or green paint. Turned legs or plain square legs usually furnished these tables with the necessary support. Due to their present scarcity, it takes some energetic searching to locate a 19th-century lazy Susan table. Lazy Susan table value guide: maple, pine top, original Amish blue paint, turned legs, circa 1870, $1,050.

LEATHERWORK. In the southwestern part of the country where metal was practically nonexistent prior to 1850, hides were often used as a suitable substitute. Collectors covet early rawhide winnowing sieves, door pulls, trunks, buckets, tobacco flasks and boxes. Deerskin coats were worn by both the military and civilian population. Buckskin or rawhide were also utilized in crafting bridles, pouches and cartridge boxes. Leather hats and leggings were among the other items in the clothing category. Saddles and shields in various forms were crafted with care by artisans learned in leatherwork. Tanned buck and buffalo skins proved ideal for shoes, grain sacks, breeches, shirts and even for artistically painted panels. Leatherwork value guide: rawhide-covered trunk, brass bound, $150; buffalo-skin shirt, circa 1880, $110.

LEHNWARE. This term is used in connection with woodenware articles made and decorated by Joseph Long Lehn (1798–1892) of Lancaster County, Pennsylvania. Once he abandoned his love affair with Mother Earth, this farmer turned his thoughts to wiling away the hours working on woodenware. Cups, goblets, spice boxes, egg cups and other woodenware necessities were turned and painted by him. According to reports, some chairs and large pieces also commanded his attention. He decorated his ware in a freehand style, often employing a grayish pink background enlivened with a strawberry motif. As the years began to take their toll, Mr. Lehn surrendered to Father Time by utilizing decalcomanias. Lehnware value guide: goblet, decalcomanias, $100.

LEMON SQUEEZERS. Many of the earliest handmade wooden squeezers resembled meat pounders, with their turned handles and corrugated heads. Of course, the amount of juice extracted by this primitive grinding method was minimal. The hinged wooden squeezer extracted the juice by pressing the cut lemon between the two sections. It appeared in various versions. Some specimens had holes bored through the hollowed section to catch the precious drippings. This type was factory produced at a later date of all wood or iron. Fancier examples boasted iron, metal or ironstone heads. Patented extractors in both reamer and hinged types flooded the market between 1850 and 1900. Such name models as "American Queen," "New Boss," "Standard" and "Yankee Lidon" really kept the juices flowing. Clear and colored glass reamers dating from the turn of the century add zest to any collection of lemon squeezers. Lemon squeezer value guide: cast iron, marked "Boss," $25; cast iron and wood, "Pearl," $25; cast iron, glass insert, "Williams," circa 1890, $20; maple, 11" long, $15.

LIBRARY TABLES. Walnut library tables were a specialty of cabinetmakers residing in New Jersey and Pennsylvania. Quite often one served as a kitchen table in a rural household, although pine versions were made expressly for this purpose. If the drawers of a walnut table show excessive signs of wear, its use as a kitchen piece is substantiated. Sometimes the drawers of a library table were of different widths, but usually they were fitted with oversized knobs. Tabletops ranged between four and six feet in length and were always removable. Some were made of two boards held together by butterfly catches. Most tops had molded edges and rounded ends. A gracefully scalloped skirt is an indication of a superior library table. Library table value guide: pine, two drawers, two-board top, scalloped skirt, simple turnings, 50" long, 33" wide, 29" high, $575.

LIFT-TOP COMMODE. Nothing lifts the spirits of a country antique person faster than locating a fine 19th-century lift-top commode. This style commode was equipped with an overhanging lid easily lifted to reveal a full-size well approximately fourteen inches deep. There was a small off-center drawer on most examples for storing towels or soaps. A door or doors in the lower portion provided a storage compartment. Naturally, variations abound on these bedroom pieces as small and large models were handmade and factory produced in the preplumbing period. A washbowl or pitcher could be stored in the well area to prevent the water from freezing when Jack Frost made an unexpected visit in the middle of the night. The cupboard was suitable for storing a slop jar or chamber pot. Nowadays, these sought-after pieces hold just about everything but a washstand set. Lift-top commode value guide: pine, painted, 14″ deep well, one drawer, one door, circa 1880, $170.

LINEN PRESSES. This two-part furniture form consisted of an upper cupboard and a lower chest of drawers. The slightly smaller upper section fitted into the raised molding on the lower portion. Linens were stored in the linen press, which had solid doors usually hung with H-shaped or butt hinges. Mahogany, cherry, maple, poplar or pine were used in its construction, as were various combinations of hard and soft woods. Widely crafted, it was a particular favorite with country cabinetmakers of New Jersey, New York and Pennsylvania. Cupboard interiors were fitted with either shelves or sliding trays. Ornamentation varied in accordance with the skill of the craftsman, the finer examples displaying detailed decorative trim. Bracket feet or short cabriole brackets with claw-and-ball feet supported the imposing linen press. Linen press value guide: cherry, two doors, plain panels in upper section, three drawers in lower section, cock-beaded edges, willow brasses, circa 1820, $1,800.

LOOP-BACK WINDSOR CHAIRS. From the mid-1700s onward capable American chairmakers exhibited their expertise by crafting superior loop-back Windsor chairs. Commonly known as "stick chairs," Windsors had a light and airy appearance which belied their strength and durability. Although New England chairmakers excelled in producing them, loop-back chairs were also crafted in other sections of the country. This type of Windsor had the spindles enclosed within a single piece of wood. The bar found across the back on the hoop-back style was missing. Most chairs had seven to nine spindles, saddle seats and turned legs braced by a stretcher. As with other Windsors, they were painted to conceal the various woods used in their construction. Some people deplored the white-painted Windsors, but obviously not Benjamin Franklin, who placed an order for two dozen of them. Loop-back Windsor value guide: armchair, brace back, curly maple and mahogany, turned spindles and legs, seven-spindle back, $425; side chair, hickory spindles, maple legs, seven-spindle back, turned legs, circa 1830, $350.

LOW-BACK WINDSOR CHAIRS. The vogue for Windsor chairs quickly spread north from Philadelphia in the mid-1700s, becoming fashionable in New York and New England. The Declaration of Independence was composed by Thomas Jefferson while he sat in a Windsor chair. The low-back style was aptly named as it had short spindles and a semicircular top rail and arms. Some of the earliest types boasted between eleven and seventeen spindles. Later the number of spindles decreased. The blunt-arrow-shaped legs found on early chairs were eventually superseded by vase and ring or simulated bamboo turnings. They were fabricated from several kinds of wood, neatly camouflaged with a coat of paint. In the 19th century the low-back style was responsible for such offspring as the firehouse and captain's chair. Low-back Windsor chair value guide: continuous arm applied crest, thirteen spindles, saddle seat, bulbous turnings, circa 1760, $475; writing armchair, oak, painted green, sixteen spindles, turned legs, circa 1820, $430.

LOW-POST BEDS. Many early household inventories referred to low-post beds as "stump beds" or "low bedsteads." The simple bed frame consisting of posts, rails and plain low headboard was a memory piece based on English models. Their height made them

Left: Low-back Windsor chair, with back extension, 19th century; Right: Low-post bed, early 19th century

Both photographs, National Gallery of Art, Washington

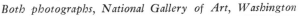

ideal for low-ceiling farmhouse bedrooms, and the style prevailed well into the 19th century. Their makers apparently ignored contemporary furniture styles, as most low-post beds were constructed with turned posts and unornamented headboards. In the American Empire period there was a slight attempt to duplicate formal styles with turned, carved or reeded posts and carved headboards. Bedmakers used available local woods such as cherry, birch or maple, frequently combined with pine or other softwoods. Low-post bed value guide: maple posts, turned, butternut headboard, stained red, circa 1840, original finish, $250; Shaker type, Mt. Lebanon, New York, maple and pine, natural finish, circa 1840, $280; spool-turned, full size rounded corners, circa 1855, $235.

M

MAHANTONGO VALLEY FURNITURE. George and Jacob Braun, Jacob Maser and John Moyer were among the members of the "Brotherhood" or "Consortia" of skilled cabinetmakers diligently practicing their profession in the Mahantongo Valley, Schuylkill County, Pennsylvania, between the 1820s and 1840s. The desks, chests, cupboards and other forms made by guild members apparently were inspired partially by Sheraton styles. Their work shows a preoccupation with turned supports and painted details. Stiles were ornamented with borders of stenciled rosettes, incorporated with typical regional motifs, primarily birds, flowers and geometric forms. This regional furniture is dearly treasured, and should never be altered despite minor deterioration of decorated areas. Mahantongo Valley furniture value guide: cupboard, two glass pane doors above two drawers, two cupboard doors, original decor, fair condition, $2,500.

MAMMY BENCHES. Simply by fitting a short settee with rockers, ingenious furniture makers conceived the marvelous mammy bench. It had a removable guard rail extending across the front, of a size to hold an infant. While baby was being rocked safely in the fenced-in area, mother could proceed to accomplish some sit-down chores. Chairmakers certainly endeavored to make motherhood easier with this combination. There was even a double mammy's bench for rocking two infants simultaneously. Since they were introduced about 1820 when painted furniture designs proved fashionable, this piece was usually subjected to painted and stenciled motifs. Decoration was of the type normally reserved for Hitchcock-type chairs. Various firms produced them in somewhat similar styles, including Lambert Hitchcock and presumably Hitchcock, Alford & Company. Mammy bench value guide: Hitchcock type, stenciled florals on top rail and stretcher, striping, plank seat, unsigned, original decor, circa 1830, $650; arrowback, painted black, stenciled top rail, florals, plank seat, striping, circa 1850, $625.

MARZIPAN MOLDS. The marchpane or marzipan mold was a favorite throughout Europe for centuries, particularly with the confectioners of Belgium. This custom prevailed among early settlers, who carved these rectangular wooden boards with intaglio designs. Most examples ranged between fifteen and thirty inches in diameter. For special celebrations or in honor of historical events, the marzipan board with its varying designs was pressed into service. They represent excellent examples of American folk sculpture. Somewhat in the same category are the springerle boards used for making Swiss and German cookies. They were divided into from six to twenty-four squares, each carved in a different design. Collectors spring to attention over the creative motifs, including birds, animals, nursery rhymes and Biblical themes. Marzipan mold value guide: floral motif, hearts, Pennsylvania, 12″, circa 1850, $265.

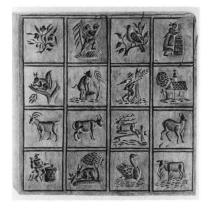

Springerle board, Pennsylvania, 19th century
National Gallery of Art, Washington

MASHERS. Mashers both large and small were whittled by an army of amateur woodworkers in the 1700s and 1800s. Those handy with a jackknife turned them out in amazing numbers, usually of pine, maple, walnut or a hardwood known as red lignum vitae. Collector interest heightens on those displaying intricately turned shafts. Within arm's reach in the kitchen were large mashers for sauerkraut or cabbage and smaller ones suitable for vegetables, potatoes, herbs or spices. Finding two early handmade examples exactly alike would be reason for rejoicing, as most handmade mashers fall into the one-of-a-kind category. A thick masher with a large flat head, known as a butter tamp, was used for packing butter into a butter box or tub. Those devoid of decoration are known within collecting circles as Shaker mashers. Toward the middle of the 19th century the round or square wire-headed potato masher with a wooden handle became a cooking companion. Masher value guide: pine, sauerkraut masher, $18; Shaker, mushroom shape, $20; walnut, potato masher, $12; maple, herb masher, 4″ tall, $12.

MASSACHUSETTS SHELF CLOCKS. In the late 17th and early 18th centuries, Massachusetts boasted some of America's foremost clockmakers. The famous Willards and others active in this region made a special type of shelf clock, commonly called a Massachusetts shelf clock. Benjamin Willard's son Aaron was known to have been highly successful with this style timepiece, retiring in 1823 when he was succeeded by his sons. This particular shelf clock, produced principally between 1800 and 1830, had a thirty-hour or eight-day brass movement. The clock face was housed in a square case, with a square pendulum case beneath. Occasionally they were made as striking clocks. Due to their unique shape, they are also referred to as half-clock, case-on-case or box-on-box clocks. Massachusetts shelf clock value guide: Johnathan Wilder, thirty-hour movement, kidney dial, circa 1820, $850.

MATCH HOLDERS. Just watch a collector's face light up at the sight of a metal, glass or ceramic match holder, which reached their peak of popularity in America following the Civil War. It should come as no surprise that their mass production coincided with the distribution of low-cost friction matches. Glasshouses made them in various designs and in some of the most famous pressed patterns of the period. Matches were stored in pressed-glass boots, shoes and slippers, plus various other equally whimsical shapes. The cast-iron versions covered a wide range of motifs, with heavy emphasis on floral and animal subjects. Should one wish to specialize, the bisque types alone would fill a china cabinet. Small match safes were also made to be carried in a person's pocket. Match holder value guide: glass, bear's head, $35; milk glass, Uncle Sam's hat, $30; iron, dog with tree bark, $25; iron, devil's head and leaves, $20.

MEAT POUNDERS. Antique woodenware is admired by collectors who appreciate its light weight, smoothness and patina. A common cooking accessory certain to be found in the Colonial kitchen was the wooden meat pounder. Also known as a steak mauler, it was used in preparing meat. These wooden mallets were made in different sizes, often with corrugated or pyramid-shaped heads. The indentations on the head of the mallet caused increased friction while the meat was being pounded. These early tenderizers sold for fifteen cents each in woodenware catalogues of the late 1800s. Another innovation during this period was the combination meat tenderer and ice pick attached to a hammerlike handle. Meat pounder value guide: corrugated tapered head, circa 1840, $20.

MILK CUPBOARDS. This country kitchen piece was presumably a specialty of the Pennsylvania woodworker. These pieces, of single-unit construction, generally date from the mid-19th century. Since it was purely utilitarian, there was no attempt on the part of the maker to furnish it with any decorative accents. A representative version had upper and lower doors of equal size and depth separated by two side-by-side doors. Minor variations occurred according to individual design. Most had wooden latches and door pulls and cast-iron butt hinges. Fortify yourself before embarking on an expedition for one as they are in short supply. Milk cupboard value guide: pine, two doors, wooden pulls and latches, circa 1860, $550.

MIRROR CLOCKS. Chauncey Jerome scored a coup in clockmaking when he combined a mirror and a clock in a single object about 1826. For some unknown reason he named it a "bronze looking-glass clock," despite the fact that bronze was not involved in its production. Any timepiece having a mirror as a conspicuous feature of the case is known as a looking-glass or mirror clock. Other craftsmen quickly copied his idea with notable success. Several clockmakers active in New Hampshire have been credited with a highly regarded rectangular looking-glass clock. Their weight-driven eight-day brass movement clocks with plain or scrolled tops and bottoms fetch substantial sums. Gradually, other makers marketed mirror clocks, thus enabling one to check the time and the ravages of time in one quick glance. Mirror clock value guide: Silas Hoadley, stenciled splat and columns, mirror beneath dial, $975.

MONKEY JUGS. Hideous is the word to best describe the rather grotesque monkey jug, also known as voodoo or slave jugs. The latter name stems from the fact that some were made by plantation slaves in the mid-19th century. Although the form was known earlier, most monkey jugs date from the mid-1800s. These vessels, designed to hold liquids, were always crafted from local inexpensive clays. Stoneware, redware or brownware types were produced with or without a glaze. Each jug showed a rather awesome profile with a large protruding nose, prominent ears, round eyes and open mouth and teeth. Possibly their makers were trying to exhibit a sense of humor, as the jugs were hardly designed for beauty. Some of the potteries marked them with an incised name, leaving one to ponder whether it represents the maker or the owner. Monkey jug value guide: brownware, handle, fair condition, $335.

MORTARS AND PESTLES. In the pre-electric blender or mixer era, the mortar and pestle was employed to grind, pound, crush or beat a variety of foods. Apothecary shops also used them in pulverizing various preparations. Since they were subjected to vigorous abuse, their makers endeavored to make them as durable as possi-

Monkey jug, pottery, 19th century

National Gallery of Art, Washington

Left: Wooden mortars and pestles, late 18th century; Right: Pewter mug, 18th century

Both photographs, National Gallery of Art, Washington

ble. The substance was placed in the mortar and pulverized by the pestle. They were made of many materials, including wood, brass, bronze and agate. Some were quite small, while others measured up to three feet or more in height. Cooks and pharmacists always kept them close at hand in several different sizes. Many were bowl-shaped, although some bell-shaped models occasionally surface. Mortar and pestle value guide: wooden, maple, 7″ tall, 4½″ wide, $60; wooden, original yellow paint, 8″ tall, 5″ wide, $55; brass, round bail handle, 4″ tall, 3″ wide, $55; iron, pedestal base, 6″ tall, 4″ wide, $40.

MUGS. Mugs of silver, pewter and wood were made by country craftsmen well into the middle of the 19th century. This handled drinking vessel made without a cover was a familiar sight in taverns and homes. The wooden examples were composed either of staves bound by iron or hickory hoops or crafted from a single piece of wood. Colonial inventories often listed silver or pewter mugs as "pots." A bulbous type silver mug was also called a "cann." Many present-day collectors use this term in describing a similarly shaped pewter vessel. On rare occasions a craftsman departed from the standard straight-sided shape by fashioning a barrel-shaped mug, which was certain to draw an admiring glance from a fellow im-biber. Although English mugs were often used as measures, with the capacity stamped toward the top edge, few American-made examples exist. Mug value guide: pewter, J. Dunham, circa 1870, $225; pewter, American, unmarked, baluster shaped, $120.

N

NANTUCKET LIGHTSHIP BASKETS. Basket collectors are constantly on the lookout for splint baskets crafted by seamen associated with the Nantucket lightship. This style basket with its broad bottom had vertical splints of ash, hickory or oak strengthened toward the top by hoops. Round or oval baskets were made in nested sizes, some with flat tops or tight-fitting covers. They were crafted with and without handles. Many were produced during the latter part of the 19th century. Originally they had a natural finish, but those of a later date were varnished. The age can be nailed down somewhat by examining the nails. On the earliest examples copper or iron nails and tacks were utilized, whereas later baskets displayed brass tacks. Nantucket lightship basket value guide: handled, round, 6″ diameter, $185.

NEEDLEWORK PICTURES. Ladies with a knack for needlework derived many of their needlework picture designs from early engravings. The artistically rendered needlepoint work completely covered the canvas frequently in the form of florals, landscape scenes or coats of arms. Toward the early 1800s silk motifs were worked on a satin ground. Frequently the maker enhanced portions of the picture with handpainted details in either oils or water colors. Heads and hands were often completed in this manner rather than being accomplished with a needle. Raised Berlin work kept ladies in stitches during the mid-19th century. Initially patterns were engraved and handpainted, but eventually colored designs were stamped on the background. Wool stitches were employed to create Berlin wool-work pictures, which covered a multitude of subject matter ranging from George Washington to Mary Queen of Scots. Needlework picture value guide: embroidery, watercolor details, portrait with florals, circa 1820, $325; embroidery, florals and butterflies, framed 20″ x 16″, circa 1830, $250.

NEW ENGLAND WINDSOR ARMCHAIRS. New England chairmakers excelled in crafting this style armchair, made from the 1780s onward. It was a variation of the hoop-back Windsor, with the semicircular horizontal rail omitted. The curved back enclosing the spindles also formed the arms in one continuous piece of bent wood. The curving top rail and arms formed from one piece provided the New England Windsor armchair with its distinguishing feature. Many makers included a small comb or braces. At the point where the arms curved upward to form the back, breakage often occurred. Because this particular portion of the chair suffered from a structural problem, many antique examples show signs of repair in this area. New England Windsor armchair value guide: pine, maple and hickory, painted black, nine spindles, circa 1800, $730.

NOGGINS. Among the treenware treasures certain to titillate the woodenware collector are the pitchers or mugs known as noggins. These drinking vessels made with pouring lips, but without covers, were crafted from a single block of wood. The round shapes turned on a lathe are the most familiar. However, some unusual hand-carved noggins have been unearthed by aware antiquers. They were executed in exact measurements of one, two, three or four cups; thus it is understandable why the word "noggin" is also used in describing a small measure. Noggin value guide: pine, early, handcrafted, 4" tall, $155.

NURSING ROCKERS. A somewhat smaller version of the famous Boston rocker, this chair was introduced in the mid-19th century. It was a low-back rocking chair made without arms. This piece of cottage furniture invariably found its way into the bedroom area. Furniture factories making plank-bottom chairs produced these inviting rockers throughout the age of industrialization. Definitely an offshoot of the Boston rocker, it has been variously referred to as "Little Boston," "sewing rocker" and "nursing rocker." Nursing rocker value guide: stenciled decor, rolling seat, circa 1860, $185.

O

OGEE CLOCKS. Plain rectangular clocks having an ogee molding on the front were extensively produced by American clockmakers between the 1840s and early 1900s. They were made in sizes ranging from under one foot to more than four feet in height. Painted flowers in the corner of the dial or reverse painted tablet are indications of an early ogee clock. Later examples had plain or monochrome-painted dials and stencil-decorated tablets. Their army of makers supplied them to customers domestically and abroad, as thousands were exported to various parts of the world. These eight-day or thirty-hour clocks were equipped with many types of brass or wooden movements. A clock paper pasted to the inside of the case can provide information pertaining to the maker. Ogee clock value guide: Forestville, eight day, time and strike, brass movement, mahogany case, $180; Gilbert, eight day, time and strike, spring driven, $160; Seth Thomas, thirty hour, time and strike, brass movement, $155.

OPEN CUPBOARDS. Even in outlying rural areas, homemakers were anxious to have a display piece for exhibiting china, pewter or other attractive household items. The two-part open cupboard, also called an open dresser or hutch cupboard, won acceptance in the early 18th century. The early types had detailed molding and scalloping, which was somewhat simplified on later versions. They were made with either three or four open shelves of equal or graduated size, having plain or scalloped edges. A lower counter top section usually had two or more drawers above a single- or double-door cupboard. Doors were plain or paneled depending on the individual craftsman. New England workers favored plain cornices, while fancy scalloping appeared on Pennsylvania models. Some open cupboards crafted specifically for displaying pewter are known as pewter cupboards. Open cupboard value guide: pewter cupboard, pine, scalloped edges, three shelves, panel door below, original red paint, 6′ tall, $1,000; walnut, six shelves, two drawers, two doors, scalloped trim, circa 1840, $560.

OVAL BOXES. A mere mention of oval boxes invariably brings to mind the Shaker box industry. Their flawlessly constructed oval boxes have been used since the late 1790s. They were sold in graduated sizes or nests of twelve, nine, seven or five. Those constructed with a handle were called carriers. Shaker boxes can be easily recognized, for side and cover laps always pointed in the same direction. Most boxes display two to four "fingers," laps or points depending on the size of the box. Maple wood was favored, combined with covers and bases of pine. The laps were fastened with wrought-iron or copper nails. Varnished as well as painted examples hold a spell over collectors. Occasionally one may show signs of red, yellow, green or blue paint. Resist the urge to repaint one as this will detract from its salability. Oval boxes made by other woodworkers always had covers lapped in the opposite direction. Oval box value guide: Shaker, sewing box, silk lining, 7½″ x 6″, $120; Shaker, fingered, original red paint, 8″ x 6″, $110; Shaker, bentwood, copper nails, 4″ x 2″, $95.

P

PAINTED CHAIRS. Between the 1790s and 1850s practically every village had its very own maker of "fancy" chairs. The majority of these lightweight yet durable chairs were based on Classical Revival patterns. Originally they were handpainted, but later stenciled motifs proliferated. Some of the earliest chairs had a brown, pale yellow or buff background, or were grained in a manner to resemble unpainted wood. Darker colors prevailed in the second quarter of the century. Since chairmakers were anxious to market them at reasonable prices, they introduced stenciled rather than handpainted surfaces. Fruits, flowers, shells, leaves and landscapes were among the multitude of attractive motifs found on fancy chair surfaces.

Left: Painted chair, early 19th century; Right: Painted chair, curved top rail, 19th century

Many had cane or rush seats. Sheraton characteristics can be noted on the earlier specimens, while American Empire styles dominated later designs. Because Lambert Hitchcock is closely associated with them, many collectors refer to painted or fancy chairs as "Hitchcock chairs." Painted chair value guide: curly maple armchair, ladder back, rush seat, original decor, $200; maple, side chair, grained, cornucopia slat, stenciled, striping, circa 1840, $185.

PAP BOATS. Searching for an offbeat collectible? Try pap boats. These small handled boat or pear-shaped containers had long tapering spouts. Invalids and infants shared pap boats in common as feeding vessels. A type of semiliquid food was called pap, giving rise to the term "pap boat." Silversmiths made and marked pap boats in the 1700s and 1800s. Plain white and decorated ironstone feeders generally bear the name or trademark of the maker for positive identification. The porcelain and glass feeders are prized. Some collectors prefer calling them feeding cups or invalid feeders, both of which are appropriate names for these coveted containers. Acquire a pap boat as soon as possible before collectors retire them to dry dock. Pap boat value guide: silver, plain type, Tenney, New York, circa 1845, $290; glass feeder, circa 1850, $65; ironstone, circa 1860, $40.

PARLOR STOVES. Between 1820 and 1900, American foundries cast parlor stoves in interesting and imaginative shapes for town and country folk. The popularity afforded the parlor stove paralleled the availability of anthracite coal in the pre-central-heating period. They were cast in shapes designed to blend with contemporary furniture styles. Those possessing a maker's name or patent date are prized by pursuers of parlor stoves. The commemorative stoves immortalizing an important event in the nation's history, such as the Bombardment of Fort McHenry, 1814, or the General Zachary Taylor stove of 1848, are acclaimed acquisitions. The famous Franklin stove appeared in many versions during the 19th century. Openwork pierced galleries of iron or brass adorned their tops in the mid-1800s. The collector with a sense of humor should strive to acquire a dunce-cap stove, with its pronounced dunce cap. Another favorite in the middle part of the century was the parlor cook stove heavily ornamented with eye-catching designs supposedly capable of distracting the eye from its functional purpose. Parlor stove value guide: cast iron, ornamental house shape, circa 1850, $750; cast iron, scrolled decor, curving legs, 48" tall, $450.

PAUL REVERE LANTERNS. Collectors have bestowed this name on a cylindrical-shaped pierced tin lantern having a conical top. The term is misleading inasmuch as this style had absolutely no connection with Paul Revere. A true Paul Revere lantern had a square shape, stepped turrets and decorative trim. The type mistakenly known as a Paul Revere lantern was actually a farmhouse-type lantern popular in the 19th century. They could be found near the back entry; farmers relied on them to light the way between house and barn. They are quite interesting in themselves. Many have lacy pierced designs in star, sunburst, circle and diamond shapes, which cast an artistic glow. It appears that the name is here to stay, as these lanterns are revered by collectors. Paul Revere lantern value guide: pierced stars, 14" tall, $130.

PEG LAMPS. The peg lamp was so named due to its bottom stub or peg, designed to fit into a candlestick. These lamps consisted of a small reservoir usually of glass or metal having a metal burner at the top and a peg bottom. They were nighttime necessities in the early 1800s, when lamps burned whale oil or camphene. Since they were unable to stand upright without being fitted into the top of a candlestick, many proved perishable, making them anything but plentiful presently. Those designed to burn camphene generally had long wick tubes with metal caps. From the 1830s on some so-called peg lamps were permanently fitted into the candlestick by means of plaster of Paris or a similar substance. Peg lamp value guide: brass candlestick, double-wick burner, 6¾" tall, $90; tin, whale oil, clear font, 8" tall, $70.

PEMBROKE TABLES. According to legend, Thomas Chippendale originally designed this style table for the Earl of Pembroke. Mr. Chippendale referred to them as breakfast tables in his directory. George Hepplewhite gave them a stamp of approval in his furniture guide, proclaiming their many uses. Thomas Sheraton thought a Pembroke table was ideal for either a lady or gentleman to breakfast on. With such a list of credentials, is it any wonder that formal and country furniture makers found profits in Pembroke tables? The Pembroke table typically had a broad top and short leaves, exactly the reverse of other drop-leaf tables. The earliest examples had leaves twelve to fifteen inches wide, with a fixed top measuring about double the width. They had plain or serpentined rectangular leaves with out-rounded corners. Most examples had one drawer and four tapering legs braced by stretchers. By the 1800s the four turned legs were usually fitted with socket casters. Some country versions usually having vase-shaped legs with ring turnings, or spool turnings, were fabricated from assorted hardwoods. Pembroke table value guide: mahogany, Hepplewhite style, one drawer, inlaid, circa 1800, $560; cherry, oblong top, plain skirt, one drawer, square tapering legs, circa 1810, $475.

PENCIL BOXES. Before writing off this category, consider the possibility of acquiring a prized Pennsylvania slate or pencil box of the mid-1800s. Such a find is likely to exhibit painted or inlaid motifs. The pencil box with its sliding lid resembled a smaller version of the candle box. The sliding lid could be removed to reveal interior compartments, which accommodated small writing necessities. Although intended for minors, these boxes now represent major acquisitions. Most Pennsylvania woodworkers preferred crafting them of pine or walnut. While collectors crave handcrafted types, even early factory-made boxes have made their mark on collectors. Pencil box value guide: pine, sliding lid, dovetailed, original red paint, circa 1850, $30.

PENCIL-POST BEDS. One high-post bed found in country bedrooms of the late 1700s was the so-called pencil-post bed. This four-poster bed had thin six-sided posts that did indeed resemble pencils. The unique posts furnished this style bed with its individuality. Some were painted, others had a natural wood finish. The thinner the posts, the finer the bed. Sometimes the headboard was shaped in cyma scrolls. In the early 1800s, some displayed Sheraton characteristics. Pencil-post beds can be found in a variety of woods, including maple or cherry, often combined with pine. Pencil-post bed value guide: pine and maple, New England, original paint, circa 1790, $950; cherry and pine, Sheraton style, circa 1810, $630.

PENNSYLVANIA GERMAN. There is considerable collector interest in the arts and artifacts attributed to the Dutch, German and Swiss settlers of southeastern Pennsylvania. After the initial colony was founded in the 1680s, settlers scurried through the port of Philadelphia, landing squarely in Penn's land from their homeland. This migration was particularly heavy prior to the Revolutionary War. The settlers and their descendants are known as Pennsylvania German, although they refer to themselves as Pennsylvania Dutch. Between the early 1700s and mid-1800s traditional European folk designs manifested themselves in the furniture, pottery, metalwork, carvings, Frakturs and other forms originating in the area. Among the mélange of motifs were birds, animals, tulips, hearts, the tree-of-life design and variations of the six-pointed or other divided star forms. Existing specimens of Pennsylvania Ger-

Pennsylvania decorated cupboard, dated 1828

National Gallery of Art, Washington

145

man folk art are vigorously acquired by antique aficionados. Pennsylvania German value guide: beanpot, pottery, red glaze, black sponge decor, $140; bowl, slip decorated, red glaze, manganese stripe, 8¾" diameter, $165; rocker, ladder back, original green paint, $140; rye straw hamper, 24" tall, 20" wide, $120; valentine, cut paper work, watercolor, angels, flowers, circa 1810, $200.

PENNSYLVANIA PAINTED ROCKERS. A special type of rocker was made by the artisans of Pennsylvania in the mid-1800s. The prized Pennsylvania rocker was steeped in regional characteristics. It had a splat back rather than the more common spindle back; the splat extended from the top rail right down to the wooden seat. A curved central finger hole adorned the top rail, which was downcurved to join the rounded uprights. Assorted woods were utilized. Frequently these rockers were subjected to a coat of brown or black paint, after which they were ready to submit to the decorator's brush. Painted designs in breathtaking polychrome colors were applied to the top rail, splat and seat front, combined with elaborate striping. Birds, foliage, fruit, flowers and other motifs associated with the area enlivened these remarkable rockers. A matching lady's rocker and side chair were subjected to similar embellishment, making a triumphant threesome. Pennsylvania painted rocker value guide: flowers, fruit, original decor, circa 1850, $275; lady's rocker, naturalistic motif, original decor, $220.

PEPPERBOXES. Ethan Allen and partners of Massachusetts and Blunt & Syms of New York were among the leading makers of this percussion cap muzzle-loading pistol. The pepperbox evolved slowly. With various American improvements, it met with civilian and Army acceptance primarily during the 1830s and 1840s. This pistol had a series of barrels surrounding a central axis, capable of being fired in succession by a single hammer. There were both single- and double-action models, and the barrels could be revolved either manually or automatically. The number of barrels ranged from three to eighteen. People stopped packing the pepperbox once the Colt revolver shot into prominence. Pepperbox value guide: Sharps, pepperbox no. 1, four shot, 22-caliber, $400.

PEWTER. Colonial pewterers labored under difficult conditions, for they depended on England for tin supplies. England, determined to

Pewter coffee pot, Pennsylvania, early 18th
century

National Gallery of Art, Washington

control American pewter trade, placed an exorbitantly high tariff on
tin, making it more sensible to purchase pewter from them directly.
Since early pewterers worked with molds designed in their native
land, the dominant influence was English. Pewter utensils were in
daily use and could be melted down and reshaped when excessive
wear occurred. Larger pieces frequently bore the maker's name,
location or a set of hallmarks. The smaller ones generally had initials
only. Quite often a piece had the name of a sales agent. American
pewterers, free to adopt their own touchmarks, usually preferred
familiar European devices such as a crown, lamb, dove or full-
rigged ship. Following the Revolutionary War, when supplies became more available, patriotic symbols were utilized, particularly
the eagle. Circular or rectangular forms housing the maker's name
or initials gained prominence in the early 1800s. The Golden Age of
American Pewter terminated about 1850, when the demand slack-
ended due to competition from inexpensive silver, glass and ceramic
tablewares. Pewter value guide: bowl, Boardman, 8″ diameter,
$450; charger, American, unmarked, 12″ diameter, $220; coffeepot,
Smith & Co., 12″ tall, $240; plate, E. Danforth, 8″ diameter, $280.

PICTURE FRAMES. Many early looking-glass makers found
picture frames provided them with an additional source of revenue.
Advertisements began appearing for them on a regular basis in the
late 18th century. Quite naturally, the majority were custom made
with plain or carved members, generally finished in black or gilt.
Country frames tended to follow the painted decoration found on
contemporary furnishings and woodwork. Convex moldings won
approval in the early 19th century, while reeded moldings were
thought to be proper for watercolor accomplishments. Since every
proper young lady was encouraged to partake of art instruction,

147

every minor and major accomplishment was fitted with an appropriate frame. The wide flat molding found on mid-19th-century frames proved suitable for stunning stenciled or painted motifs. Ornate gilt moldings were the great American frame-up of the Victorian era, when small factories produced them in quantities. Frame value guide: stenciled, wavy lines, 12" x 10", circa 1840, $135; curly maple, handcarved, 14" x 20", $85.

PIE CRIMPERS. The reader of a 19th-century cookbook may find the pie crimper referred to as a giggling iron, jagging iron, pastry jagger, pie sealer or pie trimmer. This small utensil was always within easy reach as pies popped up on rural menus repeatedly. The pie crimper was quite versatile, performing such tasks as cutting pastry or cookies and fluting the edges of pies. There were numerous variations in its design, the most common being a short handle attached to a fluted wheel. They were usually made of a combination of materials, including wood, iron, brass, porcelain, horn and whalebone. A bone or ivory pie crimper crafted with infinite care for a wife or sweetheart by a sailor on a whaling vessel earns the edge value-wise. Any pie crimper displaying handiwork is eyed with admiration by those attracted to kitchen collectibles. Pie crimper value guide: wrought-iron pie piercer and dough cutter, $65; wrought iron, double wheeled, tooled handle, $60; brass, turned maple handle, $45.

PIE PEELS. In country areas where simple utilitarian articles reigned supreme, many pies were lifted from the oven by means of nothing more than a wooden paddle. However, the short-handled, wide-headed pie peel was usually close at hand for lifting chores. The handles were considerably shorter than those found on bread peels. The pie peel was nudged from favor when round tin pie lifters were introduced along with coal stoves. The pie fork was a two-pronged affair consisting of heavy wire with wooden or wire handles. The various improvements appealed to bakers, but from a collector's viewpoint the wooden pie peel is preferred. Pie peel value guide: wooden, stub handle, hanging, 16" long, 12" wide, $70; lifter, two tines, handle, 18" long, $18.

PIE PLATES. A new ceramic form was developed in the hands of the talented Pennsylvania potters in the 18th century. They cre-

Left: Redware sgraffito decorated pie plate; Right: Pie safe, Shaker type, 19th century

Both photographs, National Gallery of Art, Washington

ated a utensil of red earthenware in a shallow circular shape known as a pie plate or bio-schissel. Every household had several pie plates in different sizes crafted by the village potter. They employed sgraffito or slip methods of decoration, which varied according to the expertise of the craftsman. Many plates display traditional motifs, including birds, human figures, flowers, leaves and eagles. The inscriptions read like pottery prose, with emphasis on mottoes, humorous sayings, proverbs and quotations. Signed and dated specimens evoke immediate collector attention. Pie plate value guide: slipware plate, yellow slip, crosshatched wavy lines, sawtooth edge, $260; slipware plate, 10" diameter, white, green and black wavy lines, $155; slipware plate, 9½" diameter, green and brown wavy lines, $140.

PIERCED TINWARE. Numerous artistically minded tinkers marketed pierced tinware in the 19th century. A check of signed and dated pieces strengthens the belief that most wares date from between the 1830s and the 1850s. Pierced tin differs from punched tin, as a complete perforation was accomplished by piercing the surface with a chisel or nail. A chisel created a slit, while a nail produced a more esthetically pleasing hole. On some occasions the piercing was purely ornamental, but on most objects it served a utilitarian purpose. Pennsylvania perforators played it safe with standard designs, including stars, flowers, birds, eagles and animals. The Shakers shuddered if the piercing was purely decorative; they worked their geometric patterns for functional purposes only, and with amazing accuracy. Pierced tin value guide: foot warmer, pierced diamond design, wood frame, $75; cheese mold, heart shaped, footed, circa 1850, $120; grater, pierced stars, paddle shaped, $50.

PIE SAFES. The pie safe functioned as a primitive refrigerator in country kitchens of the 19th century. Basically, it was a narrow cupboard fitted with front doors, which provided a means of ventilation through pierced tin panels, screening, wooden grillwork or fabric. Baked goods, meat and other perishables were placed on the inner shelves, where they were kept fresh and hopefully protected from rodents and insects. Regional characteristics manifested themselves in these highly regarded cupboards. Those displaying pierced tin pans fetch the highest returns; the more elaborate the piercing, the higher the value. Shaker safes were pierced with the precision of a computer card. Pennsylvania piercers provided their customers with delicate piercing in rare eagle, rooster, six-pointed geometric designs or free-form scrolls or arabesques. This piece is frequently referred to as either a pie cupboard, meat safe, tin safe or kitchen safe. Pie safe value guide: pierced tin panels, Gothic pattern, circa 1850, $570; pine, pierced tin, two doors, two drawers, circa 1860, $440.

PIGGINS. Although the multipurpose piggin was a farmhouse favorite between the 1600s and 1900s, the form is fairly unfamiliar to antiquers. This wooden bucket of Scotch-Irish origin, which functioned as a milking container and dipper, was utilized for many farmhouse chores. These hooped and staved containers had one long extended stave forming the handle. Sometimes the protruding stave was quite short, while on other examples it stood eight inches high. Since the piggin handle was made without a hole, it is possible to distinguish it from its look-alike, the sap bucket. Piggin value guide: pine, staved and hooped, original yellow paint, 10″ tall, $75.

PILGRIM PERIOD (1650–1690). Although purists persist in restricting the term "Pilgrim" to the furniture of the Plymouth colonies, it has achieved a broader connotation. It is widely used in reference to American-made furniture in the Jacobean style of the 17th century. Sometimes this period is known as the Puritan Span. American colonial furniture imitated the Jacobean forms popular in England during the reign of James I (1603–1625). Oak was the chief wood, often combined with pine. These pieces of wainscot construction were ornamented with flat carving, turnings and applied moldings. Among the notable pieces produced in the Jacobean style were press cupboards, court cupboards, Brewster chairs, Carver chairs, slat-back chairs, wainscot chairs, joined stools, chests, trestle tables, table-chairs and Bible boxes. Pilgrim Period value guide: blanket chest, carved oak, Massachusetts, circa 1675, $3,700; armchair, turned maple, New England, circa 1690, $550.

PILLBOXES. Finding a small handmade or factory-produced pillbox of the 18th or 19th century is exactly what the doctor ordered to lift the spirits of a box buff. These round or oval boxes are the smallest type known in the box category. They generally measure from one to six inches in diameter. Often the early handmade versions were glued together by their makers. The Shakers used wire or thread as fasteners for some of the early pillboxes, typically made of shaved maple wood combined with pine tops and bottoms. Tiny machine-made nails often distinguish a later factory-made pillbox. Occasionally they were stamped or labeled with a product name accompanied by choice copy proclaiming its curative powers. Labeled boxes are actively acquired by people who appreciate Americana advertising memorabilia. Pillbox value guide: maple with pine top, Shaker, $55; "Dr. Phelps Compound Tomato Pills," label intact, $45.

PIPE BOXES. Colonial woodworkers obliged the pipe-smoking set by fabricating an array of simply constructed pipe trays and pipe boxes. Most were specifically designed to accommodate long-stemmed clay pipes, known as "Churchwarden pipes." The pipe tray was a long box with a sliding lid, which opened to reveal two long sections and a small end compartment for storing puffing paraphernalia. There were also beautifully proportioned hanging wall pipe boxes. This form consisted of an open box into which the pipe was placed bowl end down, with a smaller drawer below for holding tobacco. Although many models were similarly designed, no two were ever exactly alike. Some minor differences included those made with scroll tops, two drawers or extremely shallow wells. Pipe boxes summon the seekers who crave a challenge due to their diversity. Pipe box value guide: pine, scroll type, two drawers, dovetailed, painted, original decor, circa 1790, $750; pine, primitive type, 15" high, 5" deep, 7" wide, circa 1800, $225.

PLANK-BOTTOM CHAIRS. Local cabinetmakers experienced an economic pinch when furniture factories started shipping plank-bottom chairs into outlying areas in the 1830s. For the duration of the century these inexpensive chairs resembling the graceful Philadelphia Windsors sold in substantial numbers. They were usually purchased in sets of six. Plank-bottom chairs were manufactured with half spindle, full spindle, splat backs, arrow backs or balloon backs. Such chairs could be bought either in a natural finish or painted. People in rural Pennsylvania areas preferred buying them in a natural condition. After giving each chair a coat of paint in a chosen color, they proceeded to embellish them with typical verve in a rainbow of colors. The stenciled or free-hand decorations were executed in bird, fruit and floral designs indicative of the region. The antique examples show a mellowing of color attained only through age. Therefore, resist the urge to repaint these so-called "kitchen Windsors." Plank-bottom chair value guide: half-spindle back, plank seat, stenciled florals, balloon striping, circa 1850, $155.

PLATE WARMERS. Among the treasured items designed by American tinsmiths of the late 18th century are the cupboards or sets of shelves utilized as plate warmers. Cupboard types supported by Queen Anne legs and ornamented with brass handles on the sides are extremely rare. The cupboard door opened to reveal a series of shelves and an open back. Plates to be warmed were set on the shelves, with the open back toward the fire. After the plates had been heated, they were removed by the front door. There were several different versions operating on the same principle. Some were painted or decorated with gold lines or simple patterns. A tin bonnet is a small warming device with a curved cover, open side and top handle for warming a single plate of food set on the hearth. Plate warmer value guide: tin, cupboard type, two shelves, fair condition, $180.

PORRINGER TABLES. This collector-named table has project-ing corners which are as round as porringers. Thus the name por-ringer table is most fitting. Often the rounded corners proved ideal for supporting candlesticks. Those having vase-turned legs and stretchers suggest characteristics identified with the William and Mary period (1690–1720). However, it is always important to re-member that country furniture makers held tenaciously to styles long after they had been abandoned by urban cabinetmakers. A deep cyma-curved skirt makes one of these occasional tables doubly attractive. Some porringer tables suggest a simplified version of Queen Anne styles. Maple alone or combined with cherry was the preferred wood. Porringer tops can also be found on some coveted candlestands. Porringer table value guide: maple, scalloped skirt, cabriole legs, claw-and-ball feet, circa 1760, $2,100.

PORRINGERS. When the words "pease porridge hot, pease por-ridge cold" echoed around the kitchen table, mother always reached for the ever-present porringer in the 1700s and 1800s. This small circular bowl with a single flat handle was used for serving liquid and semiliquid food. It was made in silver, wood and pewter, with most examples ranging from 2½ inches to 6 inches in diameter. The smaller versions were made with smaller family members in mind. Simple country folk preferred pewter porringers, their preference being guided by the economical advantages involved. The shallow bodies on these pieces remained unchanged, but the handles varied according to the maker and region. Fancy openwork and pierced designs reminiscent of porringers made in England met with con-sumer acceptance in New England. The solid or tab handle display-ing traditionally Continental characteristics proved popular in Pennsylvania and other areas populated by people from Central Europe. Porringer value guide: pewter, American, unmarked, 3½" diameter, $160; silver, Gorham & Co., 5" diameter, $120; pewter, Reed & Barton, pierced handle, $100.

POTTERY BANKS. Collector interest in antique banks is com-pounded daily. Pursuers of pottery banks positively shudder to think how many of them were broken in order to free their contents. Potters pleased young depositors with banks in familiar beehive, animal, bird, house, boat or jug shapes. Beautifully modeled bird finials were perched atop many versions. Thrift-minded Benjamin

Franklin would have approved of the gray and cream colored stoneware banks. Many were spontaneously painted with cobalt blue designs or scratched motifs. The animal finials appeared in sufficient numbers to fill a zoo. Eventually glass and metal banks popped onto toy emporium shelves, making the pottery examples somewhat obsolete. The tin and iron still or mechanical banks have a legion of admirers, but for the country antiques collector pottery banks never lose their lure. Pottery bank value guide: stoneware, jug shape, $120; redware, beehive shape, $85.

POTTERY GREASE LAMPS. Any representative collection of American lighting accessories would be incomplete without one or more pottery grease lamps. Village potters working with local clays made them of redware or stoneware. Numerous variations occur, but generally the form consisted of an open reservoir supported by a standard with a saucer base and one or more handles. Most models ranged between three and seven inches in height. They were made with or without a wick rest, spout or wick cover. Signed or dated examples offer a guide to age or origin, but unsigned examples are impossible to authenticate. Although pottery grease lamps were fairly common between about 1770 and 1870, existing specimens rarely come to light. Pottery grease lamp value guide: redware, dark brown glaze, 6″ tall, $175.

POWDER HORNS. American hunters relied on powder horns for carrying gunpowder prior to the introduction of the brass powder flask in the second quarter of the 19th century. The horns were usually crafted from the horns of bullocks, cows or oxen, with most versions ranging between ten and twenty inches in length. Although the majority were made at home, some were sold commercially by gunsmiths or hornsmiths. The engraving was more skillfully conceived on the commercial models. Collectors clamor for powder horns having engraved motifs in such varied forms as maps, historical events, flags, eagles, animals, leaves, flowers, ships, battle scenes and Masonic emblems. Interest is also keen on specimens bearing a name, date, rhyme or inscription. Powder horn value guide: engraved eagle, foliage, circa 1810, $265; plain, pewter spout, 12″ long, $55.

PRESENTATION QUILTS. This type of quilt is a lasting testimonial that quilting bees were more than merely gossip sessions.

Each member of a group made one or more quilt blocks, which were then assembled at a quilting bee. The pieced or appliquéd block was often signed in India ink by its maker. Once the various designs had been arranged and quilted, a truly impressive piece of needlecraft emerged. Many of these mid-19th-century pieces were signed or ·dated. Such quilts were made especially for persons held in esteem in a community: a minister, minister's wife or bride might be the lucky recipient of such a quilt. They are also known as album, friendship, autograph or bride's quilts. Presentation quilt value guide: geometric pattern, 70" x 80", signed blocks, date 1860, $275.

PRESS CUPBOARDS. The press cupboard produced primarily between about 1650 and 1700 bears little resemblance to the present-day cupboard. The piece is quite similar in design to the court cupboard. However, the press cupboard had drawers or compartments in both the upper and lower sections. On the court cupboard the upper section is closed, the bottom open. The principal purpose of the press cupboard with its roomy drawers and cupboard section was for storing clothing. The name was supposedly derived from the drawers which served as a "press," somewhat like a clothes press. It is believed that the press cupboard evolved from the court cupboard. The more elaborate examples, seldom offered for sale nowadays, were ornamented with a variety of Tudor and Jacobean ornaments. Extremely rare.

PUNCHED TINWARE. Can there possibly be a finer testimonial for punched tinware than the account records of tinsmith B. Shade of Pennsylvania, who listed George Washington as a customer for this ware in the 1790s? This method of repoussé decoration was achieved by using various tools or punches on the inside surface of the metal capable of punching, but not piercing, the tin. Each indentation appeared in repoussé on the outer surface, ultimately forming the desired design. One miscalculation and the entire undertaking became a disaster. Many types of tinware surrendered to this form of ornamentation, particularly coffeepots. Savored by collectors are the specimens showing a maker's name, customer's name or date. Some skilled craftsmen executed presentation pieces, which were frequently presented to a pair of newly-weds. The surface of punched tinware originating in Pennsylvania was enlivened with eagles, hearts, stars, barn symbols, leaves and other traditional themes. Punched tinware value guide: coffeepot, birds and flowers, dated 1855, $1,650; coffeepot, tulips and hearts, Pennsylvania, circa 1860, $1,200.

PURITAN THREE-LEGGED CHAIRS. Students of antiques are particularly interested in the three-legged chair, known to be one of the earliest types made in America. Seldom can one be found outside a museum, but a knowledge of this early style can prove beneficial to both beginning and advanced collectors. The famous Harvard chair used by the president of Harvard in bestowing degrees is the best-known three-legged chair in existence. Since they date from the mid-1600s, restoration work can be noted on many surviving specimens. They were chiefly made in New England of oak or other hardwoods. Although the style and turnings varied slightly, the three legs braced by a rectangular stretcher furnished this chair with its distinguishing feature. Puritan three-legged chair value guide: oak, turned posts, wooden seat, turned stretchers, partially restored, $875.

Q

QUEEN ANNE SPLAT-BACK CHAIRS. Queen Anne herself would have approved of the sturdily constructed chairs which originated in country workshops during the period bearing her name. The curving lines found on Queen Anne style (1720–1750) proved challenging to chairmakers. Subtle changes can be noted as the transition was made from William and Mary styles. Some chairs had stretchers, which were eventually eliminated as curved legs were found to furnish ample support. Collector interest is keen on those possessing Queen Anne characteristics. These include the undulating vase-shaped splat extending to the chair seat, the curved chair back often with a concave curve in the center portion, and the cabriole legs terminating in a Dutch foot or later in a claw-and-ball foot. Provincial versions generally had rush seats and were crafted from locally available hardwoods. Queen Anne splat-back chair value guide: side chair, maple, rush seat, original paint, circa 1760, $385.

QUILL BOXES. The long feathers plucked from the wings of crows, geese and other fine-feathered friends were used for writing and drawing. Storing them between writing chores was a solution simply solved with the aid of a quill box. In urban areas where money was more plentiful, quills were often stored in beautifully inlaid wood, or engraved silver boxes. However, in rural counting-houses quills were placed in wall boxes similar to pipe boxes. Sometimes they reposed in tills or flat boxes having sliding lids or lift-type tops. Such boxes were simply made, without ornamentation, as their purpose was primarily utilitarian. Quill box value guide: pine, hanging type, primitive, $75.

QUILTS. Questers do a quick step at the sight of an antique quilt. There are those who proclaim that the important years of bedquilts extended from about 1750 to 1860. But due to increased demand, even late 19th- and early 20th-century quilts are becoming collectible. Most quilts encountered by the casual browser are of the appliquéd or patchwork type. Embroidered quilts have all but vanished from the marketplace. The type of quilt crafted by sewing pieces of fabric to the backing is known as an appliquéd quilt. Patchwork quilts, a salvage craft depending on odd-shaped pieces of

Left: Appliqued quilt, Pennsylvania German, 19th century; Right: Quilt, black design with grapevine border, 19th century

Both photographs, National Gallery of Art, Washington

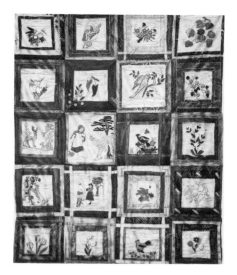

Left: Quilt, twenty pictorial squares, 19th century; Right: Crazy quilt, late 19th century

Both photographs, National Gallery of Art, Washington

remnants sewn together, lined and quilted was an innovation of the late 18th century. The colorful crazy quilt was a late Victorian version of the patchwork quilt. If differentiating between old and new poses a problem, there are several avenues of investigation open to the novice. Old quilts almost always show signs of wear, stains or fading. Machine stitching can also offer a clue to age. However, the sniff test is one of the best as they usually have a musty odor from years of attic living. Quilt value guide: appliqué, flowers, sun and birds, dated 1865, 76″ square, $175; patchwork, diamond pattern, red, black, gray and white, 78″ square, circa 1880, $120.

R

RACHET STANDS. This type of candlestand had a notched shaft which permitted the candle to be adjusted to various heights. Most rachet stands were made with a crossarm for holding candles rather than having a tabletop. Many were made with crossbar feet in the 18th and 19th centuries. The notched shaft was held in place at the desired height by various means, including a wooden peg, pawl or wrought-iron hasp. Although these candlestands were made in a variety of styles, the notched shaft provided the all-important feature. Rachet stand value guide: oak, two-candle type, $185.

RAG RUGS. Country-crafted rag rugs created from worn-out rags and remnants are lasting proof that second hand is not necessarily second best. People with a fondness for folk art floor coverings favor these handmade items. In many rural areas the rag rug was the only rug covering a bare floor well into the 1800s. Resourceful homemakers realized that unusable textiles could be cut or torn into half-inch strips and woven on a handloom. Since narrow looms made narrow rugs, several pieces were sewn together to cover a larger area. Sometimes a woman took her discards to a local weaver, who custom designed a rug to her specifications. He offered assurances that the completed carpet would differ from the one found on the neighbor's floor. Recycling in the antique manner is evident in the tongue, button, patchwork, shaggy, braided, crocheted, knitted and other romantic rag rugs of yesteryear. Rag rug value guide: small size, 30" x 24", multicolored, soft shades, fair condition, $225.

RAISED COMPARTMENT DESKS. The eminent legislators of the initial legislature of the state of Wisconsin in 1848 used this style desk, a specialty of midwestern cabinetmakers. The identifying feature was the raised recessed open or closed compartment at the rear of the sloping-lid desk. On the open-compartment version there was a spacious open area and account book pigeonholes. The closed model had two full-width shelves, flanked by variously sized pigeonholes above one or more shallow drawers. When the piece was made in two parts, it generally had a full-width drawer beneath the sloping lid. Such desks were supported by either plain or turned legs. Raised compartment desk value guide: open type, one drawer, turned legs, circa 1850, $565.

RAISIN SEEDERS. The Enterprise Grape & Raisin Seeder, No. 36, patented in 1895 by the Enterprise Manufacturing Co. of Philadelphia, Pennsylvania, removed more than its share of seeds around the turn of the century. It bore the inscription "wet the raisins." According to the maker, these crank-handled machines broke existing records by seeding a pound of raisins in five minutes. This made the earlier homemade wooden models obsolete. Cast-iron seeders were overworked during December, when they made a bounty of raisin-filled holiday treats. Look for a maker's name, patent date or other information molded into the cast-iron as a dating guide. The raisin seeder rummager may be rewarded by finding a smaller version, which performed its seeding service with the aid of a lever. It pressed the raisins vigorously against sturdy wires through which the seeds ultimately passed. Raisin seeder value guide: Enterprise Grape and Raisin Seeder, cast iron, $22; The Gem, cast iron, Patent 1895, $20.

RECTANGULAR MIRRORS. The multipurpose rectangular mirror was winning country customers from the 1840s onward. It was simply made with a single panel of glass housed in an oblong frame having mitered corners. They were made in various sizes ranging from two to five feet tall and one to three feet wide. The earlier types made by local cabinetmakers or small furniture factories of rosewood, mahogany and black walnut were more intricately molded than later models. Eventually many made them of pine, which was gilded or painted to resemble rosewood or black walnut. When the frame was permitted to remain in a natural finish, added detail was often achieved by surrounding the mirror panel with a narrow beaded or concave gilt molding. Rectangular mirror value guide: walnut, 3′ x 2′, natural finish, $75.

REDWARE. Although the common red clay for producing redware was available in many areas along the eastern seaboard, this type of pottery is often associated with Pennsylvania, New York and

Redware presentation platter, dated 1823
National Gallery of Art, Washington

New Jersey. It burned at a low temperature, forming a soft porous body somewhat reddish brown in color. The rather dull surface was treated to glazing, which provided a protective coating and also gave some brilliance to the piece. Various colored glazes were achieved through different potting techniques. There were unglazed objects and others only partially glazed. Slip-decorated pieces are acquired with zeal by country antique buffs, particularly dated or elaborately decorated pieces. The sgraffito-ornamented redware principally made as presentation pieces by Pennsylvania potters always creates a stir among redware rummagers. Redware value guide: seated dog, red-orange glaze, streaked with brown, circa 1861, $300; mold, cornbread, 8", $290; flower pot, yellow glaze, Pennsylvania, $100; pouring mug, manganese glaze, ribbed at base, $45.

REFLECTOR OVENS. One of the new cooking conveniences being widely touted by tinsmiths of the 1780s was the reflector oven. The heat from the hearth reflected from the top and the back of these tin ovens, thereby heating the food from every angle. Commonly known as tin kitchens, they came in various sizes, ranging from one to three feet in length. These portable covered spits or roasting jacks underwent various minor improvements as their makers endeavored to impress the public with their durability and maintenance-free operation. The half-cylinder model set on four legs with an iron spit running through the oven was widely marketed. A strong selling point was the fact that they were constructed in a manner to prevent grease from spattering on the hearth or on the homemaker. Tin biscuit ovens operating on the reflector principle were among the other important new cooking accessories. The later charcoal-burning biscuit ovens were generally reserved for baking crackers. Reflector oven value guide: tin, 2' high, circa 1810, $85.

REMINGTON REVOLVERS. Eliphalet Remington Jr. was preoccupied with flint- and percussion-type rifles for civilians and Army use prior to developing his first pistol in 1849. It met with only moderate success. An improved model was offered in 1856, resembling the Colt pistol and vying with it in favor. During the height of hostilities in the Civil War, this gunsmith supplied the government with 128,000 Remington revolvers. This figure did not represent those sold privately to individuals, attesting to widespread reliance on the Remington. Remington revolver value guide: Elliot, ring trigger, 32-caliber, $390.

RESTORATION CHAIRS. The cane chair with its extensive carving and turning reigned supreme as a favorite in England during the reign of Charles II (1660–1685). American chairmakers borrowed the design from their English cousins with slight simplifications. Any chair in this category has a distinctive seat and partial back of cane. Since cane proved highly perishable, locating one with its original caning is improbable, if not impossible. Even when such a chair sports a newly caned, upholstered or leather replacement seat, it ranks as a super sitter. Often the front legs and feet were executed in the well-known "Flemish scroll." According to legend, such a chair accompanied William Penn to America. Restoration chair value guide: maple, armchair, caned panel, caned seat, restored, circa 1710, $975.

RETABLOS. The retablos is a religious picture painted by a santero on a wood panel over a gesso ground. From the mid-17th century on, they were painted by anonymous southwestern craftsmen. Smaller sizes were designated for home use, while larger ones adorned church altars. The santero learned the craft of painting on panels of cottonwood or pine originally from Mexican priests. Dating a retablo can pose a problem, for few were dated or signed. Each artist gave his own interpretation to the subject matter, with many being quite crude and primitive. The animated figures with exaggerated mannerisms associated with earlier works became more subdued on later renditions. Retablos value guide: pine board, gesso covered, religious figure, medium size, New Mexico, circa 1880, $450.

ROCKING CHAIRS. This truly American development in the furniture field evolved during the 18th century. Two types of rocking chairs exist: the converted models and those originally made with rockers. By the early 1800s most were being constructed with rockers. Many early rockers were armless. The Shakers were among the first people to realize the importance of this furniture form; they used them in their retiring rooms. Throughout the 19th century manufacturers supplied them in sufficient numbers to keep America

Rocking chair, stenciled, American Empire
style, circa 1830

National Gallery of Art, Washington

rocking. While the seat was usually made of pine, other parts of the chair had assorted available hardwoods. Initially the rockers extended an equal distance from the front and the rear. In the early 1800s the rockers became longer on the rear of the chair. The greater distance the rear rockers project, the later the chair. All the various types of antique rocking chairs made in America are assured of arousing interest. Rocking chair value guide: maple, arrow back, stenciled, circa 1840, $230; maple, fiddleback Boston, natural finish, $165; maple, cane seat and back, $160; sewing, plank seat, $115.

ROCKINGHAM. American brownware or Rockingham, with its light buff body and solid or mottled brown glaze, is indeed the ware that is closely allied with Bennington, Vermont. Naturally, collectors endeavor to attribute each and every piece to the potters of Bennington, but, alas, it was also produced elsewhere. Trying to document an unmarked piece can furrow the brow of an authority. Following a successful showing at the New York Crystal Palace Exhibition of 1853, dozens of prominent American factories produced it for the duration of the century. Ordinary household articles and extraordinary ones such as tobies, pitchers, Apostle wares, Rebekah at the Well teapots, coachman's bottles, poodle dogs, hound-handled pitchers and statuary pieces are among the remarkable remembrances of Rockingham. Rockinghamware value guide: cup and saucer, large size, 1850s, $60; inkwell, shell-shaped, circa 1840, $85; milk pan, $40; pitcher, octagonal panels, 10″ tall, $50.

ROD-BACK WINDSOR CHAIRS. Chairmakers in various sections of the country made rod-back Windsor chairs throughout the 19th century. Some were left in a natural finish while others were ornamented in the manner of "fancy chairs." The sloping back usually had a straight top rail housing five to seven rod spindles, often with bamboo ringings. Their saddle seats were either square or shield-shaped. Bamboo turnings usually occurred on the splayed legs, which were braced by stretchers. There were rod-back side chairs and armchairs. Inexpensive lightweight rod-back Windsors were handcrafted and factory produced by the score with slight modifications. Rod-back Windsor chair value guide: maple and hickory, five spindles, bamboo turnings, straight top, circa 1830, $165; four spindles, kitchen type, circa 1875, $70.

ROLLING PINS. The earliest wooden rolling pins were handleless. Later, one and eventually two handles were added for obvious reasons. Their makers utilized durable woods such as maple, mahogany or cherry. Smaller sizes measuring less than five inches in length were made for junior family members. Adult sizes were larger, with some examples ranging up to three feet in length. Smith, Mason & Co. of Vermont and the Crystal Rolling Pin Company of Massachusetts were among the woodworking firms rolling them out in the late 19th century. Rolling pins were made of numerous materials, including ivory, glass, china and horn. China emporiums offered blue and white Delft or Meissen onion pattern designs in the closing decades of the 1800s. Rolling pin value guide: porcelain, blue and white onion pattern, $45; maple, handleless, 2″ diameter, $25; pine, tapering ends, $20.

ROLL-TOP DESKS. The tambour roll-top desk came into prominence in America during the Hepplewhite and Sheraton periods. It proved more practical than the earlier cylinder desk since it conserved space. A tambour is a series of small wooden strips adhered to a canvas or strong cloth. Because this procedure proved too complicated for untrained woodworkers in country areas, roll-top desks failed to reach outlying regions in any quantity prior to their mass production by late-19th-century furniture factories. Frequently they were fabricated from such woods as walnut, cherry or mahogany. Furniture factories centered in and around Grand Rapids, Michigan, supplied them in ever-increasing numbers to country customers following the Centennial Exposition of 1876. Roll-top desk value guide: oak, 38″ wide, circa 1880, $600.

ROPE BEDS. Before the introduction of slat beds with springs in the early 1800s, mattresses were supported by a network of ropes. Such beds are known as rope beds. The rope was either wound around knobs on the bed rail or was threaded through holes in the bed rail. There were wooden bed wrenches or keys to tighten the webbing when it became slack. Sometimes a bed had a piece of sacking or stout canvas roped in a similar manner to provide resiliency. When the roping was stretched tightly on beds without bed screws, it also held the posts and rails firmly in position. Rope beds were commonplace in country regions well into the 19th century. Rope bed value guide: high-post, curly maple, shaped headboard, urn finials, $475; low-post, maple, three-quarter size, original paint, $265.

RUSHLIGHT HOLDERS. Rushes impregnated with grease were used in lieu of candles for illumination throughout Great Britain for centuries. The fat-soaked rushes were placed to burn in plier-shaped holders of iron, with wooden blocks or tripod bases known as rushlights. The lighted rushes being held by the prongs or clips furnished scant light after dark. Sometimes the actual holder is called a "rush light." If you have a burning desire to own a rushlight holder, patience is advised as they are extremely scarce. Rushlight holder value guide: wrought iron, wooden base, $95.

RUSTIC MIRRORS. Bringing a touch of the outdoors indoors in the late 19th century was the factory-made rustic mirror. The rectangular frame surrounding the mirror panel achieved its individuality when the semicircular top was skillfully carved to represent naturalistic branches. An intermingling of twigs and leaves continued down both sides of these rustic remembrances. Frame makers depleted their inventories by shipping them into rural regions repeatedly. They generally measured approximately 20″ high and 14″ wide. Assorted hardwoods were used in their construction, with some being stained to resemble walnut. The rustic mirror blended beautifully with cottage furnishings of yesteryear. Rustic mirror value guide: black walnut, circa 1875, $65.

S

SADIRONS. Prior to the introduction of the sadiron in the late
18th century, work-weary homemakers struggled with box irons.
They held a heated brick, slug of metal or hot coals. Early handwrought sadirons had a decorative handle attached at only one
point. Slightly more available to the casual collector are the 19th-
century cast-iron types having weight, date, patent information and
manufacturer's mark molded into the iron. A standard form evolved
as various factories produced them with a handle attached to the
triangular base at two points. The Enterprise Manufacturing Company of Philadelphia did their utmost to ease ironing chores with
their Mrs. Potts Double-Pointed irons. Gas irons, charcoal-burning
irons and others with fonts for holding oil were among the improved
types resting on ironing boards in the latter part of the century.
Sadiron value guide: child's, detachable, cast iron, $6; Mrs. Potts
cast iron, $7; charcoal, self-heating, $9.

SADWARE. A knowledge of pewter jargon can enable even the
novice to trade more effectively in the antiques field. The term
"sadware" is used to denote such articles as a plate, dish or charger.
The difference between a plate, dish or charger is primarily one of
size. A plate measures up to twelve inches in diameter and a dish up
to eighteen inches, while a charger exceeds eighteen inches in diameter. Any large pewter platter measuring approximately twenty-
six inches in diameter is referred to as a "boar's head platter." The
term "Cardinal's hat" is used in describing a deep dish with a broad
rim. A piece of sadware engraved with wedding motifs is known as a
marriage plate. The platen plate has a rather broad rim and was
often utilized during church communion services. Other terms such
as hexagonal rim and narrow rim are self-explanatory. Sadware
value guide: dish, Samuel Danforth, 11½″ diameter, $390; plate,
E. Burns, 8″ diameter, circa 1815, $275; charger, American, un-
marked, molded rim, circa 1840, $135.

SALEM ROCKERS. At first glance the Salem rocker might be mistaken for the better known Boston rocker. But upon closer examination a difference may be noted in the shape of the seat: while the Boston seat curves up in the back and down in the front, the seat of the Salem is absolutely flat. This has caused some collectors to call it a flat-seat Boston. From the early 1800s many factories made both style rockers, usually ornamenting them with similar stenciled motifs. When a Salem rocker still has its original decoration intact, the value edges even higher. Collectors find Salem rockers positively bewitching. Salem rocker value guide: black paint, stenciled headpiece, seven spindles, circa 1840, $245.

SALT BOXES. The lowly salt box with its slanting cover was elevated to a lofty status in architectural quarters when houses with steeply sloping roofs were nicknamed "salt boxes." Long before the salt shaker reached tabletops in the mid-1800s, the salt box of wood, copper, pottery or pewter could be found hanging near the fireplace. There were some tabletop models, but generally salt was stored in a wall-type container, hung as close to the hearth as possible to keep the contents free from excessive moisture. These square or semiround boxes with hinged sloping lids appeared in many styles. The wooden examples were plain or fancy depending on their origin. One whittled in Pennsylvania was more likely to display carved motifs or colored designs, sometimes including a name or date. In the late 1800s the blue and white pottery salt box with a wooden lid appeared in eye-catching designs. Salt box value guide: walnut, hanging, hinged cover, one drawer, dovetailed construction, $90; pine, wall type, two compartments, cover, $70; porcelain, blue and white decor, hinged wooden lid, circa 1890, $45.

Pennsylvania decorated salt box, dated 1797

National Gallery of Art, Washington

SAMPLERS. Sentimental samplers were attempted at an early age by young ladies anxious to show their proficiency with needlework. Originally they were quite narrow, generally measuring approximately eight inches in width. By the late 18th century the larger, more familiar shapes appeared. Homespun materials were used on early samplers, with most makers concentrating their efforts on alphabet arrangements, sometimes enhanced by attractive borders. Several different rows of alphabet letters were often accompanied by one or more rows of numerals. From the mid-18th century on, pictorial scenes, mottoes and inscriptions were skillfully executed by studious young stitchers. Other sampler subject matter included maps, historical events, portraits and architectural forms. Fortunately, many were signed and dated by their justifiably proud owners. Sampler value guide: church, trees, figures, Ellen Marsden, 1849, 27" wide, 23" tall, $150; the Lord's Prayer, floral designs, dated 1835, 16" wide, 14" tall, $130.

SANDWICH GLASS. The Boston and Sandwich Glass Company was founded by Deming Jarves in 1825. He had formerly been in the employ of the New England Glass Company. The new firm immediately established itself as a leader in glasswares, enjoying this position until it ceased operating due to financial difficulties in 1888. Collectors compete for examples of superior Sandwich glass, which includes a full range of products in pressed, lacy, blown three-mold, engraved, cut and art glass. Their lovely lacy glass characterized by relief designs against a stippled background brought them acclaim between the 1820s and 1840s. The term "Sandwich" has become synomous with pressed glass due to the firm's vast contribution in this field. Glowing accolades have been bestowed upon their glasswares, and deservedly so. Sandwich glass value guide: plate, Roman rosette, 7½" diameter, $75; salt dip, lacy flint, $60; bowl, lacy oak leaf, 6½" diameter, $50; tieback, opalescent, pewter stem, 3", $45; cup plate, heart pattern, $18.

SANTEROS. Stunning images originating in the Spanish southwest are among the most treasured pieces of American folk art. "Santo," from the Spanish word meaning saint, also denotes a holy image executed in any media. The craftsmen who created and repaired these images were known as santeros. A santero usually learned his craft from a teacher-priest. Images of holy persons or religious objects were crafted from local materials. Pictures, figures and other religiously oriented articles were conceived of wood, metal, paint, plaster or in printed pictures. Painted panels covered with gesso are known as retablos. A bulto is a free-standing statuette of one or more figures carved in the round. Amateur and professional santeros rarely signed their output, making attribution difficult. Auction attendees have been known to engage in spirited bidding to obtain the work of a santero. Santero value guide: pine cross, applied tin and wood ornaments, 12" tall, circa 1870, $290.

SAP BUCKETS. When maple sugar ruled as the sweetener prior to commercially produced cane sugar, the trusty sap bucket stood ready for service near the maple tree. Sap flowed from the bark via hollow wooden tubs, known as spiles, into the staved and hooped sap bucket. A single extended stave with a hole bored near the top end formed the handle. The hole in the handle permitted it to hang from the spile. Sap buckets characteristically tapered from the top rather than the bottom. By the mid-1800s woodworking establishments were sweetening their earnings by manufacturing low-cost sap buckets. These buckets, once used to catch sap, presently catch collectors. Sap bucket value guide: pine, staved with metal hoops, 10" high, $35.

SAUSAGE STUFFERS. The earliest tin sausage guns with wooden plungers were made in various sizes. Smaller sizes were ideal for home use, while others measuring up to four feet in length performed their duty in commercial establishments. They all operated on somewhat the same principle: the sausage mixture was packed into a tin tube and ejected into the skin casing by means of a wooden plunger. The do-it-yourselfer set had a banner day with sausage stuffers, fashioning some boxlike arrangements where the plunger was activated by a wheel or crank. By the 19th century patented cast-iron models performed so efficiently that would-be inventors relinquished their pursuit of better-performing sausage guns. Sausage stuffer value guide: cast-iron, Enterprise Manufacturing Company, $40; tin, decorated, turned wooden plunger, 17" high, $30.

SAWBUCK TABLES. The X-shaped trestles resembling a sawbuck frame provide this table with its unusual name. The earliest examples dating from the late 1600s had thick two- or three-board tops supported by two X-shaped trestles. These tables, usually made of oak, were braced by a stretcher morticed through the crossing. Between 1700 and 1800 the majority of sawbuck tables had two-board pine tops generally with cleated ends. The X-shaped trestles were lighter and had chamfered edges. One or two stretchers were utilized at a height whereby they could double as footrests. During this era, oak, pine or walnut tops were often combined with an understructure of local hardwoods. Those originating in the 1800s were simplified. The trestles were noticeably lighter, chamfered edges disappeared and the tables became shorter. Shaker sawbuck tables reflect the spirit of simplicity inherent in their pieces. Sawbuck table value guide: pine, 4' long, 30" wide, chamfered X-shaped trestle, circa 1810, $875; walnut, breadboard ends, scrubbed top, Shaker type, circa 1860, $750.

SCALES. Beam scales, platform scales, dial scales and spring scales were in general use throughout the 19th century. Perhaps the earliest was the wrought-iron even-balance scale, with a center fulcrum and two arms of equal length. Somewhat later this type was produced in cast iron with a center post. Steelyard scales have been in use since antiquity. Collector interest in the old-fashioned counter-top scoop scale with a brass or tin scoop has resulted in a flood of reproductions. The Columbia Family Scale of sheet steel finished in black enamel with gilt decorations was widely touted in the late 19th century. Portable platform scales on wheels with a capacity of 600 pounds were listed in hardware catalogues at sixteen dollars each. Jones of Binghamton used a cloverleaf trademark on their "Cloverleaf" scale around the turn of the century. Scale value guide: counter type, even balance, tin scoop, 8-pound capacity, circa 1880, $95; Chatillon spring balance, round brass dial plate, $35.

SCHOOLMASTER'S DESKS. Country cabinetmakers had an exclusive on the schoolmaster's desk, which was crafted by them throughout the 19th century. It was typically made with a slope-front boxlike area supported by long legs, with or without a back rail, drawer or lower shelf. Some had small feet, others no feet. Their makers failed to adhere to any particular formula but always provided the owner with ample storage space beneath the lift-top lid. This area was of a size to hold essential stationery supplies and various important papers. Locally available hardwoods and softwoods were used in the construction. Nowadays the schoolmaster's desk is viewed with far more admiration from collectors than it was by reluctant school youngsters of yesteryear. Schoolmaster's desk value guide: cherry, back rail, one drawer, lower shelf, circa 1840, $325; pine, black paint, one drawer, turned legs, circa 1850, $265.

SCHRANKS. In Pennsylvania German communities a massive wardrobe resembling a Dutch kas was called a schrank. Skilled cabinetmakers fabricated them primarily between the early 1700s and mid-1800s. A schrank was typically crafted with two doors above two drawers. On the interior portion were inner shelves and pegs for holding clothing. They rested on various types of supports, and since they were constructed in various sections, assembling or dismantling one was quite simple. A walnut schrank possessing detailed inlay or applied carving, combined with other decorative elements, represents the ultimate achievement in American cabinetwork. Handsome decorated schranks painted in soft hues with polychrome folk art motifs are likewise prized. A maker's name and date generally appears on a schrank designated for a dowry. Schrank value guide: pine, painted florals, original decor, circa 1830, $3,400.

SCONCES. Sconces were originally sold in pairs, but nowadays they are often sold singly. The sconce is a bracket attached to a wall by means of a backplate. Some were made to hold a single candle while others held two or more. Backplates were generally made of mirror glass, pewter, tin, brass or silver. Most were simply designed, ranging from six to twelve inches in height. Tin sconces were often

Tin sconce, Pennsylvania, 18th century
National Gallery of Art, Washington

found hanging on farmhouse walls, as they were somewhat less expensive than other metal versions. Although the backplates appeared in varying designs, the simplest type held candles in country regions. Sconce value guide: tin, crimped top, hole for hanging, 12″ tall, pair, $240; brass, single candle, 8″ tall, pair, $110.

SCOOPS. Regardless of size or shape, any handcrafted scoop is a newsworthy acquisition. They were made in endless variety, as their makers required only a block of wood, a knife and some spare time. Scoops with fancy handles usually bring fancier prices. The craftsman who conceived the original two-way scoop, with a scoop at one end and a stirrer at the opposite end, is unknown, but widely copied. Large apple butter scoops often measuring up to fifteen inches in length were made by able-bodied woodworkers including the Shakers. For removing soft soap from the barrel there were rectangular and handleless shell-shaped models designated for flour. Cranberry, winnowing and blueberry scoops all lightened the farmer's workload. Any scoop seeker who wishes to diversify should investigate the interesting variety available in hornware and metalware. Scoop value guide: apple butter scoop, burl and tiger maple, carved, heart design, $145; brass, store scoop, 10″ long, $40; copper, 6″ long, $25; tin, wooden handle, 10″ long, $20.

SCREW-TYPE CANDLESTANDS. The candlestand surrendered to progress in the early 1700s when the screw-type version was introduced. Now it was possible to adjust both the candle arm and the table to a desired height. Durable maple was often chosen as the wood, since it resisted breakage. Dating one can be difficult since the form remained in vogue in country regions indefinitely. As a general rule, the earliest types were often the plainest. Some stands had their legs turned in imitation of Windsor chair legs. Detailed turnings and intricate screw mechanisms are indications of a finely crafted example. Much like its fellow furniture forms, the screw-type candlestand came under the decorator's brush when the vogue for painted furniture persisted in the first decade of the 19th century. Screw-type candlestand value guide: maple, turned legs, round top, two candle arms, circa 1810, $420; maple, painted black, gold striping, circa 1815, $385.

SCRUBBING STICKS. On washday the sturdy wooden scrubbing stick was pressed into service by busy homemakers of the 1700s and early 1800s. These scrubbers of European origin, also referred to as mangle boards or scrubboards, were the forerunners of the present-day washboard. Although they varied in size, most models measured four to six inches in width and from one to two feet in length. One side of the wooden slab remained flat while the reverse side was cut with corrugations, which provided indentations for rubbing the clothes back and forth. Sometimes the corrugations were made on a slant, and some had rather pronounced points. A short handle or a hand hold on the flat surface enabled the user to obtain a firm grip for those vigorous pressing and squeezing chores. Scrubbing stick value guide: maple, handmade, slanted corrugations, $85.

SECRETARY DESKS. The tambour secretary with its sliding shutters was the rage of the Hepplewhite and Sheraton periods. Formal furniture makers excelled in crafting these handsome pieces. However, they were too costly for country folk, and untrained woodworkers in rural areas simply could not master the intricacies of tambour work. As an alternative, they offered their customers a secretary desk having cupboard doors rather than tambour shutters. The completed form consisted of an upper cupboard section with either solid wood or glass doors, and a tablelike lower section with one or more drawers. There was no attempt to conform to any set guidelines, as the form varied slightly depending on its origin. Their makers fabricated them from native woods such as cherry, maple, birch or walnut. Secretary desk value guide: walnut and pine,

Secretary desk, cathedral windows, 19th century

National Gallery of Art, Washington

cathedral panel doors, one drawer, circa 1830, $1,050; cherry, wooden doors, no drawers, Southwest origin, circa 1840, $985.

SETTEES. Presumably the earliest American settee was of the wainscot type having a solid seat and back. From the late 18th century on, they were a specialty of Windsor chairmakers. The earliest and finest examples had shaped seats, thin spindles, turned stretchers and other traces of dignified handwork. This form experienced widespread acceptance during the 19th century. They usually had wooden or cane seats measuring between three and seven feet in length. Many were enlargements of Windsor chair styles, notably the rod-back, comb-back, low-back and bow-back forms. Their makers ornamented them with handsome painted and stenciled decorations and gold striping, making them absolutely irresistible. Lambert Hitchcock and his successors marketed some sensationally ornamented settees in the 1830s and 1840s. Settee value guide: arrow-back, twenty-three spindles, stenciled, 4' long, $830; fiddle-back, painted black, plank seat, circa 1840, $800; rod-back, pine, painted blue, 6' long, $740.

SETTLE BEDS. New England furniture makers borrowed this gem of an idea from their French-Canadian neighbors. Therefore, a number of existing settle beds are thought to have originated in Canada. With an eye to conserving valuable room space, some ingenious woodworker uncorked this bit of ingenuity, which functioned as a bed by night and a settle by day. The seat area could be tilted forward to form a high-sided box. It could be converted into a bed with the aid of a feather mattress or some straw. Whether or not this afforded the slumberer an undisturbed night's sleep is questionable. Latching on to an early settle bed with original painted designs is better than catching forty winks. Settle bed value guide: pine, original blue paint, $765.

SETTLES. The high solid back and wide sides of the settle protected the user from chilly drafts in the 17th and 18th centuries. This piece was usually found close to the hearth. Since it had been known in rural English cottages at an earlier date, furniture makers reconstructed the form from memory. Craftsmen simply could not settle on one specific style, thereby resulting in some minor construction variations. Some had wide protruding sides forming the armrests and a hooded top. A storage unit was often placed under the seat with either a lift-top or drawers. Softwoods proved most popular, and many were treated to a coat of green, blue or red paint. One interesting innovation was the curved back settle upon which two people could sit slightly facing each other. Those having a paneled back or center armrest display eminent handwork. Settle value guide: pine, paneled back, original red paint, center armrest, circa 1730, $1,600; pine, original green paint, New England, circa 1740, $1,400.

SEWING TABLES. Trying to find an antique sewing table is definitely easier than locating a needle in a haystack, as they have survived in surprisingly large numbers. Many versions had a silk bag below, often to hide a wooden box. However, both the bag and the box may be missing on antique specimens. Seamstresses displayed their sewing skills on models possessing Hepplewhite, Sheraton or American Empire influences. A mention should be made of the Martha Washington sewing table, as supposedly the First Lady used a worktable of this type at Mount Vernon. Country sewing tables lacked the detail found on formal models. Shaker examples were usually made of maple or cherry used singly or together. Inexpensive pedestal-base sewing tables made from black walnut or mahogany, and spool-turned stands, were available at furniture emporiums in the mid-19th century. Sewing table value guide: Shaker type, circa 1860, $300; pine and mahogany, Hepplewhite style, octagonal top, one drawer, square tapering legs, $290.

SGRAFFITO. The word sgraffito is derived from the Italian word sgraffiare, meaning to scratch. Pottery decorated with a scratched

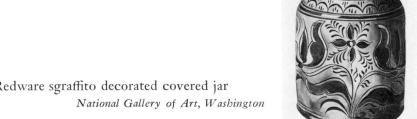

Redware sgraffito decorated covered jar
National Gallery of Art, Washington

motif is called "sgraffito ware." First the selected item was given a coat of pale clay, after which a chosen design was scratched or cut through the outer layer to reveal the color of the clay beneath. Naturally, the indentations made it rather impractical for everyday use, thus reserving it for gift or presentation items. Pennsylvania potters employed this technique on wares from the 1700s onward, although it experienced its major thrust of popularity in the 19th century. Birds, animals, flowers, hearts, inscriptions and human figures found their way onto sgraffito plates, pitchers and other utilitarian and ornamental items. Sgraffito is simply sensational, and current prices reflect collector agreement. Sgraffito value guide: pie plate, tulips, flowers, 8″ diameter, $480.

SHAKER CHAIRS. Shaker chairs rightfully deserve the superlatives cast in their direction by collectors. Practically every community produced them, with especially large numbers originating at New Lebanon, New York, renamed Mount Lebanon in 1861. Ladder-back straight or side chairs and rocking chairs were among the earliest forms designed for domestic use and for public sale. In the latter part of the 19th century, chair catalogues listed numerous designs, including bentwoods and spindle-backs. They were typically made with rush, cane, wood-splint or fabric-taped seats. Side chairs were made for men and women, with the latter being somewhat lower. Originally chairs were stained red, but later they had a natural finish. Acorn-shaped finials provide a distinguishing feature atop the back posts. Another style peculiar to the Shakers is the curved dowel bar attached to the rear posts, known as a cushion rail. They were sold through direct factory sales and by sales outlets in major cities. Shaker chair value guide: child's chair, armless, red paint, original decor, $275; armchair, large size, acorn finial, domed mushroom arm, taped seat and back, $260; dining chair, two slats, 25″ high, $225.

SHAKER COLLECTIBLES. Mother Ann Lee arrived in America with exactly eight disciples in 1774. About 1787 the first commune was founded at New Lebanon, followed by a number of others in the early 1800s. By 1850 eighteen conclaves were active, with a total population of approximately 6,000 Believers. During their most productive period they were involved in numerous industries which brought wealth to their self-supporting communities.

Shirred Shaker rug, 19th century
National Gallery of Art, Washington

Their herbal medicine and seed business prospered, as did their chairmaking activities. Presently collectors compete diligently for any item, large or small, attributed to the Shakers. Boxes, clocks, stoves, baskets, sieves, swifts and other articles made or used by them bring premium prices on the antique marketplace. Credit must be given to the Shakers for numerous inventions and improvements. They were pioneers in packaging seeds in small packages and in the medicinal herb industry. Among other notable accomplishments were the clothespin, self-acting cheese press, improved washing machine, cut nails, a pea sheller and a butter worker. Constantly striving for perfection, they were ever alert to devices that would save time and labor. Shaker collectibles value guide: basket, rectangular splint, 10" x 14", $40; box, oval, 4" x 6", $45; funnel holder, wooden, $110; cider press, $70; laundry stove, cast iron, $475; sugar bucket, wooden with cover, $55.

SHAKER FURNITURE. Simple Shaker furniture, known and loved for its simplicity and purity of form, truly appears to have been divinely inspired. It was devoid of ornamentation and possessed a minimum of turning. Pine was perhaps the most popular wood, but cherry, ash, hickory, apple, pear and maple were also used. Cherry was widely favored for tabletops. Ash and hickory were utilized for bent forms, including rockers, slats and arms. Each piece of furniture was finished in a high degree of excellence. Originally, pieces were stained or painted red, but later a natural finish was preferred. Shaker beds were a mere three feet wide, with low headboards and footboards. They were painted green and came equipped with wooden rollers. Trestle, sawbuck, ironing, drop-leaf, sewing, oval and bread-cutting tables all originated in Shaker communities. Their candlestands are always in demand. The finest woods available were used in crafting bureaus, chests, cupboards, counters,

Left: Shaker chest of drawers, 19th century; Center: Shaker drop-leaf table, 19th century; Right: Shaker cupboard, 19th century
Bottom left: Shaker pine chest, 19th century; Right: Shaker three-drawer table, 19th century

cabinets, blanket boxes, washstands, writing desks and other case pieces. Collectors believe in the furniture crafted by the Believers. Shaker furniture value guide: bed, maple, rope, painted green, $295; cupboard, pine, two doors, bottom two drawers, natural finish, $1,750; spinning wheel, $365; worktable, pine and cherry, red stain, original, $480.

SHAKER ROCKERS. The Shakers were among the first to fully exploit the advantages of the rocking chair in America. They were placed in the "retiring" room originally for the elderly or immobile, but later practically every room had one. Although relatively few were produced prior to 1800, by the second quarter of the 19th century they were enjoying widespread acceptance. A common Shaker rocking chair, one made without arms, cost one dollar in 1831. Some collectors prefer classifying them according to their distinguishing characteristics. The five major types are the scrolled arm, mushroom post, rolled arm, cushion rail and sewing rocker. They were typically made with one rung at the rear and two at the front and sides. Tapes or braid woven in a checkerboard pattern replaced earlier splint seats about 1830. Shaker rocker value guide: sewing rocker, taped seat and back, drawer beneath seat, $390; armed rocker, cyma-curved arms, five-slat back, $340; armless rocker, four slats, taped seat, $285.

SHERATON FANCY CHAIRS. The fad for Sheraton fancy chairs originated in England, reaching American shores in the late 18th century. Although the public admired them, they were too expensive for people of limited means. This prompted American chairmakers to copy the idea, and by the early 19th century fancy chairs were being mass-produced at affordable prices. The so-called Sheraton fancy chair was characterized by tapering front legs curved out slightly at the base, terminating in knob feet. They usually had rounded front rush seats and a back which featured a slight backward curve. Backs were generally composed of several rows of delicate splats and straight-line rectangular top rails. Small wooden balls appeared between the rows of splats and on the front stretcher. Originally, they were handpainted, but eventually stenciled surfaces were combined with gilt or gold striping. Sheraton fancy chair value guide: maple, shield-shaped back, painted florals, gilded, circa 1810,

Shaker rocker, 19th century
National Gallery of Art, Washington

179

Tavern sign, hand-painted, 18th century

Cigar-store Indian, 19th century

Both photographs, National Gallery of Art, Washington

$240; maple, painted yellow, handlegrip-decorated crest rail, rush seat, green trim, original decor, $230.

SHOP SIGNS. All the trade signs and shop figures once viewed along main streets in the 18th and 19th centuries are attractive acquisitions. This includes such standbys as the barber's pole, optician's eyeglasses, fishmonger's fish and cobbler's boots. The earliest free-swinging symbols were the work of wood-carvers. Later the signboard replaced the trade symbol, these being primarily the work of carpenters and sign painters. Since few were signed by their makers, research is required before age can be determined. Many painters reserved their major artistic thrust for fine-quality tavern or inn signs. Shop figures are fast sellers with fanciers of American folk art, particularly the cigar-store Indian carvings of 19th-century origin. Shop sign value guide: optician's sign, spectacles and eyes, carved wood, 19th century, $1,200; cigar-store figure, Indian squaw, 6' tall, $4,000.

SHOW TOWELS. A show towel is a long narrow linen panel richly embroidered by its maker with justifiable pride. They once hung on doors in the Pennsylvania area, just as they had in Europe centuries before. These towels were pretty as well as practical. When guests arrived, a slightly soiled towel was covered with a show towel. The earliest towels, embroidered in cross-stitch, show soft muted colors; after aniline-dyed yarns were introduced in the 1840s, the colors became bolder. Also, new stitching techniques were developed by experimental needlewomen. Names, initials and dates are commonly found on these treasured towels. Those destined as part of the linen dowry always bear the maker's name and a date. The wide range of traditional motifs favored by ladies swift of needle bear a resemblance to samplers of Pennsylvania origin. Show towel value guide: embroidered, tulips, hearts, stars, circa 1830, $55.

SIEVES. Collectors spend leisure hours sifting through farmhouse possessions searching for sieves. Smaller versions sifted medicine powders; medium sizes, flour; larger versions, charcoal. The earliest horsehair sieve had a mat woven on a frame from the hair of a cow's tail or a horse's mane. The mats were then set in oval or round hooped frames, usually of pine, maple, oak or ash. One was occasionally fitted with a single or double wooden cover. Hair mats were gradually supplanted by silk bolting cloth or wire. Other sieves resembling colanders were made of pierced copper, tin or brass. The square-shaped, sturdily constructed charcoal sieve had an oak frame and an ash splint sifter. The so-called riddle was a Shaker sieve specialty for sifting seeds or wheat, having a brass wire mat. Their oval double-covered examples are doubly pleasing to the sieve seeker. Patented tin sifters proliferated throughout the 19th century, when such pantry pleasers as the Hunter Sifter, the Magic Flour Sifter and the Acme Sifter were distributed. Sieve value guide: maple, round, early hair type, 10″ diameter, $65; Shaker type, brass wire mat, $45; Shaker type, horsehair, 5″ diameter, $40.

SILVER. America was blessed with capable craftsmen, many of whom were practicing the art of silversmithing during the latter part of the 17th century. New England, New York and Pennsylvania had their share of silversmiths, and in the early 18th century they were joined by others working in Maryland, Virginia and the Carolinas. In the post-Revolutionary War period, silversmiths opened workshops in various outlying areas. The work of the silversmith, or goldsmith as he preferred calling himself, was dominated by the English influence. However, in each locality some regional flavor manifested itself. The crafted pieces tended to follow contemporary

Both photographs, National Gallery of Art, Washington
Left: Silver tankard, New England, mid-18th century; Right: Silver teapot, early 18th century

furniture designs. Because the output was primarily custom-made, silversmiths served as both designers and craftsmen. Taking tremendous pride in their work, they usually signed their pieces with a name or initials, often appearing within an oval, shield, rectangular, star or heart-shaped device. The age of the individual silversmith was doomed when machine-made objects were introduced in the 1840s. Silver value guide: bread tray, sterling, unmarked, $70; cream jug, marked Kirk, $185; spoon, rat-tail, American, circa 1750, $70; sugar tongs, plain, $50.

SKILLETS. In the colonial period this kitchen utensil was also known as a pipkin or poset. These small pots with long handles were made of copper, iron, bronze or brass. The earlier the skillet, the smaller. Originally they were quite small, with wand or rod-type handles and three short legs. Later the form was expanded as they became broader and rounder. In the 1700s they were being made by many iron furnaces in New York, New Jersey and Pennsylvania. Many coppersmiths also advertised them at an early date. Skillet value guide: cast iron, straight handle, three legs, 7″ diameter, $45.

SKIMMERS. One utensil certain to be found hanging by the kitchen fireplace was the skimmer. It was used to remove cream as it formed on the surface of the milk. A widely known model featured a long iron handle attached to a perforated pan of copper, tinned iron or brass. The type featuring a ring handle was known as a flit.

Busy separators often chose oval or shell-shaped wooden skimmers, generally made of pine. Frequently, an ambidextrous worker demonstrated separating skills by using a skimmer in each hand. The fine-quality creamware skimmers from the famous Wedgwood factory in England seldom reached small-town country stores in the 19th century. However, inexpensive wirework skimmers retailing for a mere eighteen cents each were reordered repeatedly by general store shopkeepers. Skimmer value guide: brass, wrought-iron handle, ring end, 20" long, $55; iron, 19" long, $22.

SLEEVE BOARDS. In the pre-permanent press period the sleeve board was an essential ironing adjunct. These wooden boards of pine, maple or oak were about one inch thick and just wide enough to accommodate a sleeve. Sleeves could be slipped on or off these boards so easily that they made ironing a cheerful chore. The boards stood on their own base whether homemade or factory-produced. Later patented models capable of being attached to existing ironing boards were widely advertised. Sleeve boards were luring customers in hardware store catalogues around the turn of the century, inexpensively priced at under a dollar each. Sleeve board value guide: circa 1880, $20.

SLEIGH BEDS. Formal furniture makers introduced this decidedly different low-post bed resembling a sleigh or horse-drawn cutter about 1820. It had a headboard and footboard of equal height, with curving top rails amply supported by flaring cyma-curved legs terminating in a heavy block foot. Many models were fitted with casters. Formal furniture makers and early factories advertised them in veneered mahogany during the American Empire period. Naturally, country cabinetmakers adapted the design, simplifying it in the transition. They favored local softwoods such as pine, which was frequently painted to simulate mahogany. The newly invented iron bed latch securely held the bed parts in place. Sleigh beds slid into rural bedrooms in the second quarter of the 19th century. Sleigh bed value guide: walnut, sleigh-shaped, circa 1845, $330.

SLEIGH BELLS. Beautifully sounding brass or iron sleigh bells appeared in over twenty different sizes during the 19th century. Factories centered in New England marketed them in sizes ranging from seven-eighths of an inch up to three and three-quarter inches in diameter. Brass examples are preferred, along with any bearing a maker's name, initials or date. Leather straps carried a varying number of them depending on the size of the bell. Bells attached by cotter pins are earlier than those secured by rivets. Full or partially full strings warrant collector appreciation. Ball-shaped bells are more common than bell or acorn shapes. The town of East Hampton, Connecticut, became known for its fine-quality sleigh bells through the efforts of such industry giants as William Barton and the still-existing Bevin Brothers Manufacturing Company. Sleigh bell value guide: brass, 78" strap, thirty bells, $110; iron, original strap, thirty bells, $75.

SLIPWARE. Slip-decorated redware was achieved by tracing motifs on the piece with diluted clay of a creamy consistency in a contrasting color. It was made in America from the mid-1700s, but was afforded its finest expression on the creative pieces of Pennsylvania origin. Originally the potters in this region imported clays specifically for this purpose, but later it was made entirely in America. Sometimes the slip decoration was confined to simply lines and dots, while on other items motifs, inscriptions, flowers, birds, animals and human figures were executed with a high degree of inventiveness. Any piece of slipware is salable, but special interest centers on articles possessing a name or a date or having historical significance. Those made as presentation pieces rarely slip past a knowledgeable buyer. Slipware value guide: loaf dish, vivid glaze and slip, 14" diameter, $150; bowl, yellow and red slip, 5" diameter, $135; plate, wavy lines, 10" diameter, $150.

SMITH AND WESSON. Horace Smith and Daniel Wesson, two capable gunsmiths active in the mid-1800s, pooled their resources to gain fame and fortune in the firearms field. Among their contributions was a new repeating pistol plus a rifle with an improved cartridge. The repeating mechanism they developed eventually evolved into the Volcanic pistols and rifles of 1855. Further revision of these pistols by B. Tyler Henry resulted in the concept for the famous Henry and Winchester rifles. The cartridge revolving arms produced by the partners in the 1850s provided their business with a much needed shot in the arm. Smith & Wesson value guide: Ladysmiths 2nd model, $560.

SMOOTHING BOARDS. In the pre-flatiron era the wooden smoothing board, European in origin, was called upon to perform pressing chores. These wooden boards, measuring up to thirty-six inches in length, were slightly curved. Some were entirely flat while others had a corrugated side. The corrugations were rounded rather than pointed, thus differing slightly from the sharp-pointed scrubbing stick. A carved flatiron-shaped handle adorned the flat side of most boards. Here the craftsman displayed his knack with a knife by carving delicate designs, often accompanied by a date. Most models had a knob at the other end so the user could grip the board with both hands. Smoothing board value guide: flatiron handle, one corrugated side, $70.

SOAPSTONE. This bluish gray soft rock having a smooth surface, similar to soap, was originally known as potstone in the 17th and 18th centuries. Because it could be easily turned on a lathe or cut with a saw or knife Colonial craftsmen fashioned it into various utilitarian objects. Its heat resisting quality made it suitable for cooking vessels. Colonial kitchens boasted soapstone sinks, stoves, pots, pans, flatirons, trivets, griddles and mortars and pestles. By fitting a soapstone slab with a wood or metal handle it functioned as a portable warmer. Soapstone seekers worked up a lather over intricately carved ornamental objects such as bookends or tobacco jars. Many pieces originated along the Atlantic coast where soapstone was found in substantial amounts. Soapstone value guide: foot-warmer, metal handle, circa 1830, $90; kettle, circa 1790, $175; trivet, rectangular, circa 1800, $35.

SOUTH JERSEY GLASS. This type of free-blown glassware is associated with Casper Wistar's glasshouse in southern New Jersey, founded in 1739. The factory remained active until the Revolutionary War brought about its financial collapse. South Jersey glass can be characterized by the lily pad design, threading, quilling and prunts (small blobs of applied glass). Factory workers produced these so-called off-hand pieces for families and friends. Bowls, vases, candlesticks and pitchers have been ascribed to early glassworkers. As factory glass blowers migrated into other regions, South Jersey type glass was produced elsewhere, notably in Pennsylvania, New York, New England and Ohio. Similar decorative devices appeared on glasswares well into the 19th century, some destined for com-

Left: Ribbed cruet, South Jersey glass characteristics

Right: Picture frame, Southwestern tinware, 19th century

Both photographs, National Gallery of Art, Washington

mercial distribution. South Jersey glass value guide: pitcher, 8″ tall, lily pad decor, crimped, footed base, $260.

SOUTHWEST TINWARE. The first tin plate reached New Mexico over the Santa Fe trail in the second quarter of the 19th century. Candle sconces and tin-framed looking-glasses were among the initial items reaching the area. For the local artisan, there was no recourse but to use every piece of tin scrap in conceiving tinware. They skillfully pieced together pieces of tin scrap salvaged from tin cans. Window glass and wallpaper were also new commodities; when combined on a piece of Southwest tinware, they suggest a date of production subsequent to the mid-1840s. All-over pierced designs and cut-out fins were employed as decorative devices on this regional tinware possessing enormous charm. Southwest tinware value guide: picture frame, 14″ x 12″, circa 1880, $235.

SPARKING LAMPS. These small glass or metal lamps were designed to burn a small amount of oil. They are often referred to as "squat lamps" or "tavern lamps." The latter term originated from their extensive use in taverns, where a guest often carried one to light the way to his room after an evening of imbibing. Since it burned only a small supply of oil, the possibility of any mishap was greatly reduced; should the user fall asleep before extinguishing the light, it slowly burned itself out. These lamps were often miniature versions of larger models, with most measuring between three and eight inches tall. Sparking lamps were lit by a young maiden who had a gentleman caller. When the light flickered out, it was a signal for the suitor to depart posthaste. Sparking lamp value guide: glass, amber, 6" tall, $130; pewter, saucer base, handle, circa 1840, $175.

SPATTERWARE. This provincial pottery pleaser dating from the early 1800s, also known as spongeware, originated in the Staffordshire district of England. Country folk adored this brightly stippled ware executed in vivid shades of red, yellow, brown, green or black. The term "spatter" does not correctly describe the technique employed. Each piece was dabbed with a paint-soaked sponge or similar object. The amount of sponging varied in accordance with the potter. There were over forty freehand patterns used as center subjects, with Peacock, Star, Schoolhouse and Tulip being the best known. Spatterware dinner and tea services, platters and other tabletop necessities were made, but were rarely marked by English potters. This colorful tableware was exported from England, Scotland and Wales during the 19th century. Spatterware value guide: creamer, 6" high, Tulip pattern, $160; pitcher, 7" high, flowers, blue and pink, $240; sugar bowl, blue peafowl, $220; teapot, Rainbow pattern, $300.

SPICE BOXES. In the 1700s spice boxes were usually crafted by a family member or the village carpenter. As coopers set up shop in outlying areas, round or oval spice boxes in single or graduated sizes were stenciled with the name of the contents for easy identification. The Shakers showed a distinct preference for oval spice boxes with fingered joints. They were made in graduated sizes, generally in groups of five, seven, nine or ten. Since complete sets are seldom found, even single boxes of Shaker origin command collector interest. The spice box scavenger delights in acquiring an example from the Pennsylvania area, where these kitchen staples were enlivened with traditional folk motifs. A dated example is certain to fetch a substantial figure. Competing for consumer approval in the 1800s were the lightweight, but durable, stenciled or japanned tin spice containers. These round, square or oblong boxes, often made with hinged lids, held a series of small containers lettered with the name of the contents. Spice box value guide: tin, round, hinged lid, six containers, japanned, $50; lift lid, handmade, pine, original blue paint, $40.

SPICE CHESTS. Early spice chests vary in workmanship as they were designed by cabinetmakers, carpenters or family handymen. Precious spices were stored in them, and the finest examples came equipped with locks. Most were designed to hang on the wall or to stand on a table, but there were some very luxurious ones resembling small highboys. The form varied somewhat, with many having six, nine or twelve drawers. There were plain, painted and carved chests of various sizes, often bearing initials or a date. Dated types are generally thought to have been presented as gifts on special occasions. The choice of wood depended almost solely on what was available locally at the time of construction. Spice chests are fast sellers in any season. Spice chest value guide: pine, twelve drawers, porcelain knobs, dovetailed, original blue paint, $90; oak, six drawers, wooden pulls, hanging type, $70.

SPICE GRINDERS. Exotic spices arrived by the boatload to the shores of America from faraway ports such as the West Indies. Small wooden spice grinders were made in two parts, each with a series of tiny steel points. When the two pieces were fitted together and turned, the teeth automatically crushed the spices. In the 19th century japanned tin examples operating on somewhat the same principle were marketed. Another wooden grinder was shaped like a small coffee mill. It was activated by an iron crank handle which set the inner teeth in motion, thereby grinding the spices. The powdered spices were deposited and removed through a small pull-out drawer. Spice grinder value guide: wooden, two parts, $35; tin, japanned, circa 1860, $18.

SPINDLE-BACK SIDE CHAIRS. In the latter part of the 19th century the turned spindle-back side chair was an inexpensive piece of cottage furniture. Many were sold as a part of a cottage bedroom set. The slightly concave top rail had a scroll-arched lower edge which accommodated the spindles comprising the open back. Generally two or four spindles, vase, knob and ring-turned, could be found between the top rail and the cross slat. The back uprights usually displayed vase-and-ring turnings. They had cane seats and turned legs braced by a stretcher. If the chair has retained its original painted decoration and striping, the price jumps accordingly. The maple examples are heavier than those made of lightweight pine. Spindle-back side chair value guide: pine, cane seat, circa 1880, $80.

SPINNER, DAVID. David Spinner was one of the most proficient potters practicing his chosen profession in Bucks County, Pennsylvania, at the dawning of the 19th century. Obviously, he was inspired by prints of the period, as his incised earthenware designs depict such subjects as fashionably dressed ladies, soldiers and hunting scenes. Undoubtedly these sgraffito images would probably draw a mixed reaction from art critics, but they do possess a pleasing peasant quality. Local townspeople considered Spinner quite an accomplished artist. Signed specimens exist; some wares were marked "David Spinner Potter" or "David Spinner his Make." This potter broke with tradition by writing his inscriptions in English rather than German. Extremely rare.

SPINNING WHEELS. Surely one of the most decorative accessories to be found in Early American furniture is the spinning wheel. Practically every home had a spinning wheel, generally passed down from generation to generation. The whirling spinning wheel was a familiar sound in Colonial homes. Made by local carpenters, it varied only slightly in form over the years. Although it was treated with utmost care, locating one in working condition can be rather difficult. However, since many are purchased primarily for display, size and condition are often of principal concern. Spinning was accomplished on a large wheel, while flax was spun on a smaller wheel called a Saxon wheel. In rural areas women and men often shared spinning chores, but in wealthier homes, servants listened to the song of the spinning wheel. Spinning wheel value guide: child's flax wheel, $220; maple and pine, original green paint, circa 1820, $260.

SPLAT-BACK WINDSOR CHAIRS. Abraham Lincoln supposedly sold a chair of this type to a neighbor shortly before embarking to Washington for his inauguration in 1860. The solid vase-shaped center splat is wider than that found on the earlier and more elegant pierced splat associated with English Windsors. This style chair was made with a flaring rectangular seat. It had splayed tapering legs braced by a box stretcher. The solid one-piece seats were often made of pine or other softwoods, while other parts were constructed of various hardwoods. These farmhouse favorites of the mid-19th century were painted or stained and usually highlighted with striping. Splat-back Windsor chair value guide: pine, grained, gilt striping, circa 1870, $130.

Shaker laundry basket
National Gallery of Art, Washington

SPLINT BASKETS. The majority of American baskets, whether handmade or factory-produced, were made of splint. They were crafted with thin flexible strips of wood, notably ash, oak, hickory or poplar. The cross-hatch weave was far more popular than the hexagon weave. Only a small percentage of baskets were marked by their makers; thus dating can be perplexing. The earliest baskets were made of heavy splint and hand-forged or square-headed cut nails. Natural binding materials were utilized in their construction, and many show signs of tool marks. A factory-made example had machine or wire nails, thin splint, metal bail handles and bindings of thread, raffia or string. Earlier handcrafted baskets are eagerly acquired as they are true one-of-a-kinds. Splint basket value guide: Shaker laundry basket, $130; egg, 10" high including handle, $25; berry, handled, 4" x 4½", $20.

SPONGEWARE. Flea-market shoppers are familiar with this coarse type of late white earthenware daubed in blue, blue-green, blue-brown and other colors. Blue and white pieces generate greatest collector excitement. This late ware should not be confused with the earlier and more valuable spatterware. Country kitchens became brighter when eye-appealing spongeware appeared in the late 1800s and early 1900s. This comparative newcomer has acquired a legion of admirers who search for mixing bowls, cups and saucers, cookie jars, teapots, butter crocks, toilet sets, jugs, plates, platters and other utilitarian articles. The term spongeware originated because the decoration was often achieved with the application of a color-soaked sponge. Spongeware value guide: cup and saucer, blue and brown, $40; pitcher, blue and brown, 9" tall, $70; sugar bowl, blue and white, $45; mixing bowl, blue and white, 12" diameter, $45.

SPOOL BEDS. The spool-turned bed proved to be the sleeper of the 19th century, thanks to their mass distribution by cottage furniture factories. Low-post styles featuring button or spool turnings became farmhouse favorites as early as the 1830s. By the 1840s furniture factory catalogues illustrated them in various sizes, often with a headboard and footboard of equal height. On other models the headboard was slightly higher than the footboard. These beds are easy to recognize despite the minor variations in overall construction due to the ever-present spool-turnings. The side pieces were secured with bedscrews or bed latches. About 1850 a spool bed with rounded corners was developed, coinciding with the enormously successful American tour of the Swedish nightingale, Jenny Lind. Out of deference to this talented songstress, they were nicknamed Jenny Lind beds. Spool bed value guide: black walnut, low-post, 40" high, spool-turned posts, circa 1870, $220; maple, low-post, button-turned finials, 6' long, 4' wide, $190.

SPOOL FURNITURE. The elaborately turned spool furniture of the 19th century represents another coveted category of Country furniture. It bore a resemblance to the earlier 17th-century Flemish or Elizabethan styles. It was made by cabinetmakers in the first quarter of the century, but later spool furniture became America's first mass-produced style. There were various types of turnings, including bobbin, sausage, knob, spool, button and vase-and-ring. Furniture factory catalogues bulged beyond belief with spool-turned beds, tables, cribs, cradles, towel racks, chairs, shaving stands, settees and stools. Black walnut, maple, mahogany, cherry, poplar and birch were the preferred woods, with the finer woods left in a natural finish and others treated to staining or painting. Between the 1820s and 1880s spool furniture threaded its way into every nook and cranny. Spool furniture value guide: mahogany drop-leaf table, rectangular, 42" x 60", six spool-turned legs, $475; cherry chest of drawers, four drawers, 42" high, 38" wide, circa 1860, $220; walnut footstool, circa 1870, $85.

SPOOL-TURNED CRIBS. Between the 1840s and 1880s infants were lifted in and out of stunning spool-turned cribs. Local cabinetmakers vied with small furniture factories for cradle customers. Despite the slight variations in design, the ever-present spool-turned posts provide the distinguishing feature. When mahogany was utilized, the fenced-in portion between the posts was comprised of upright strips. On black walnut versions the posts and spindles were both elaborately turned. One side of the crib was usually hinged. Spool-turned furniture seekers do a double take over the double-width size designed to accommodate twins. Spool-turned crib value guide: black walnut, 26" high, 36" wide, circa 1850, $250.

SPOOL-TURNED SOFAS. One of the scarce forms in spool-turned furniture is the open or upholstered-back sofa. Its production was chiefly confined to early furniture factories operating in New England during the 1840s and 1850s. They were typically made with spool-turned posts, the rear ones terminating in spool-turned finials. A repeating curve usually adorned the lower edge of the seat rail. The open ends had spool-turned arms exactly the same height as the chair back. These simply turned spool sofas, usually made of cherry, birch, maple or black walnut, measured approximately six feet in length. Spool-turned sofa value guide: maple, open back, 6'2" long, 20" deep, circa 1855, $485.

STEEPLE CLOCKS. American clockmakers developed this style shelf clock to compliment Gothic Revival styles prevalent in the mid-1800s. Small Connecticut clockmakers specialized in producing them in numerous sizes and shapes. The pointed top and pillars terminating in pointed finials furnished these clocks with their distinctive look. There were both round and sharp-topped Gothic clocks, the sharp type being known as a "steeple clock." Those possessing a clockmaker's label can be easily identified. The stunning steeple clock was a clock with its own point of view. Steeple clock value guide: Birge and Fuller, double steeple, stenciled tablet, circa 1845, $250; New Haven Clock Company, painted tablet, 22" high, $225.

STEVENS, ZACHARIAH BECKETT. Can a young blacksmith turned tinsmith find fame and fortune in a little town in Maine? Yes, is the answer, if the gentleman in question is America's best-known practitioner of painted tinware: Zachariah Beckett Stevens. The town of Stevens Plains, Maine, became a thriving tin center in the

Apple tray, Zachariah Stevens style, 19th century

Steeple clock, New England, 19th century

Both photographs, National Gallery of Art, Washington

1800s thanks to this talented craftsman who opened a tin shop there in 1798. His business flourished as traveling peddlers sold his wares over hill and dale. Uncle Zach, as he was known to the townsfolk, had the master's touch on tinware. Using white, red, yellow and black backgrounds, he proceeded to paint in soft, warmly realistic colors. The intricate borders defied comparison with other country painters, as he combined different colored brush strokes with berries and leaves on many pieces. Two large vermilion cherries can be found on some Stevens specimens. His two sons, Alfred and Samuel, operated the business from 1830 until 1842, when the tin shop was closed due to a serious fire. Lovers of American folk art deservedly cast accolades in the direction of this magnificent man from Maine. Extremely rare.

STIEGEL, HENRY WILLIAM. This gentleman hardly had time to catch his breath after arriving in Lancaster County, Pennsylvania, from Germany when he opened a successful iron foundry. In 1763 he turned his efforts to glassmaking, and by 1765 he was the proud owner of three active glasshouses. Two of them were located in Manheim, a town he founded. Stiegel imported skilled workmen from Europe, who proceeded to ornament glass with engraved and enameled motifs in the Continental tradition. Fine-quality flint glass in shades of purple, amethyst, blue and occasionally emerald green brought recognition to the glasshouse. Molded glass having ribbed, quilted or swirled patterns was another Stiegel specialty. Fame and fortune came his way, along with the complimentary title "Baron." However, overexpansion caused his downfall and eventual imprisonment for debt. By 1774 Stiegel's enterprises had ceased operating. Stiegel glass value guide: lady's cuspidor, fluted rim, Stiegel type, $350; scent bottle, swirled, twenty-rib pattern, Stiegel type, $280.

STILLS. Who do you think was responsible for supplying whiskey to the Philadelphia and Baltimore markets in the 1800s? This rather dubious honor must be bestowed upon the farmers of Pennsylvania. Tinsmiths and coppersmiths operating along the eastern seaboard advertised stills in many sizes from the late 18th century on. Many craftsmen who chose a career in copper managed to keep the wolf away from the door filling customer's orders for stills and apple butter kettles. A farmer of meager means frequently pooled resources with several associates to form a "distillery partnership." Stills always show signs of superior workmanship. A century or more ago in the still of the night there was nary an empty still. Still value guide: copper, complete, circa 1840, $150.

STONEWARE. Following the Revolutionary War this hard, nonporous pottery made from tan and gray clays fired at high temperatures found favor in America. Jars, crocks, jugs and numerous other humble household staples were made of stoneware, often saltglazed. Decorated pieces are prized. They took the form of sgraffito, low-relief ornaments, stenciled motifs or cobalt blue handpainted designs. The former was fashionable after 1825, when flowers, patriotic motifs, houses, trees, ships, birds, animals and sunbursts were among the patterns preferred by potters. Those employing freehand curlicues and scrollwork designs display artistic touches of enormous appeal to collectors. Marked pieces are very salable. Un-

Left: Stoneware jar, eagle decor, 19th century

Right: Stoneware pitcher, cobalt blue decoration

Both photographs, National Gallery of Art, Washington

194

marked specimens also fetch substantial returns although attribution is difficult due to the similarity of American-made wares. The popularity of stoneware among antiquers is every bit as durable as its name implies. Stoneware value guide: cooler, cobalt blue banding, marked Charleston, $185; crock, two handles, No. 4 within wreath, $130; pitcher, Remmey, presentation type, "D. Reed/1901," $265.

STOOLS. A stool is generally described as a seat to hold a single person. The first American-made stools dating from the 17th century were known as "joined stools," "joint stools" or "short joints." They were, as the names imply, made by joiners. There were basically two styles of stools, short ones known as footstools and larger ones designed as seats. However, minor family members often warmed themselves on footstools by the hearth. All of the country versions were loosely based on formal designs. They were constructed from native woods, with tops of wood, rush or other suitable regional materials. Upholstered seats were usually found on examples originating in urban areas. The stool searchers should be prepared to encounter such variations as the cricket stool, window stool or closet stool for hiding a chamber pot. Stool value guide: Windsor type, three legs, original green paint, $170; poplar bed stool, maple legs, circa 1810, $130; milking stool, four legs, circa 1860, $70.

STOVE PLATES. The illustrious ironmasters of Pennsylvania cast ornate stove plates primarily based on European designs for five-plate stoves. The patterns were derived from memory or copied from stove plates brought to the new country by German immigrants. Quite often the ironmaster benefited from some subtle advertising by incorporating the furnace name or a date in the design. Biblical subjects dominated the decorative themes of stove plates in the 1740s, when figures and texts were employed to illustrate Bible stories. More than one tiny tot received some pre-Sunday school training by examining a cast-iron stove plate. Agricultural and horticultural motifs combined with German inscriptions and quotations were afforded a warm reception in the 1750s and for several decades thereafter. The Hereford Furnace, Elizabeth Furnace, Mary Anne Furnace and Coalbrookdale Furnace were among the Pennsylvania-based firms creating these cast-iron masterpieces. Stove plate value guide: flowers and leaves, circa 1750, $1,100.

STRAW BASKETS. The thrifty German settlers found a multitude of uses for rye straw. They used it in thatching roofs of sheds and barns and in making baskets. When skillfully fashioned into sturdy strips and bound together with narrow strips of hickory, they created a coiled form of basketry known as shtrowkarab. Although most baskets remained undecorated, some were painted in solid shades of red, green or blue. Busy hands made rye straw fruit baskets, storage hampers, market baskets, egg baskets, church offering plates and sowers' baskets, to mention a few. The shallow coiled bread baskets in which rye bread was set to rise appeared in many sizes. They were sold by itinerant basket makers well into the late 1800s. The crafting of straw baskets, primarily rye straw, was principally confined to Pennsylvania, New Jersey and New York. Straw basket value guide: grain sower's basket, handles, $90; rye straw apple-drying basket, handle, $80; church offering plate, $65.

STRAW RUGS. At forty cents per yard, even price-conscious country dwellers could afford a piece or more of straw matting imported from some distant port in the late 1700s and 1800s. Straw rugs were extensively imported to the colonies in the pre-Revolutionary War period. Obviously they captivated consumers from all walks of life, as George Washington ordered them repeatedly for Mount Vernon. When the straw mat hit the farmhouse floor, it automatically signaled the arrival of summer. Commercially-made straw carpeting was a novelty, as most other country floor coverings were entirely homemade. Despite the modest cost of straw rugs, some people in outlying areas actually attempted to craft their own natural-fiber floor coverings. Straw matting suddenly showed an upsurge in popularity following the Philadelphia Centennial Exposition of 1876, when the Japanese influence spread through town and country. Straw rug value guide: oval, 48″ long, 36″ wide, slightly worn, circa 1830, $85.

STRIPED RUGS. W. P. Sprague celebrated the opening of America's first carpet factory in Philadelphia, Pennsylvania, in 1791 by designing a carpet at his new establishment for the United States Senate Chamber. His effort prompted Alexander Hamilton to recommend imposing a tariff on imported carpets as a stimulus to domestic production. As might be expected, the birth of the carpet industry went unheralded in country communities, where women spent long hours sitting before hand looms crafting simple striped rugs, which are synonymous with country living in the 1800s. They were made of wool combined with cotton or flax tow colored with domestic dyes, which produced soft muted colors. The yarn was either homespun or woven by a village weaver or itinerant weaver. A factory-made striped rug can be recognized by a tighter texture and by bolder colors achieved from chemical dyes. Shaker rug-makers were encouraged to limit the striping to two colors, such as red and green or butternut and gray. Striped rug value guide: red, yellow and blue stripes, 40" long, 24" wide, good condition, circa 1850, $190.

SUGAR BOXES. Box buffs become box buyers whenever a round- or oval-lidded receptacle for storing sugar or meal is uncovered. Small quantities of sugar or meal were transferred to pantry boxes from barrels or tubs. The nested oval Shaker boxes for storing these items display a precise uniformity. Their boxes with finger seams and lapped covers were usually secured with copper or wrought-iron rivets. Those made by other boxmakers show handwork which varies depending on the deftness of the artisan. The round and oval boxes for sugar and meal are somewhat smaller than those made to hold herbs. Wooden pegs and hand-forged nails are indications that the box was handmade rather than factory-produced. Sugar box value guide: early handmade, round, 12" diameter, cover, $90; Shaker, oval, small size, $55.

SUGAR BUCKETS. The staved and hooped sugar bucket with its bail handle and cover was a receptable born out of necessity like other members of the bucket family. Originally they were crafted by homesteaders, later by coopers and ultimately by woodworking factories. Two hoops are an indication of an early handmade bucket; later three hoops were favored. These receptacles, which often measured up to two feet in height, had close-fitting, overlap-ping tops. Hooping was originally accomplished by strips of wood, while factory-made models show iron bindings. Since pine failed to transmit any odor to foodstuffs, it was the favored wood. The bail handle was usually of ash or hickory. These buckets were usually converted into market baskets on market days by resourceful homemakers. Sugar bucket value guide: pine, red and gray paint, 14" high, $55.

SUGAR CHESTS. Southern carpenters, plantation handymen or cabinetmakers active below the Mason-Dixon line made sugar chests from the mid-1700s on. They utilized cherry, walnut or other native hardwoods. A rectangular, slightly overhanging lid concealed the inner storage area, which measured between twelve and fifteen inches deep. This area was divided into compartments or bins for storing sugar, spices, teas and other commodities. The largest compartment was usually reserved for the sugar supply. Their makers fitted them with keyholes to reduce the possibility of petty theft. A full-width drawer along the base of the piece below the well area was also fitted with a keyhole. The drawers had two glass, brass or mushroom-turned wooden knobs. Sugar chest value guide: cherry, dovetailed drawer, wooden knobs, 38" high, 18" wide, circa 1830, $725.

SWIFTS. Flea market shoppers come to a fast halt at the sight of the old-fashioned yarn winder known as a swift, also referred to as a sing devil or turn. Most swifts were made of wood. However, some intricately carved scrimshaw examples were crafted by sailors out of desperation, to break the monotony of long seafaring journeys. Sometimes in an outburst of patriotism, their proud makers stained them red, white and blue. A Shaker-made table-model swift, held together by wooden screws, collapsed or expanded in the same manner as an umbrella. Swift value guide: Shaker table type, $130.

SWIGLERS. Practically everyone is familiar with the term "a swig of rum," but who ever heard of a swigler? Well, the small cylindrical wooden keg known as a swigler was just large enough to hold a swig or two of whiskey. Although some swiglers measured up to eight inches, most models were somewhat smaller. Many were constructed of staves, making them similar in design to larger members of the keg family tree. Another type of swigler was fashioned from a hollowed-out piece of wood. This type had two heads set at either end, which expanded when wet to form a watertight opening. Swiglers were also made of pottery and stoneware, but since all examples rate as rarities, be prepared to engage in some spirited bartering before buying. Swigler value guide: wood, 7" tall, early, $85.

T

TANKARDS. The staved and hooped wooden tankard with its cover was known to have been the proper vessel for a very potent drink. Eventually drum-shaped tankards were introduced for those who felt inclined to participate in some frivolity. Any early wooden tankard is certain to whet the appetite of a woodenware seeker. Pewterers concentrated on straight-sided flat-lidded tankards in the early 18th century. Eventually the tulip shape with its double-C scroll handle and concave molded base provided a bit of competition. In the later part of the 1700s some straight-sided tankards sported double-domed lids. A tankard is likely to bear the touchmark of one of America's master pewterers. However, finely crafted unmarked pieces also merit consideration. Tankard value guide: wooden, staved and hooped, with cover, $125; pewter, American, unmarked, 14″ tall, circa 1820, $250.

TAVERN TABLES. The term tavern table is a modern phrase encompassing a group of small portable tables found in inns, taverns and homes from the late 1600s onward. In each succeeding period there was an attempt to construct them in a manner to blend with contemporary furniture styles. Therefore, the variety is endless. They may be found with rectangular, round, square or oval tops. Support was generally furnished by four turned legs, although some three-legged tables were crafted. Tavern tables were constructed with or without a drawer. Two or three board tops and turned legs braced by an H-shaped or box stretcher appeared on early Jacobean or William and Mary examples. The stretcher disappeared during the Queen Anne period, when slightly tapering legs terminated in a pad foot. Cleated tops and breadboard ends were utilized by 19th-century tablemakers. Drawers were absent on later models, but stretchers reappeared. Black or red paint covered them, in an effort to conceal the assorted hard and soft woods used in their construc-

Tea caddy, toleware, 19th century
National Gallery of Art, Washington

tion. Tavern table value guide: pine, oval top, triangular frame, stained, circa 1750, $850; pine top, maple frame, one drawer, turned legs, round top, New England, circa 1790, $800; pine, rectangular breadboard top, maple understructure, turned legs, stretchers, circa 1780, $750.

TEA CADDIES. The plain old country tea canister made by many American tinsmiths was once known by the fancy term "tea caddy." These covered containers were made to hold a pound or more of a specific brand of tea. When tea was originally imported from the Orient, porcelain caddies were the first to appear. As tea became less expensive in the mid-1700s, tea canisters were made of wood, horn, silver, copper, pewter and other materials. Nine times out of ten the country tea drinker ordered her tea canister from the local tinsmith, or whitesmith. The most exciting examples possessed painted or stenciled motifs derived from nature's wonderland. A serious collector will pay substantially more for a tea caddy having a minimum amount of original decoration than for a recently re-painted specimen. Tea caddy value guide: tin, Queen Anne style, original painted decor, 5″ tall, $220; tin, stenciled florals, 8″ tall, circa 1860, $140.

TEAKETTLES. Collectors come to a slow boil anytime they miss an opportunity to buy an early teakettle of copper, iron, brass or tin. The copper kettle, enduringly favored in Europe, achieved a decidedly American appearance in the hands of skilled Pennsylvania and New York coppersmiths, who developed the fling gooseneck style with a swinging handle. They can often be recognized by examining the bottom, which was often cut from a separate piece and joined to the sides of the kettle by tooth edges. Copper teakettles with dovetailed seams were made in sizes ranging from a pint up to two gallons. A maker's name or address, generally found stamped on the top side of the handle, generates additional collector interest. For those who simply could not afford any other type of kettle, there were inexpensive iron ones made in numerous sizes. Thanks to a band of roving peddlers, the spun brass teakettle introduced in the early 1850s reached outlying areas in record-breaking time. Aluminum and agateware teakettles were among the newfangled utensils enticing country customers in the closing decades of the 19th century. Teakettle value guide: copper, dovetailed, gooseneck spout, unmarked, $160; brass, gooseneck spout, footed, $70; iron, sliding cover, $40.

TELEPHONES. Alexander Graham Bell deserves recognition for transforming the country store into a communications center. Very often the wall telephone found in the store was the town's only one. The old-fashioned crank telephone having an oak or walnut case and metal parts is now the talk of the flea market set. Black enamel or nickel originally covered the brass parts. They varied little in appearance, although some had cathedral tops rather than straight ones. If one is found with its brass or bronze plate or shield intact, examine it for the maker's name or trademark. The Western Electric Manufacturing Company, Stromberg-Carlson Manufacturing Company and Kellogg Manufacturing Company were among the early industry giants. Telephone value guide: oak case, "Kellogg," circa 1900, $120; oak case, Northern Electric Co., $90.

TEN-PLATE STOVES. Thomas Maybury cast the first American cooking stove at the famous Hereford Furnace of Bucks County, Pennsylvania, in 1761. Goodbye, fireplace cooking! These ten-plate stoves were developed from the six-plate stoves. This permitted the insertion of a cook oven. The extra plates were utilized at the top and bottom of the oven and at the two side doors. Although the early cook stoves came equipped with a stovepipe, they lacked removable stove lids. They may appear primitive by modern standards but proved ideal in preparing ole'-time fixin's of the late 1700s. While the six-plate stove was a self-contained heating unit, the addi-

Eli Terry clock, hand-stenciled, circa 1825
National Gallery of Art, Washington

tional four plates converted the ten-plate stove into a heating, cooking and baking combination. Extremely rare.

TERRY, ELI. Because of the inventiveness of clockmaker Eli Terry, many country folk were able to afford a shelf clock for the first time in the early 1800s. After serving his apprenticeship, Terry founded his establishment in 1893 in Plymouth, Connecticut. Initially he made brass movements for tall case clocks, but he soon became preoccupied with perfecting wooden works and with mass-marketing procedures. After experimenting with various cases, he introduced the famous "Terry Type" clock, commonly known as a Pillar and Scroll clock, about 1817. This graceful style had delicate feet, slender pillars and a double scroll or broken arch top. Over several decades it was mass-produced and widely imitated, with many versions selling at the affordable price of fifteen dollars each. Terry value guide: pillar and scroll, Terry, three brass finials, white painted dial, $2,300.

TESTER BEDS. A tester bed was made with four tall posts complete with a frame on top to hold a valance. Thus a tester is really the frame connecting the tops of the posts on a four-poster bed. The earliest Colonial beds were extremely simple, with the drapery sometimes suspended from the ceiling. More imposing tester beds fashioned primarily by skilled urban cabinetmakers made their appearance during the Queen Anne, Chippendale, Hepplewhite, Sheraton and American Empire periods. In each style the legs, posts and feet furnished the distinguishing characteristics. Formal furniture makers showed a distinct preference for mahogany. However, in rural localities maple or other plentiful woods were utilized either singly or together. The tester bed was made by provincial craftsmen in limited quantities, and without exception these examples are of plain design. These canopied confections lost favor in the 1840s, when low-post styles prevailed. Tester bed value guide: tiger maple, double size, Sheraton style, circa 1810, $825.

TILT-TOP CANDLESTANDS. The formal tilt-top table of the Chippendale period gave birth to the smaller tilt-top candlestand. Urban cabinetmakers crafted them of mahogany, while country craftsmen resorted to an assortment of native woods. The oval, square, round or oblong tops were usually flat on country renditions, although pie-crust or dish tops appeared occasionally. They attempted to emulate the turned or carved shafts and tripod claw-and-ball or other animal foot, but their efforts were usually simplified adaptations. Many examples ranged between 22" and 26" in height. While formal pieces often displayed fancy inlaid work, the country versions were pleasingly plain. By the early 1800s these stands were showing signs of the Hepplewhite influence in rural regions. Tilt-top candlestand value guide: mahogany and maple, New England, circa 1800, $425; cherry, vase-shaped standard, 26" tall, circa 1820, $380.

TILT-TOP GATE-LEG TABLES. Based on the popularity afforded the gate-leg table upon its introduction to America in the late 17th century, the development of the tilt-top gate-leg table was inevitable. This table of New England origin is also known as a foldaway or tuckaway table. When the circular top is tilted, the fixed and swinging legs nest together. In this position it proved to be a real space saver, as it could be neatly tucked against a wall. The vase-and-ring or baluster-turned legs with matching stretchers show Dutch influence. These simple yet practical tables were made of cherry or maple, stained to resemble mahogany. Tilt-top gate-leg table value guide: cherry, turned legs, stretchers, circa 1800, $1,750.

TILT-TOP TABLES. Thomas Chippendale deserves recognition for making the tilt-top table fashionable in America in the mid-1700s. A tripod table often had a top that tilted. Frequently a double-block construction, known as a bird cage, permitted the table to rotate as well as tilt. The majority of tilt-top tables were made in America by formal furniture makers, generally of mahogany. They were made in various sizes and shapes, with most formal examples displaying fine carving or inlay work. The round tops may be divided into five categories: plate tops, pie crust tops, gallery tops, tray tops and plain tops. The plain circular top was favored by rural craftsmen when they ventured into the tilt-top table arena. Country versions were usually made of maple, cherry or walnut, and can be recognized by their simplicity. Tilt-top table value guide: cherry, oval, cutout corners, pad feet, $400.

TIN CONTAINERS. President James Monroe supposedly granted a patent for preserving food in tin containers in the early 1800s. As the century advanced, numerous American firms explored this ever-growing field with continuing success. Soon country store shelves were supporting colorful containers in fanciful shapes. Attractive paper labels proved both eye-catching and customer-catching. The labels alone are fascinating collectibles, particularly those mentioning the Shakers. Elaborately designed paper labels bring astonishingly high prices. Any lithographed can is desirable, especially those having illustrated advertisements. The more unusual the shape, the higher the value. Roly Poly cans and Huntley Palmer Biscuit tins are assured of attracting the attention of a tin container buff. Purchasing a fine can or container of 19th-century origin can easily put a dent in the bank balance. Tin container value guide: Tobacco, Roly Poly, Mayo's Brownie, $230; gunpowder, Hercules, No. 25, $18; coffee, DeSoto, original label, $15; tea, Arbuckle, $14.

TINDERBOXES. Before friction matches were introduced in the late 1820s, lighting a candle or lamp proved somewhat troublesome. A sensible solution was to use a tinderbox, which held tinder, an easily ignited substance, and the flint and steel to produce the spark. Since they were primarily homemade items, the variety is endless. There were pocket and hanging versions, and others called pistol boxes into which a spark fell when a trigger was pulled. They were made with and without a candle socket in the cover. Designed as utilitarian items, most examples were devoid of ornamentation. However, there was an elaborate silver type available with a double steel edge striking nameplate for the man who had everything. Tinderbox value guide: one compartment, candleholder top, $175.

TINWARE. Tinware played an important role in provincial areas, where it was used as a substitute for silver. The tinsmith, or white-smith, supplied plain and decorated tinware to his clientele. Many Yankee peddlers roamed the countryside selling tinware in regions lacking shopping facilities. Plain tinware articles were always in demand, one tinsmith listing seventy-five different items in a 1793 advertisement. Many pieces were crafted for use in the kitchen, by the hearth or for lighting. Heavy tinplate was found suitable for cooking objects, while light tinplate served for ornamental pieces. In the early 1800s decorated tinware came into vogue, with pieces being handpainted, stenciled or japanned. The antique examples always show a mellowing of color, and every effort should be made to preserve the original decoration and finish. Punched and pierced designs proliferated throughout the 19th century, particularly in the Pennsylvania area. Tinware value guide: dipper, 14" long, $15; dinner horn, $30; milk can, handled, $16; washstand set, two pieces, japanned, circa 1870, $100.

TOASTERS. The village blacksmith exhibited his expertise by crafting a variety of down-hearth style toasters for the colonists. These early wrought-iron toasters rarely pop up along the antique byways nowadays. Some were simple grids or clamps attached to long handles for toasting bread by the fireplace. The long arms were a safeguard against toasting the hand along with the bread. Many workers in iron embellished the toasters with attractive motifs. Sometimes the slices of bread were held between two small fences with a swiveling head, allowing the bread to be easily toasted on both sides. There were hand-held styles plus footed and standing models. No toaster collection would be complete without one or more factory-made specimens dating from the 19th century. These later improved types frequently bear a factory mark or trademark, making identification possible. Toaster value guide: iron, hand-crafted, swiveling head, footed, loop design, $155; "knoblock Pyramid Toaster," circa 1900, $20.

TODDY STICKS. The small turned toddy stick was used to crush the sugar and lemon for a drink of flip or toddy. These sticks, measuring approximately seven to nine inches in length, also did double duty as stirrers. A toddy, a warm drink frequently enjoyed during leisure hours spent in front of the fireplace, was made of sugar, lemon and hot water spiked with a bit of rum, brandy, whiskey or gin. A flip was another drink enjoyed by colonial imbibers. The sticks cause a stir among woodenware collectors and can be found with flat, corrugated and ball-shaped heads, among others. If the neck of the head shows excessive wear, it indicates that the toddy stick also served as a wheel driver in turning a spinning wheel. Toddy stick value guide: cherry, turned, 10" long, $18; maple, turned, 13" long, $24.

TONGUE RUGS. Expensive imported carpets could be found on the floors of stately city homes prior to 1800, but rarely did one find its way to a rural community. In outlying areas only scrap rugs ingeniously fashioned from tattered textiles covered bare wooden floors. Discarded materials were accumulated by thrifty homemakers-turned-rugmakers and cut up for a carpet. One of the earliest homemade American floor coverings was the appropriately named tongue rug, which consisted of overlapping pieces of tongue-shaped cloth. The overlapping tongues of discarded remnants completely covered the background fabric. Those who rummage after rag rugs speak in hallowed terms of these floor coverings, which were still found on farmhouse floors well into the 1800s. Tongue rug value guide: small size, soft muted colors, circa 1830, $195.

TOOLS. Never fail to examine the area under the flea market table if antique tools are on your shopping list. This area has yielded its share of bargains in anvils, axes, bodkins, chisels, files, gimlets or hammers. Earlier handcrafted tools are treasured, but even later factory types warrant consideration. Forms varied only slightly over the years; thus dating can be difficult. Hand tools once found in a household or farmer's chest bring handsome returns. Since each trade had its own tools, the variety is limitless. The carpenter's adze appeared in many patterns, with either long or short handles. Woodworking planes are sometimes located bearing a date or initials. A maker's name or trademark suggests a date of production into the 19th century. Tools value guide: blacksmith's tongs, wrought iron, 16" long, $20; carpenter's calipers, wrought iron, 18" long, $35; cooper's croze, red paint, V-blade, $60; molding plane, double blade, $15.

TOWEL BAR WASHSTANDS. Although the towel bar washstand is often thought of as a 19th-century bedroom piece, it was often crafted by cabinetmakers of the 18th century. This type of open washstand generally had either a rectangular or square top and a plain or slightly arched gallery piece at the rear. If the towel bar ends were spool-turned; the legs followed a similar design. As a rule it had a small drawer and a lower shelf. Sometimes a hole was cut in the center to hold a washbowl, since the pitcher rested on a lower shelf. Cabinetmakers active in the early 19th century made them from locally found hardwoods, while later in the century factory versions were mass-produced. A chest of drawers with towel bar ends was another form favored during the Victorian era. Towel bar washstand value guide: maple, rectangular top, one drawer, lower shelf, 34" high, $95; walnut, spool-turned legs and towel bars, one drawer, circa 1870, $165.

TOWEL RACKS. The 19th-century towel rack continues to hold a spell over collectors. These sought-after pieces were often included in a complete set of bedroom cottage furniture. Mahogany and rosewood were used on the earlier examples. Later, other woods including black walnut, cherry, maple and birch were utilized. They were often painted to blend with existing bedroom furniture. The number of horizontal rods varied according to the maker. A favorite style of the late 1800s had the framework supported by open trestle ends. Another towel hanger of the period was the spool-turned version comprised entirely of slender turned parts. Towel rack value guide: cherry, trestle type, 30" high, circa 1870, $55; walnut, spool-turned, painted brown, circa 1880, $48.

TOYS. Charming folk toys were designed by carvers and carpenters-turned-toymakers in country regions during the 18th and 19th centuries. Wilhelm Schimmel, Aaron Mountz and George Huguenin were among the talented woodcarvers contributing miniatures for minor's merriment. Animals, birds, figures, Noah's arks, marionettes, puppets, dolls, and dollhouse articles all vied for valuable playroom space. Hobbyhorses were designed and constructed for children of all ages, with varying types of rocker action. Animated toys were in short supply until the whirligig and other toys conceived with mechanical contrivances appeared. Bellows toys based on earlier German prototypes reached a high degree of excellence in the hands of Pennsylvania toymakers. Mass-production methods developed in the late 19th century brought about the introduction of mechanical toys. The earlier handcrafted playthings

Left: Folk toy, Noah's ark and animals, 19th century; Right: Wooden rocking horse

immediately fell to the bottom of the toy trunk, awaiting redis-covery by folk toy fanciers. Toys value guide: hobbyhorse, painted, on platform with rollers, circa 1840, $240; lamb pull toy, circa 1850, $120; Noah's ark, handcarved, sixty pieces, ark, $350; squeak toy, cat on platform, $90.

TRAMMELS. The trammel provided the fireplace with a touch of interesting artistry furnished by the village blacksmith. It was an adjustable rack or rachet designed to hold pots or kettles over the fireplace from a crane or lug pole. The lug pole was a heavy wooden bar used in early fireplaces at a desired distance from the intense heat. Some very long trammels were used for holding cooking uten-sils from the lug pole. The trammel functioned as a primitive pot-holder. When a more convenient swinging iron crane replaced the lug pole, trammels continued operating in their normal function. Any dated specimen is definitely a trammel to be treasured. Hearts, scrolls and other designs distinguish a superior trammel from a common one. Many lighting devices were fitted with wrought-iron trammels so they could be easily adjusted for height. Trammel value guide: two ring hooks, hand-forged, 60" long, circa 1780, $65; iron, four adjustments for fireplace kettle, $60.

TRAMP ART. Toward the latter part of the 19th century, in-genious hoboes wandered about the hinterlands edge or notch carv-ing a remarkable number of objects in so-called Tramp Art. Here is onc of the few categories of American folk art where prices are not prohibitive. Empty cigar boxes were used by these roaming carvers, who traded or peddled the completed object for room, board or a handout. Bureau boxes, comb and brush sets, picture frames, mirrors and similar smaller items are more likely to be found than larger furniture forms. Rarely was the printing on the cigar box removed; in fact, the lithographed labels lent a touch of color to the finished object. Tramp art pieces proved extremely perishable, and many were discarded by owners who found them distasteful. Time has been kind to them, as collectors acknowledge tramp art as folk art. Tramp art value guide: bureau box, red velvet lining, $35; picture frame, notched edges, 14" x 20", $55; sewing case, $28.

TRAPS. Nowadays, if you offer a fine antique trap for sale the world may not beat a path to your door, but a trap collector surely will. They were an absolute necessity in rural areas, both for protection and for catching game. Many early wooden traps were handcrafted by the homesteader. Others of either iron or steel could be purchased from the village blacksmith. Daniel Boone was known to have made and repaired traps in Missouri. Any early handcrafted example possessing a maker's name is assured of immediate sale. Traps were widely used and made by fur trappers. Originally they furnished their own traps, but when fur companies were established, they supplied them to their trappers. Many fur companies had their own trapmakers. In the second half of the 19th century, trap manufacturers were springing up in various localities, including Sewell Newhouse of New York State and Blake, Lamb and Company of Connecticut. Trap value guide: fly trap, glass, beehive shape, $80; bear trap, wrought iron, $75; rat, "Star," $10.

TREENWARE. Treenware or woodenware was extensively used in rural households well into the 19th century. Treen, the ancient plural of tree, was handcrafted with primitive tools. Plates, platters, trenchers, bowls, mugs, dippers, ladles and other kitchen utensils were hand-turned, gouged or whittled by settlers, following an Old World tradition known for centuries on the Continent. Common household articles were designed from maple, pine, birch, oak, ash, beech, hickory or basswood. American treenware can be recognized by its simplicity; European pieces tended to be more elaborate. Dating a piece is a problem as similar forms remained fashionable in-

Maple dipper, 18th century
National Gallery of Art, Washington

definitely. American treenware is treasured. Treenware value guide: bowl, molded edge, 20″ diameter, circa 1830, $375; chalice, cherry, 8″ high, $135; spoon, 14″ long, $30.

TRENCHERS. The wooden plate or platter called a trencher experienced widespread use in America from the landing of the Pilgrims well into the 1800s in rural areas. While more affluent city dwellers preferred china or pewter, country folk fashioned wooden utensils by means of simple carpentry or turning. When new trenchers were needed they were often made by a family member. Round and square trenchers measuring between five and fourteen inches in diameter were made with flat or depressed areas for serving food. Many households could not afford the luxury of a trencher for every diner; thus two people often ate from the same one; they were nicknamed trenchmates. The small indentation in the corner of a trencher was used to hold salt. On English examples the owner's name was sometimes stamped on the rim, but this practice was rarely employed on American-made specimens. Farm tables were set with trenchers made of ash, beech, birch, maple or other available woods. The English custom of using the reverse side of the trencher for a second course gave rise to the term "dinner side and pie side." Trencher value guide: pine, deep rim, 10″ diameter, $120.

TRESTLE-FOOT GATE-LEG TABLES. This interesting and ingenious variation of the standard gate-leg table was introduced by American furniture makers in the late 1600s. It can be recognized by the trestle feet supporting the end legs. Some unusual examples supported the top leaves with a single gate rather than the usual two gates. Turned legs and matching stretchers are indications of superior workmanship. When the center fixed leaf was narrow, the table folded very flat against the wall. The trestle feet, usually ranging about 10" wide, prevented these tables from tipping over. Trestle-foot gate-leg table value guide: cherry, turned legs, stretchers, circa 1710, $1,400.

TRESTLE TABLES. When trestle tables first appeared on Pilgrim inventories in the mid-1600s they were called a "table board with frame." The one-board plank tops on the early examples measured up to six feet in length. However, since diners sat on only one side of the table, many measured about two feet in width. Support was furnished by two or three T-shaped trestles, each of which rested on a shoe foot. A single wide flat stretcher connected the trestles. Eventually the trestle table became somewhat plainer and lighter in weight. Two board tops prevailed, with most examples ranging between four and five feet in length. Shaker versions had warp-resisting breadboard ends and two or three pedestal trestles resting on an arch foot or shoe foot. Trestle table value guide: pine and maple, one board top, T-shaped trestles, 18th century, $1,550; Shaker, white oak and ash, stained red, circa 1850, $875.

TRIPOD CANDLESTANDS. The familiar tripod candlestand with its turned shaft surmounted by a top came into widespread acceptance in the 1700s. Formal furniture makers introduced the concept, which was quickly copied by country carpenters. The tops were made in various sizes and shapes, with most rural makers favoring flat tops. Local woods were utilized in rural areas, including cherry, birch and maple. The tripod foot can provide a clue to age, for makers attempted to craft them in the prevailing furniture style. Therefore, Queen Anne, Chippendale, Sheraton, Hepplewhite or Empire influences may be noted in their construction. All the Shaker communities made them with either peg feet, spider feet or snake feet. Tripod candlestand value guide: maple top, cherry legs, porringer top, $450; Shaker, cherry top, maple legs, round top, circa 1860, $400.

TRIVETS. Originally trivets were made by the village blacksmith. Some of the earliest types had a flat brass top and a design often incorporating the owner's initials. Three-legged trivets for holding utensils by the hearth had typical heart and barn symbols

Left: Circular cast-iron trivet, 19th century; Right: Wrought-iron trivet, 18th century

when they originated in Pennsylvania. Eventually the trivet business was transferred from the blacksmith to the cast-iron foundry. These foundries never floundered in creating new and exciting patterns throughout the 19th century. They controlled the market somewhat after 1850. The simple eagle, star and patriotic motifs were replaced by more intricately fashioned designs after 1850. Victorian tastes demanded ever-fancier trivets, and firms obliged with elaborate naturalistic fruits and flowers, fraternal and portrait designs. Some foundries found it profitable to include their name or trademark, thus benefiting from some subtle advertising. Trivet value guide: wrought iron, penny feet, two cross-bars, $165; wrought iron, heart design, footed, $155; cast iron, Jenny Lind, $40; cast iron eagle and wreath, $20.

TRUNDLE BEDS. The trundle bed was a real space saver as it was low enough to be rolled under another bed when not in use. At night it was brought from its daytime hiding place. The term "trundle" or "truckle" refers to a child's or servant's bed. Strong cords or ropes were laced around the pegs or knobs along the rails to support a mattress. Despite the fact that these beds were little more than frames for mattresses, their short posts displayed simple turnings of a type found on many early low-post beds. Trundle bed value guide: maple, turned posts, circa 1820, $195.

TRUNKS. Following the Revolutionary War, cabinetmakers, brushmakers and other craftsmen began advertising trunk work. Saddlers seem to have gained a monopoly on them sometime in the early 19th century. Small pine trunks covered with horsehair, paper, leather or canvas were often ornamented with brass upholsterer's nails artistically arranged in a chosen pattern. Deerskin, pigskin, sheepskin and oxhide were all used to cover early trunks. They were either flat or had rounded tops, and remained in vogue until the mid-1800s. Jenny Lind arrived in America about 1850 with a leather trunk which curved in the center; before she had time to place it in her dressing room, it was being copied and became known as the Jenny Lind trunk. The Saratoga and General Grant trunks were among the fashionable traveling companions of the 1880s. Often the newspaper lining can offer a guide to dating. Trunk value guide: sheepskin trunk, circa 1840, $190; Jenny Lind trunk, newspaper lined, circa 1860, $150.

TUBS Although local coopers crafted tons of wooden tubs, these containers for holding liquids proved highly perishable. Thus surviving specimens rate as rarities. Round and oval tubs were staved and hooped similar to buckets. Two extra-long staves with handle holes sufficed as handles. The staves were generally strengthened with either iron or wooden hoops. On the earliest models the wooden hooped ends were tucked under. Tubs were made in many sizes, and undoubtedly some functioned for purposes other than originally intended. Large maple-sugar tubs with tight-fitting overlapping lids often measured up to three feet in height. Butter tubs also had overlapping tops but were somewhat smaller than maple-sugar tubs. Cream was stored in a receptacle known as a sour-cream tub. The present scarcity of handmade tubs has caused collector interest to shift to factory-made examples. Tub value guide: sugar tub, circa 1840, $55; sour-cream tub, circa 1860, $50; tar tub, circa 1870, $40.

TUCKAWAY-TRESTLE TABLES. New England furniture makers are credited with this space-saving design crafted by them primarily in the late 1600s and early 1700s. A narrow central fixed leaf and two drop leaves formed the top, which was either round, oblong or oval. The fixed leaf was attached directly to the trestle uprights, which were braced by a stretcher. When it was time to tuck away this trestle table, the leaves were lowered and the table occupied precious little floor space. Tuckaway-trestle tables of maple or walnut are best known, although occasionally a top of pine was used along with an understructure of hardwood. Tuckaway-trestle table value guide: pine, maple understructure, round top, New England, circa 1700, $1,200.

U

UNDER-THE-EAVES BEDS. Simple low-post under-the-eaves beds introduced in the late 1600s were still gracing country bedrooms a century later. This style typically had short head posts, rail-high foot posts and a plain headboard. Rails were always bored with rope holes or had small rope knobs to accommodate the rope lacings upon which a feather or straw tick rested. Standing a mere thirty-six inches high, it measured slightly over six feet in length and approximately four feet in width. They were constructed from assorted hard and soft woods, such as a headboard of pine combined with posts of maple or birch. The form remained virtually unchanged, although the posts became heavier and often terminated in cone-shaped turnings on later examples. Many later beds were painted red, green or blue. Under-the-eaves bed value guide: basswood headboard, birch posts, original red paint, circa 1830, $230.

UNICORN CHESTS. The unicorn was employed as a decorative device by Pennsylvania cabinetmakers, particularly on pieces decorated for a dowry. It had been known as a symbol of piety and virtue, as well as a guardian of maidenhood, since medieval times. The arrangement of the panels and amount of ornamentation varied according to the individual designer. The backgrounds were either painted or handsomely stippled. Sometimes the center panel of unicorns was flanked by panels of mounted horsemen framed by urns and tulips. Painted panels and sides were artistically executed by incorporating the unicorn motif with variously colored flowers, leaves, hearts, birds, angels and other traditional Pennsylvania motifs. A dowry-decorated chest is almost certain to have the name of the owner and a date, unless some foolhardy person has attempted to repaint the piece (which seriously affects its selling price). Unicorn chest value guide: three panels, center unicorn, urns, tulips, circa 1820, $5,600.

URN STANDS. Formal furniture makers made urn stands in many styles, but they remain a rarity in country furniture styles. From the late 1700s onward, skilled craftsmen working in outlying areas crafted them in very limited quantities. This is unfortunate as urn stands can be adapted to present-day interiors as decorative accents; these bygones make excellent plant stands. The plain circular tops, generally measuring about 17″ in diameter, were supported by a sturdy post. Widely spread legs gave the necessary leg span to furnish solid support. Their graceful appearance belied their strength, as these stands held heavy and cumbersome objects without tipping over. Circular-top pedestal stands generally made of black walnut, maple or ash were factory-made favorites of the 1870s and 1880s. Urn stand value guide: maple, pedestal type, circa 1880, $110.

V

VICTORIAN CHESTS OF DRAWERS. The chest of drawers was a standard piece in a set of Victorian bedroom furniture, whether made with or without a mirror. It was subjected to the various Revival styles of the era. The earlier chests frequently exhibit signs of handcraftmanship, as they were made by cabinetmakers. Hand-cut dovetails and roughly smoothed drawer bottoms and backboards are indications of a finely crafted chest. A typical chest of drawers made between the 1840s and 1890s had three or four drawers, all full width with the exception of the top one, which sometimes had two half-width drawers. Factory-made types had a back composed of five to seven vertically placed overlapping pieces. There were spool-turned and painted or grained cottage-furniture versions made by numerous factories. Some were fitted with marble tops, and all examples came equipped with casters. Victorian chest of drawers value guide: pine, four drawers, paneled sides, bracket feet, original brasses, circa 1850, $230; walnut, three drawers, low block foot, leafage and scroll handles, circa 1875, $210.

VORSCHIFTS. Fortunate indeed was the Pennsylvania school pupil gifted with an elaborately handwritten manuscript called a vorschift by his schoolmaster. The purpose of it was ostensibly to teach children German script alphabets and numerals. However, it also served to demonstrate the schoolmaster's writing skills. This forerunner of the 19th-century copy book was often presented as a reward of merit. A prominent feature of the vorschift was the pious maxim which occupied considerable space and on which the schoolmaster waxed poetically. Needless to say, such manuscripts were dearly treasured by their recipients and passed from one generation to the next. Vorschift value guide: birds and flowers, elaborate capital letters, floral border, dated 1821, $1,375.

W

WAFER IRONS. The wafer iron was a cast-iron cooking necessity in the days of fireplace cooking. This utensil was guaranteed to draw a happy response from minor family members. These cast-iron contrivances consisted of two griddles measuring approximately six inches in diameter attached to a long pincerlike arm. Wafer irons were made in oval, round or rectangular shapes. Those wise in the way of old wafers declare that the heart-shaped irons were usually presented to a bride. The griddles were engraved with various motifs which formed raised designs on the wafers, making them both decorative and eye appealing. Wafer tongs is another acceptable name for these 18th-century hearthside utensils. Wafer irons value guide: wrought iron, hearts, 18″ handle, $100.

WAFFLE IRONS. Waffles had been used in European religious ceremonies centuries before the first settlers reached the shores of America. Therefore it is not surprising that these utensils could be found near the colonial hearth in square, round, rectangular, oblong and heart shapes. The early irons had long pincerlike handles for holding the waffles over the fire. Examine any early example with care, as dated specimens are known to exist. When the coal stove replaced fireplace cooking, new and improved waffle irons were marketed in ever-increasing numbers. Many coal-stove irons were fitted with ball-and-socket joints enabling them to be turned over easily. Some of the grids imprinted waffles with glance-worthy star, heart and geometric patterns. Improved models were manufactured by the Griswold Manufacturing Company of Pennsylvania, Wagner Manufacturing Company of Ohio and the Fanner Manufacturing Company of Ohio in the late 1800s. Waffle iron value guide: geometric pattern, wrought iron, long handle, early, $65; Griswold waffle iron, circa 1885, $24.

WAGON SEATS. From the late 1700s on, the auxiliary wagon seat was found in wagons transporting family members to destinations both near and far. They characteristically had short legs to conform to the depth of the wagon. Thus the wagon seat resembled a pair of short slat-back armchairs. The three turned uprights generally terminated in simple steeple, knob or ball finials. Two or three slightly concave splats formed the double back. Most examples were made with rush or splint seats. Occasionally the seats were made in two sections, but such versions rate as rarities. A Pennsylvania wagon seat displaying a cutout heart motif·on the back, or a child's wagon seat, are other fortunate finds. Wagon seats were customarily crafted from durable native hardwoods. Wagon seat value guide: hickory, rush seat, spindle back, turned arms, circa 1840, $375.

Wagon seat, cut-out heart design, Pennsylvania, late 18th century

National Gallery of Art, Washington

WAG-ON-WALL CLOCKS. Skilled cabinetmakers of the 18th century concentrated on custom-made tall-case clocks, but less capable workers devised simple hang-up, or wag-on-wall, clocks. Far less expensive than tall-case examples, they found favor with the less affluent. Such clocks were made by the Blaidsell family of Massachusetts. The term wag-on-wall was applied to any clock having the pendulum and weights exposed. A mere fifteen dollars purchased the movements, but most cases cost an additional five to twenty-five dollars. Therefore, many people hung the movement on the wall until sufficient funds were acquired to buy the case. As a deterrent to dust, some clocks were fitted with plain hoods. Striking a bargain on a wag-on-wall clock will surely set the tongues wagging at the local clock collectors' club. Wag-on-wall clock value guide: porcelain dial, ornate pendulum, 58″ long, $575; wooden face, scalloped, floral decor, circa 1840, $450.

WAINSCOT CHAIRS. Early wainscot chairs are a tribute to chairmakers of the Pilgrim period. Rarely found outside a museum, they deserve consideration due to their historical significance. American chairmakers borrowed the design from English models about 1650. So impressive is the wainscot chair that many colleges own such a chair, using it primarily for ceremonial occasions. The word "wainscot" originally meant the finest grade of oak wood, the very type from which these chairs were made. They were crafted with plain or carved wooden panel backs, having a straight top rail or carved or arched cresting. Sometimes the carving in low relief extended to the seat rail. These chairs had rectangular wooden seats and legs braced by heavy box stretchers. The front legs were usually turned, often terminating in ball feet. Due to restoration work, the original wooden seat and back are often replaced by one of leather. Wainscot chair value guide: oak, wooden seat, box stretcher, turned ball feet, New England, $2,600.

WALL BOXES. Any box crafted to hang or rest against a wall can be classified as a wall box. They were made from the 17th century on by woodworkers who rarely failed to dovetail their output. Even when nails were available, dovetailing occurred on these pieces. Originally the form consisted of a box without a lid; later a lid was added, and eventually one or more drawers. As time elapsed some were made solely of drawers. When a maker wished to exploit

Wall-type corner cupboard, Pennsylvania, 18th century

National Gallery of Art, Washington

his way with woods, he enlarged the size of the knob to correspond with the size of the drawer. Look for signs of superior workmanship, such as thumbnail molding or other detailed handwork. Painted or stenciled boxes were executed with alacrity by Pennsylvania artisans. Wall box value guide: candle, painted red, dovetailed, $160; spice, pine, eight drawers, dovetailed, porcelain knobs, circa 1870, $85; salt, pine, dovetailed, original blue paint, $80.

WALL CUPBOARDS. Many present-day collectors are searching for small hanging cupboards designed specifically to be hung on a wall or in a corner. Even the earliest Colonial pine hanging cupboards are likely to show signs of dignified handwork such as front and side panels or moldings. As a guide to dating, most early examples had solid wooden doors, while in later examples glass-paned doors became fashionable. There were numerous varieties of open or closed hanging cupboards combining shelves and drawers, or simply composed of small drawers. Arched or diamond-shaped panels denote admirable cabinetmaking skills. Iron bolts with large heads securing the hinges usually indicate a piece of Pennsylvania origin. Makers in this region also indulged themselves in elaborate carved motifs. Wall cupboard value guide: pine, 34" high, raised panel door, dovetailed drawer, $385; pine, one door, one drawer, 24" high, Pennsylvania, circa 1860, $325.

WASH BENCHES. The wash bench could usually be found stationed against the farmhouse wall directly outside the back door. Because of extended exposure to the elements, the original paint has often been removed. Since it was designed to hold heavy buckets of water, woodworkers generally strengthened the wash bench by bracing the legs. This functional form appeared in a variety of styles, usually devoid of any decorative treatment. Occasionally a narrow apron was included beneath the seat with scrolled ends. A bit of refinishing can convert any antique wash bench into a proper resting place for plants or people. Wash bench value guide: poplar top, maple understructure, original blue paint, $140.

WASH STICKS. Before washing machines were developed, a wooden bat or wash stick was utilized on washday from the 1600s onward. After the wash had been placed in a tub of warm water, the stick acted as an agitator by means of manual power. Those intrigued by the lure of antique woodenware search for intricately carved examples. Naturally, the amount of detail found on a stick varied in accordance with the woodworking skills of its creator. A homesteader endowed with artistic ability often carved a stationary captive ring from the same piece of wood, which increased agitation and decreased aggravation. If a wash stick was unavailable, often a sturdy tree branch served as a suitable substitute. Wash stick value guide: maple, handmade, captive ring, $85.

WASHBOARDS. When the primitive scrubbing stick was supplanted by the wooden washboard, work-weary washers heaved a sigh of relief. By the middle of the 19th century wooden washboards with corrugated or spool-shaped scrubbing areas were being manufactured in America. Although the all-wood models were marketed until the closing decades of the century, the metal-faced types became Monday morning musts. Zinc-faced, glass, brass and Rockingham pottery washboards are possible finds in this category. Diligent scrubbers had their ups and downs on such name washboards as Labor-Saver, Brass King, Universal and Soap Saver. Even the large family-size models were bargain priced at $1 each around the turn of the century. Washboard value guide: Glass Duke, Wayne Manufacturing Co., $18; Rockingham pottery, wooden frame, circa 1850, $135; pine, handmade, early, $70; Glass Duke, Wayne Manufacturing Co., $18; Labor Saver, aluminum, $15.

WASHING MACHINES. Practically every home inventor experimented with a wooden washing machine destined to make scrubbing sticks, wash kettles and washtubs obsolete in the 1700s and early 1800s. Do not be surprised if you stumble upon one of these oblong or square boxes containing mangle arms in a barn at the next country auction. Although the first American patent for a washing machine was not granted until 1805, there are enough homemade versions to fill several museums. Because many primitive models stood on legs and rocked, they were called cradles. By the middle of the 19th century, wooden washing machines were being advertised by many factories. Collectors rotate toward these early washing machines made by such pioneer makers as Moses Flanders of Vermont, Moreland & Co. of Kentucky, A. H. Filner of Wisconsin and the Blackstone Manufacturing Co. of New York. Washing machine value guide: Mission Washer, hardwood, steel braces, $135; Pan American Washer, four legs, hardwood, Blackstone Manufacturing Co., Jamestown, New York, $160.

WASHSTANDS. Before the advent of modern-day plumbing facilities, washstands were bedroom necessities for holding a bowl and pitcher. Open washstands of the handcrafted type enjoyed prolonged popularity in America until the mid-19th century, when their production shifted to furniture factories. Country craftsmen fabricated them in an almost endless variety, with the majority having a square or rectangular top, a single drawer and a lower shelf. Frequently a hole was placed in the center of the top to accommodate a washbowl, while the pitcher rested on the lower shelf. Corner washstands with three legs and triangular tops rate as rarities. The enclosed type usually had a single- or double-door cupboard beneath one or more drawers and was carved or painted to blend with existing pieces. Marble-top versions are prized. Washstand value guide: curly maple, one drawer, cupboard base, circa 1840, $220; walnut, cupboard base, marble-top, circa 1880, $275; pine, painted black, grained, hole in top, lower shelf with drawer beneath, $190.

WASHTUBS. The staved and hooped wooden washtubs made by many American coopers were constructed in a manner similar to buckets. They typically had an inset bottom and two short staved handles complete with handle holes. The Niagara Pail and Tub Factory of New York shipped them into rural communities. Other active tubmakers of the mid-1800s were John Crawford of New York, Ellis Watson of New York and Michael Hillrich of Kentucky. These woodworkers encountered some unexpected competition when coal ranges brought about the introduction of oval copper and tin wash boilers. There were also cast-iron wash boilers lined in porcelain to tempt the tub buyer. Washtub value guide: pine, circa 1870, $35.

WATER BUCKETS. Nowadays antique water buckets hold magazines, potted plants, refuse or just about anything other than water. A century or two ago they were used for storing or carrying water after it had been extracted from the well. A water bucket can be recognized by two protruding staves to which the strap handle was attached. The two extended staves proved invaluable when the bucket was turned upside down for drying, as they enabled it to be raised off the ground. These staved containers were made with sturdy hoops and without covers. There were straight-sided buckets and others that tapered slightly toward the bottom. Locked laps or laps tucked under are indications of an early handmade specimen. Later factory-made examples had nailed laps or iron hoops. Unfortunately, water buckets appear far more frequently on canvases reflecting country life a century or more ago than they do in antique shops. Water bucket value guide: staved, locked laps, early, $75.

WEATHER VANES. Folk art fanciers fan out in all directions searching for these barn or rooftop weather predictors. The earliest and consequently the most desirable ones were handcrafted by a carpenter or farmer. Metal and wooden vane designs were typically

Left: Weather vane, rooster, 19th century; Right: Horse and jockey copper weather vane

Both photographs, National Gallery of Art, Washington

Left: "Liberty" copper weather vane, Right. Horse copper weather vane

based on familiar European themes. Farmers showed a distinct preference for roosters or motifs depicting livestock. Horses with or without vehicles did more than their share of playing host to the wind. Nautical outlines ran rampant in coastal areas. Some craftsmen sought inspiration from mythological, historical or Biblical subject matter. Handcrafted weather vanes reigned supreme from their lofty perches until the mid-1800s. Thereafter, mass-produced three-dimensional designs stamped from zinc or copper supplanted the earlier versions. Weather vane value guide: wood, rooster, circa 1790, $2,200; copper, American eagle, circa 1855, $1,800; iron, American Indian atop a horse, $1,400; tin, standing cow, $750.

WELL BUCKETS. The well bucket once used in drawing water from the well still draws collector interest. Since they were subjected to considerable punishment, their makers constructed them of oak staves bound with riveted iron bands. The iron handles were secured with rings attached to the side staves. Despite an attempt to make them durable, these buckets suffered such heavy usage that deterioration was inevitable. As well buckets were being lowered into wells in country regions, earnings climbed ever higher for such woodenware manufacturers as Spencer Rowe of Baltimore, Maryland; Tamm & Mayer of St. Louis, Missouri; and C. L. Wagoner of Statesville, North Carolina. Well bucket value guide: oak staves, iron bands, circa 1860, $55.

WELSH DRESSERS. This special type of provincial dresser was closely associated with the Welsh settlers of Pennsylvania. It was based on a dresser known in England during the Jacobean period. This piece was actually composed of two cupboards, a lower one that was closed and an upper one that was open. They were always made in two pieces. The stationary shelves on the top section generally had spoon notches, plate grooves and guard rails, especially those of Pennsylvania origin. The upper section was elaborately scalloped. Cabinetmakers originally fabricated them of oak, but later assorted native woods were favored. Pennsylvania dressers are prized, particularly those constructed of walnut or cherry. Welsh dresser value guide: cherry, two shelves upper section, two drawers above, two doors lower section, guard rails, circa 1810, $1,750.

WHALE-OIL LAMPS. The whale-oil or "common" lamp designed to burn whale oil was popular from about 1787 until after the Civil War in America. John Miles of Birmingham patented his "Agitable lamp" in 1787, and it was immediately adapted to the needs of Americans, who appreciated its economical and clean-burning advantages. It was composed of a reservoir with a snugly fitting burner, complete with one or more round wicks. Such lamps were made of numerous materials, including pewter, tin, brass and blown or pressed glass. Those with pressed-glass bases were extensively manufactured by American glasshouses from the late 1820s onward. The pressed designs were similar to those found on tableware articles. Whale-oil lamp value guide: pewter, marked "Dunham," 8″ tall, $265; brass, two burner, 8″ tall, $100; flint glass, Bull's-eye pattern, 8½″ tall, $85; tin, two wicks, $75.

Left: Whale oil lamp, early 19th century

Far left: Whale oil lamp, glass font, early 19th century

Both photographs, National Gallery of Art, Washington

WILLARD CLOCKMAKERS. Benjamin Willard served his apprenticeship in clockmaking to Benjamin Cheney before returning home to Grafton, Massachusetts, in 1765. After establishing a shop in the family homestead, he was promptly joined by brothers Simon, Ephraim and Aaron. They became capable clockmakers, one and all, fanning out in the direction of Lexington and Boston. The so-called Willard or Boston school of clockmakers garnered raves for their innovative timepieces. Ever striving for perfection and new avenues of experiment, their fame increased by the hour as they marketed grandfather, banjo, lighthouse, lyre, girandole and shelf clocks. Simon led the way with his achievements, including the banjo and lighthouse clocks. Ephraim achieved success with his magnificent grandfather clocks. Aaron added further luster to the Willard name with his Massachusetts Shelf Clock. Aaron Jr. and Henry quickly followed in their father's footsteps, and it was Aaron Jr. who was credited with designing the lyre clock. The Willard name is revered in clockmaking circles. Willard clockmakers value guide: banjo clock, Aaron Willard, Federal period, mahogany parcel gilt case, $2,200; shelf clock, Simon Willard, eight-day striking, églomisé panels, $5,700.

WILLIAM AND MARY STYLE. Important changes occurred in American furniture forms during the William and Mary period (1690–1720). The period, named for the English monarchs, featured patterns derived from baroque themes. Furniture produced during this period was characterized by graceful, lighter proportions and the use of finely grained woods, notably walnut. Carved C-scrolls and S-scrolls, serpentine stretchers, pierced cresting, ball-, bun- or turnip-shaped feet and brass teardrop drawer handles became fashionable. Woven cane and japanning grained favor with cabinetmakers and customers alike. Among the new forms introduced during this period were the highboy, lowboy, day bed, slant-table desk, gate-leg table, butterfly table, tavern table and easy chair. Some chairs had upholstered or caned seats and backs, and in general were more comfortable than earlier styles. Country cabinetmakers were influenced by William and Mary styles well into the 18th century. William and Mary style value guide: highboy, walnut, 40" high, 6' 2" tall, circa 1810, $3,200; tavern table, oak, breadboard ends, one drawer, round top, circa 1790, $1,550.

WILLOW BASKETS. Agricultural magazines were encouraging farmers to plant groves of willow trees in the 1800s to meet the ever-increasing demand from willow manufacturers. With a minimum amount of cooperation from Mother Nature, it was possible to establish a grove of willow trees in just five short years. Willow baskets were made in smaller quantities in America than splint baskets, for the material for crafting them was not as readily available, coupled with the fact that they required more skill on the part of the maker. The cross-hatch weave was more widely employed than the octagon weave. While some baskets were made solely of willow, commonly known as wicker, some examples were combined with splint. Many factories made fancy wicker baskets of every description in the late 1800s. They were usually painted in several different colors destined primarily for domestic use. Willow basket value guide: clothes hamper with cover, $65; bonnet basket, rose colored, $40; fruit basket, oval, loop handle, $30.

WINCHESTER RIFLES. Oliver F. Winchester was right on target when he assumed ownership of the old Volcanic Repeating Arms Company, which had become insolvent in 1857. The new firm, known as the New Haven Arms Company, continued making arms bearing the Volcanic name. Winchester named Benjamin Tyler Henry as operating manager, and under his guise the Henry Rifle was introduced in 1860. A name change occurred in 1866, when the firm became known as the Winchester Repeating Arms Company. The initial rifle to bear the famous Winchester name was their model 1866 or 66. Everyone within earshot was impressed with this triumph and with the subsequent 73 and 76 models. Oliver was an avid gun collector, sharing a hobby appreciated by many currently. Winchester rifle value guide: model 1866, 44-caliber, $420.

WINDSOR CHAIRS. Philadelphia chairmakers introduced Windsor chairs to America in the 1720s. These chairs first gained favor in the town of Windsor, situated in the Berkshire district of England; it is for this reason that they are so named. The chairs became instant winners. A century later over one hundred Windsor chairmakers were supplying them to customers in various localities. These so-called stick chairs were typically constructed with solid plank seats, spindle backs, turned splayed legs and well-designed stretchers. Windsor chairs were graceful in appearance but very

Windsor writing armchair, comb-back
style, circa 1810

durable. Crafted from assorted hard and soft woods, they were
painted Indian red, dark green, brown, black, yellow or white to
conceal the various types of wood. Numerous varieties were marketed, but the six basic types are the low-back, fan-back, comb-
back, hoop-back, loop-back and New England armchair. The center
ridge was higher on the finest Windsor chairs. Count the number of
spindles on the back, as the best chairs have the most spindles. Nine-
spindle chairs are prized as are those with boldly splayed legs.
Windsor chair value guide: bow-back armchair, blunt arrow feet,
saddle seat, Pennsylvania, 18th century, $575; comb-back armchair,
nine spindles, New England, original green paint, $540; fan-back
side chair, pine and ash, six spindles, circa 1820, $350.

WINNOWING BASKETS. Seasoned basket collectors capable of
separating the wheat from the chaff are able to identify splint winnowing baskets. They were frequently elliptical in shape, often having hickory frames and handles. While primarily used for
winnowing grain, they also saw action in other fields, as farmers
used them in shucking peas and beans. The splint baskets were more
desirable than those made entirely of wood, which often proved too
fragile for such chores. The fact that every handmade basket is a
true one-of-a-kind challenges the collecting instinct of the dedicated
antiquer. Winnowing basket value guide: splint, oval shape, 16″
diameter, $60.

WIREWARE. Items conceived of wire are known as wireware,
wirework or wire goods. Although they had been used on a limited

basis at an earlier date, those manufactured in the latter part of the 19th century are generally encountered by casual browsers. One can accumulate a stunning array of wireware without seriously endangering the economic condition of the family. Woods, Sherwood & Company of Massachusetts was a principal manufacturer of utilitarian and decorative objects. Company catalogues contain familiar and unusual objects such as oyster broilers, corn poppers, wheel mousetraps, cross toasters, soap holders and fly traps. Wickedly wonderful wirework patterns were created for compotes, epergnes, baskets and other pieces. Furniture forms delightfully designed from wire were also offered to customers in the closing decades of the century. Wirework value guide: dish drainer, $18; vegetable skimmer, wooden handle, $15; coffeepot stand, $12; egg boiler, $10.

WOODCARVINGS. All of the various wooden objects whittled for pleasure or profit currently entice collectors. Most whittlers have remained anonymous, but others such as Wilhelm Schimmel, Aaron Mountz, George Hugenin and Noah Weis are known by their recognizable carvings. Pieces of importance to antiquers include those which have been carved, whittled, turned or scratch-carved. Many utilitarian objects lent themselves to a decorative surface, such as marzipan boards, springerle boards, dippers, ladles and bowls. Toys, sculptured figures, garden ornaments, trade signs, figureheads and eagles by the dozens were produced by untrained, but not untalented, craftsmen. Wandering woodcarvers who traded their wares for food or lodging are responsible for a tremendous output of woodcarvings. Often the original paint may be worn or missing, but

Far left: Rooster woodcarving, 19th century

Left: Woodcarving, "Whipping Post, Delaware Justice"

Both photographs, National Gallery of Art, Washington

Left to right: Carved maple-sugar mold; Handcrafted wooden strainer; Batter mixer, wooden handles; Wooden spoon rack, early 19th century

rarely will this deter a buyer from acquiring either a primitive or a professionally conceived woodcarving. Woodcarvings value guide: eagle, wings spread, 14″ high, circa 1880, $640; hen, original paint, $120.

WOODEN LOG CHAIRS. The hollowed-out log, crudely crafted into a chair, is hardly capable of winning any awards in the comfort department. But it does transmit a warm rustic feeling reminiscent of the Old West. Exactly when and where the first chair of this type originated is unknown. However, its popularity in America coincided with the westward movement of the 19th century. The majority had solid log-shaped bases and high curved solid backs. The seat was derived from a pine board. These rustic reminders of yesteryear are a lasting tribute to their makers' ingenuity. Wooden log chair value guide: maple, bulbous shape, pine seat, circa 1860, $325.

WOODENWARE. By the early 18th century woodenware was being produced on a commercial basis in America by men known as coopers. There were several different classifications of craftsmen. Tight coopers made large-size kegs and casks for holding liquids, while dry coopers limited their wares to barrels or kegs for holding dry commodities. Another group known as white coopers, or dish turners, confined their output to small household items, plates, bowls, spoons and pitchers, commonly called treen. Woodenware collectors search for hand-shaped pieces, particularly those having incised or handpainted designs or initials and a date. Finely turned pieces, which are handsomely proportioned, also find instant buyers. Items crafted of burl are always considered best. Old pieces frequently show tool marks, stains, signs of heavy usage and a patina which distinguishes them from modern wares. Pennsylvania and Shaker woodenware articles are always salable. Woodenware value guide: bowl, burl, 12" diameter, $130; Nutcracker, cat's head, circa 1880, $80; Shaker spoonholder, pine, $60; chopping bowl, original blue paint, 12" diameter, $55.

WOOLWINDERS. This handy wooden device, capable of winding wool or yarn into tangle-free skeins, appeared in various models. Most common was the X-shaped form attached to a spindle, which in turn was set into a simply constructed pedestal stand. Most types were supported by four short legs. Sometimes the X-shape part was composed of two crossed bars. A representative collection of early woolwinders would certainly demonstrate the versatility of their makers, as humble versions were handcrafted by homesteaders in various sections of the country. A wooden object resembling a double-ended anchor, known as a niddy-noddy, was utilized for winding yarn into a skein. Woolwinder value guide: pine with table attachment, six adjustable spokes, $55; niddy-noddy, $35.

WORKBAGS. Sedulous sewers used cloth sewers' sacks or workbags as extra pockets for holding sewing materials. Bags in various sizes having creative crewelwork designs, or embroidered in the flame stitch, were either pinned to an apron or hung from the shoulder to facilitate sewing chores. Those approaching handbag size were often taken on trips so that busy fingers could chalk up extra sewing mileage. Purportedly those having large circular bases or small inner pockets cut fumbling time to a minimum. Most workbags were suspended by a broad ribbon or plaited cord, and antique examples are certain to show signs of wear from almost daily use. A type of chair having a workbag attached to the area beneath the seat is known as a workbag chair. Workbag value guide: crewelwork designs, flowers and leaves, medium size, $110.

WRIGGLEWORK. In the 1600s and 1700s a chased type of decoration known as "flechin" was employed by artisans in Switzerland and Germany. This type of engraving occurs rarely on American-made pewter but does adorn a limited amount of treasured tinware. Wrigglework sustained itself as an art form in America due primarily to the patient craftsmen of Pennsylvania. These competent workers incised a design on the bare metal by painstakingly tapping a chisel or suitable sharp instrument with a hammer. The chisel was moved slowly following each tap of the hammer to form a series of short zigzag line strokes, ultimately creating the desired pattern. Initials and dates were sometimes incorporated into the design by talented craftsmen. Wriggled tinware displayed motifs similar to those found on Pennsylvania Frakturs and coverlets. Wrigglework value guide: tin, bureau box, tulips, stars, 5″ x 4″, circa 1840, $370.

WRITING-ARM WINDSOR CHAIRS. This variation of the Windsor chair had one arm equipped with a stationary or pivoting shelf of a size to serve as a writing surface. This addition, developed in the mid-1700s, met with enthusiastic response, particularly in schools and colleges. The extended writing shelf appeared on numerous types of Windsor chairs, including the rod-back, arrow-back, comb-back and low-back styles. The fixed tablet was sometimes supported by several spindles, and occasionally a small drawer was to be found below the writing arm or the seat. Any chair having a left-handed writing arm is a rarity. Thomas Jefferson is known to have perfected a special type of writing-arm Windsor with a revolving seat. Writing-arm Windsor chair value guide: bow-back armchair, original red paint, circa 1800, $650.

WROUGHT IRON. Since the blacksmith rarely signed his work, the collector has a difficult task in trying to distinguish American-made wrought-iron wares from close-resembling imports. The problem is compounded since many early ironworkers were trained in England. Wrought-iron pieces made during the 17th and 18th centuries were extremely simple. These purely utilitarian objects were crafted with considerable restraint. Soft malleable wrought iron was worked or formed by the blacksmith into a strong product that resisted corrosion. Settlers often complained about the high cost of wrought iron. Yet they were dependent upon the blacksmith for many items, including tools, implements, hardware, locks, latches, lighting devices and fireplace and kitchen equipment. A collector should familiarize himself with the categories of wrought iron, as opportunities exist for specialization. Wrought iron value guide: spatula, brass inlaid eagle, $250; strainer marked "J.W.," $180; fork, cutout Pennsylvania heart, $125; ladle, copper bowl, marked "S. Beihler," $80.

Y

YELLOWWARE. In the 19th century many of the same potters engaged in producing redware and Rockingham also made yellowware. Inexpensive yellowware was marketed in a full range of utilitarian items, as homemakers walked out of country stores carrying mixing bowls, cups, plates, molds, teapots, tureens and other tabletop necessities. When the body was covered with a transparent glaze it intensified the buff to deep yellowware color; thus the name yellowware is most fitting. While relief or molded decorations were rarely utilized, some pieces had a contrasting colored white, black, blue or brown band. Unfortunately, few potters bothered to mark this simple kitchen pottery, although it was extensively produced around East Liverpool, Ohio, principally between 1830 and 1900. Any piece of yellowware produced in Bennington, Vermont, is certain to warrant substantial returns. Yellowware value guide: pudding mold, ear-of-corn, $80; teapot, blue band, $65; pitcher, white band, 12" tall, $40; pie plate, 8" diameter, $24.

YOKES. Yokes in various sizes were used on practically a daily basis before the development of modern transportation. Small goose yokes were approximately sixteen inches in length. Even goats were fitted with single-type yokes when used as a means of transportation. Somewhat rarer are the dumbbell-shaped turkey yokes usually pressed into service when minor family members decided to view the countryside from a cart or wagon. The most familiar type of yoke is, of course, the ox yoke. Some measured up to five feet in length; pine or oak were the popular woods. Joseph Jackson & Sons of Tennessee and Nathan Lee of Connecticut were among the firms pulling in profits from ox yokes in the 19th century. Yoke value guide: ox, oak, complete, $120; goat, walnut, single, $75.

Z

ZOAR COLLECTIBLES. One of the most successful experiments in communal living ever attempted in America was the Zoar community of Ohio, established in 1817. This religious sect prospered over the years as they became adept in over thirty-five different arts and crafts. Some furniture forms tended to exhibit slight traces of contemporary furniture styles. Chairs, chests of drawers, rockers, tables, cupboards and other furniture forms crafted by them evoke immediate collector appreciation. Their furniture styles were simple and heavy, possessing traces of German influences. They proved

Left: Zoar plank chair, 19th century; Right: Zoar bonnet cabinet, 19th century

Both photographs, National Gallery of Art, Washington

Both photographs, National Gallery of Art, Washington

Left: Zoar wall cabinet, dated 1836; Right: Zoar decorated chair, 19th century

their resourcefulness by operating a woolen mill, printing and binding shop, tin shop and pottery. Glazed and unglazed redware articles originated at the pottery in addition to a limited production of Rockingham and yellowware. This religious sect disbanded in 1898, leaving a multitude of mementos. Shortly thereafter Zoar collectibles started soaring in value. Zoar collectibles value guide: spinning wheel, $325; rocker, plank seat, circa 1860, $235; tin teapot, circa 1850, $90.

Index

Numbers in *italics* refer to photographs.

Pewter, 146
  coffeepot, 52, 147
  mugs, 137
  sadware, 166
Pottery
  banks, 153–54
  Bell, 15–16
  Bennington, 17
  bulb jars, 29
  chalkware, 40, 41–42
  cow creamers, 65
  farmer's cups, 83–84
  Fenton, 84–85
  Gaudy Dutch, 101
  Gaudy Welsh, 101
  German blue stoneware, 101–2
  jugs, 119
  jugtown, 119–20
  pie plates, 148–49
  redware, 160–61, 160
  Rockingham, 163
  sgraffito, 175–76, 176
  slipware, 184
  spatterware, 187
  Spinner, 189
  spongeware, 190–91
  yellowware, 232
  Zoar, 233–34

Quilts, 157–58, 157, 158
  appliqué, 157
  crazy, 66, 158
  presentation, 154–55
  See also Coverlets

Records, see Certificates
Religious articles
  bultos, 29
  door lintels, 74–75
  retablos, 162
  santeros, 168–69
Rocking chairs, 162–63, 163
  American Standard, 2–3
  Boston, 20
  cane-back, 37–38
  fiddleback Boston, 85, 85
  nursing, 139
  Pennsylvania painted, 146
  Salem, 167
  Shaker, 178–79, 179

Zoar, 233–34
  See also Chairs
Rugs
  appliqué, 6
  braided, 22–23
  button, 33
  embroidered, 81
  floor cloths, 92
  Frost patterns, 98
  hooked, 112, 112
  rag, 159
  shirred Shaker, 177
  straw, 196
  striped, 196–97
  tongue, 206

Seats
  buggy, 28
  wagon, 217, 217
Silver, 181–82
  coin, 53
  tankard, 182
  teapot, 182
Stoneware, 194–95
  German blue, 101–2
  hound-handled pitchers, 113
  jar, 194
  jug, 119
  pitcher, 194
Stools, 195
  cricket, 67
  footstools, 94–95
  joint, 118–19
  spool footstool, 191
Stoves
  cannon, 38–39
  column, 54
  dumb, 79
  Dutch, 80
  five-plate, 90–91
  foot warmers, 95–96
  four-o'clock, 96
  Franklin, 97–98
  globe, 102
  parlor, 143
  plate, 195
  reflector, 161
  ten-plate, 201–2

Tables
  bedside, 13

240